THE EXPERIENCE OF COLOUR IN LORCA'S THEATRE

LEGENDA

LEGENDA is the Modern Humanities Research Association's book imprint for new research in the Humanities. Founded in 1995 by Malcolm Bowie and others within the University of Oxford, Legenda has always been a collaborative publishing enterprise, directly governed by scholars. The Modern Humanities Research Association (MHRA) joined this collaboration in 1998, became half-owner in 2004, in partnership with Maney Publishing and then Routledge, and has since 2016 been sole owner. Titles range from medieval texts to contemporary cinema and form a widely comparative view of the modern humanities, including works on Arabic, Catalan, English, French, German, Greek, Italian, Portuguese, Russian, Spanish, and Yiddish literature. Editorial boards and committees of more than 60 leading academic specialists work in collaboration with bodies such as the Society for French Studies, the British Comparative Literature Association and the Association of Hispanists of Great Britain & Ireland.

The MHRA encourages and promotes advanced study and research in the field of the modern humanities, especially modern European languages and literature, including English, and also cinema. It aims to break down the barriers between scholars working in different disciplines and to maintain the unity of humanistic scholarship. The Association fulfils this purpose through the publication of journals, bibliographies, monographs, critical editions, and the MHRA Style Guide, and by making grants in support of research. Membership is open to all who work in the Humanities, whether independent or in a University post, and the participation of younger colleagues entering the field is especially welcomed.

ALSO PUBLISHED BY THE ASSOCIATION

Critical Texts
Tudor and Stuart Translations • *New Translations* • *European Translations*
MHRA Library of Medieval Welsh Literature

MHRA Bibliographies
Publications of the Modern Humanities Research Association

The Annual Bibliography of English Language & Literature
Austrian Studies
Modern Language Review
Portuguese Studies
The Slavonic and East European Review
Working Papers in the Humanities
The Yearbook of English Studies

www.mhra.org.uk
www.legendabooks.com

STUDIES IN HISPANIC AND LUSOPHONE CULTURES

Studies in Hispanic and Lusophone Cultures are selected and edited by the Association of Hispanists of Great Britain & Ireland. The series seeks to publish the best new research in all areas of the literature, thought, history, culture, film, and languages of Spain, Spanish America, and the Portuguese-speaking world.

The Association of Hispanists of Great Britain & Ireland is a professional association which represents a very diverse discipline, in terms of both geographical coverage and objects of study. Its website showcases new work by members, and publicises jobs, conferences and grants in the field.

Founding Editor
Trevor Dadson

Editorial Committee
Chair: Professor Catherine Davies (University of London)
Professor Stephanie Dennison (University of Leeds)
Professor Sally Faulkner (University of Exeter)
Professor Andrew Ginger (Northeastern University, USA)
Professor James Mandrell (Brandeis University, USA)
Professor Hilary Owen (University of Manchester/University of Oxford)
Professor Philip Swanson (University of Sheffield)
Professor Jonathan Thacker (Exeter College, University of Oxford)

Managing Editor
Dr Graham Nelson
41 Wellington Square, Oxford OX1 2JF, UK

www.legendabooks.com/series/shlc

STUDIES IN HISPANIC AND LUSOPHONE CULTURES

The Experience of Colour in Lorca's Theatre

❖

Jade Boyd

l

LEGENDA
Studies in Hispanic and Lusophone Cultures 54
Modern Humanities Research Association
2022

Published by Legenda
an imprint of the Modern Humanities Research Association
Salisbury House, Station Road, Cambridge CB1 2LA

ISBN 978-1-83954-070-7 (HB)
ISBN 978-1-83954-071-4 (PB)

First published 2022

Copy-Editor: Dr Ellen Jones

CONTENTS

❖

In loving memory of
Derek John Watt

ACKNOWLEDGEMENTS

❖

This book is dedicated to my parents, Carrie Watt-Boyd and Steve Boyd, who made this dream possible with their emotional and financial support. It is also dedicated to my grandmother Patricia Watt, who graduated from the University of Bristol in 1976, paving the way for my own achievements there.

Thank you to all my family and friends for your encouragement and support throughout this long journey, especially Frankie and Brian Boyd, Carrie Potter, and my Bristol PhD crew: Dr Lydia Wooldridge, Dr Rebekah Locke, and Dr Sina Stuhlert.

Special thanks go to my PhD supervisors Professor Susan Harrow and Dr Sally-Ann Kitts for their expertise, commitment, and rigour. Thank you to my PhD examiners Professor Sarah Wright and Dr Rebecca Kosick for their guidance and support. This would not have been possible without you.

Thank you to the Association of Hispanists of Great Britain and Ireland and to Legenda for the 2021 Thesis Publication Prize which led to this wonderful opportunity. Thanks especially to Dr Graham Nelson and Professor Catherine Davies.

J.B., June 2022

INTRODUCTION

❖

A Theatre of Poetry in Colour

Federico Garcia Lorca's (1898–1936) powerful and experimental colour-work is a critically undernourished aspect of his craft, particularly in terms of colour's psychological, bodily, and material agency. In this study I break away from scholarly preoccupations with Lorca's sexuality, with the division of his work along temporal and stylistic lines, and with the limitations of colour symbolism. An underexplored concept often mistaken as the use of verse, 'theatre of poetry' was Lorca's vision of a holistic and multi-modal theatre which sought to create a powerful and active viewing experience and to embody key linguistic images and themes in the material staging. My in-depth readings of Lorca's ten full-length completed plays (1920–1936) through the lens of colour studies offer a methodology for exploring 'theatre of poetry' in ways which also provide a fuller understanding of Lorca's colour practice.[1] Inspired by a range of interdisciplinary readings on material and affective colour, I ask not what colour 'is' or might be in Lorca's theatre, but what colour 'does'. I examine different facets of colour in Lorca's theatre of poetry: the ways in which colour and whiteness spark and reflect characters' mental states; the role of bodily recuperations of colour in terms of Lorca's exploration of character subjectivities and of implicit colours, colours implied by object association rather than colour words, and the stabbing of the male body throughout Lorca's theatre; and the importance of object colour in terms of the materialisation of poetic themes and motifs. My study reveals Lorca's colour-work to be a pervasive, autonomous, and explosive force.

Lorca Colour Scholarship

The current field of Lorca colour scholarship is largely dominated by preoccupations with traditional colour symbolism and what colour might 'mean', with Lorca's own psychobiography and homosexuality, and with his poetry rather than his theatre, particularly the colour green. Colour symbolism forms the backbone of Gwynne Edwards's treatment of colour in his fundamental 1980 study *Lorca: The Theatre Beneath the Sand*. Whilst the importance of Edwards's reading of Lorca's theatre should not be underestimated, it does rely on traditional readings of colour symbolism in Lorca's work.[2] Edwards also considers the earlier plays *El maleficio de la mariposa* (1920) [The Butterfly's Evil Spell], *Mariana Pineda* (1925), *Amor de Don Perlimplín con Belisa en su jardín* (1925) [The Love of Don Perlimplín with Belisa in his Garden], and *La zapatera prodigiosa* (1926) [The Shoemaker's Prodigious Wife] to be 'minor works' and does not explore them in the same depth. For Edwards, black constitutes old age, death, melancholy, and the negative elements of life; white is death, the passing of time, pain, frustration, sterility, but also the positive aspects of life; blue signifies encroaching death; pink is optimism and beauty; and green is hope, freshness, and vitality. Edwards's reading of blue light as evocative of a nightmare or as creating a dream-like effect is useful, but he concludes that ultimately blue light is the signifier of death, which narrows Lorca's colour-work down to a fixed meaning. The multiple and contrasting 'meanings' of colours discussed in Edwards's study calls into question the usefulness of traditional colour symbolism as a route of critical enquiry, especially if it is considered in isolation from its other functions.

Derek Harris's 1985 study of green in Lorca's work is marked both by his listing of colour frequencies and his focus on colour symbolism. Harris argues that Lorca's use of green undergoes a semantic shift from positive to negative connotations over time, as 'the conventional positive symbolism of green, its associations with hope and vitality, become subverted [...] so that a link is made between green and the experience of love and life denied'.[3] Harris suggests that the same shift from positive to negative meanings occurs in Lorca's plays: green appears as a symbol of nature in Lorca's early works, becomes more menacing and negative in the late 1920s, and is consistently evocative of death in the 1930s.[4] Harris's analysis of green in Lorca's plays is conspicuously brief, comprising a single paragraph which does not take the richness and variety of Lorca's theatrical opus into account. Whilst Harris does consider that colour values may shift and change, he relies heavily on Lorca's personal life and presumed emotional state as the driving force behind this transformation, and suggests that one reading can be applied to Lorca's vast range of poetry and his ten completed plays. Harris's failure to consider implicit colour — the colour created by colour-object associations rather than explicit colour terms — and his reduction of the meanings of green to this linear trajectory from life to death leaves Lorca's varied and remarkable use of colour unexplored beyond a cataloguing of explicit uses of green.

Harris's study highlights another key critical trend regarding Lorca's use of colour: the tendency to see colour as the manifestation of Lorca's own psyche and his sexual struggle. Whilst I acknowledge that Lorca's homosexuality, which was illegal in Spain at the time, may have been a factor in his work, we must be careful not to invest it with too much significance. Lorca was a complex, multifaceted individual and the theme of homosexuality is not explicit in most of his work, as Federico Bonaddio tells us.[5] Robert Havard's 1972 article recognises the ambiguous nature of greenness in Lorca's work, yet also attributes this conflict to Lorca's own struggle with sexuality, reading green as the ambivalent symbol of the psychic conflict of the author.[6] Nelson Orringer takes a similar approach in his 1975 study of Lorca's poetry collection *Diván del Tamarit* (1934) [The Tamarit Divan], suggesting that its faded colour palette represents Lorca's haunting by erotic memories of failed love and a desire for self-destruction. He argues that this poetry collection 'forms a mature self-portrait mostly in white and turbid gray [as] Lorca tortures himself with the despair to which memories of unfulfilling love have driven him'.[7] This psycho-biographical approach to Lorca continues in later studies. Ryan Prout's 2000 article argues that Lorca's use of blue and green in his poetry collection *Poeta en Nueva York* (1929) [Poet in New York] signifies an identification of sexual difference and sexual minority, and the resulting stigma.[8] For Prout, the possibilities of a synaesthetic reading of colour, where the visual and non-visual senses become blended, is reduced to 'the interaction between sensory perception, memory, and emotion' sparked by Lorca's personal response to his time in the United States.[9] Emilio Peral Vega's 2015 monograph *Pierrot/Lorca: White Carnival of Black Desire* is also concerned with Lorca's personal sexuality. Whilst this study is an important source for reading the Pierrot figure — a central recurring figure in Lorca's drawings, poetry, and plays — from a colour point of view Peral Vega's reading of the Pierrot figure as an 'aesthetic encoding' of Lorca's homosexuality and the 'spokesperson for his dark side' reduces the study of white and black to the staining of the white, pure, virginal, and effeminate figure of the Pierrot with the black taint of masculinity and Lorca's 'dark love'.[10] Scholarship which focuses on Lorca's colour-work as the expression of his personal sexuality is in danger of reducing his rich use of colour to one reading and assuming a personal subjective knowledge of the author which we cannot confirm with any certainty.

The recognition of the visual nature of Lorca's work opens up some important considerations about the materiality of his colour-work, albeit one restricted to his poetry. María del Carmen Hernández Valcárcel's discussion of Lorca's poetry in *La expresión sensorial en cinco poetas del 27* (1978) [Sensorial Expression in Five Poets of '27] explores the visual sensations which Lorca captures through colour language. She draws our attention to Lorca's use of metals, minerals, and flowers in *Romancero gitano* (1928) [Gypsy Ballads],[11] concluding that 'el color late bajo esta pobre cobertura, envuelto en metáforas y símbolos admirables que proporcionan una coloración velada, pero muy rica, a los poemas' [colour beats beneath this sparse outside layer, cloaked in admirable metaphors and symbols which offer a hidden, but very rich, colouring in his poems].[12] She notes that these implicit colours are also important in Lorca's other poetry collections in the predominant motifs of blood, flowers, precious metals, and gems. The importance of object colour in Lorca's theatre of poetry is central to my analysis in Chapter Three. However, Hernández Valcárcel sees Lorca's poetry as falling into two distinct linear trajectories with the traditional divide of 'early' and 'late' work and *Poeta en Nueva York* as a complete rupture despite the prevalence of implicit colour in this collection including the motif of blood. In *Federico García Lorca: El color de la poesía* (1998) [Federico García Lorca: The Colour of Poetry] Veronica Dean-Thacker and Pedro Guerrero Ruíz build on Hernández Valcárcel's work in their exploration of the role of colour and the plastic, descriptive, and symbolic aspects of what they call Lorca's 'visualidad poética' [poetic visuality].[13] Whilst Dean-Thacker and Guerrero Ruíz do engage with colour symbolism — red as love and passion; black as death, pain, and grief; white as life, pain, and death; blue as Modernist — they acknowledge the vast sensory complexity of these symbols. Dean-Thacker and Guerrero Ruíz also recognise the diachronic development of Lorca's opus, although, disappointingly, they still read *Poeta en Nueva York* as entirely distinct from Lorca's other poetry collections. Dean-Thacker and Guerrero Ruíz's reading of colour as a sensory, luminous, and mobile force offers a useful starting point, as does their exploration of Lorca's use of abstraction and the blending of the real and unreal, his playful use of language, and his colour word games. However, their focus on how Lorca uses these colour images to reflect his inner reality and his relationship with the world often leads to a restrictive symbolic analysis. The material capacity of colour which begins to emerge in these studies highlights the need to reconsider these values of colour in Lorca's work as a holistic whole and to extend these burgeoning ideas to Lorca's theatrical works.

The limitations of a symbolic reading of Lorca's colour-work have led to a focus on other elements of his stagecraft in canonical studies of Lorca's theatre by Paul Julian Smith (1998), Sarah Wright (2000), and Paul McDermid (2007).[14] McDermid's reading of material whiteness in his exploration of love, desire, and identity in *Cristo: Una tragedia religiosa* (c. 1919–1920) [Christ: A Religious Tragedy], *Mariana Pineda*, and *Don Perlimplín*, is a valuable starting point, especially in terms of character transformations and their movement from an earthy to a celestial plane, and his analysis of *Mariana Pineda* influences my discussion of bodily colour in Chapter Two. However, the study of Lorca's theatre is in urgent need of a focus on his theatrical colour-work in its own right as a core part of his raw, immersive, and hybrid 'theatre of poetry' rather than a minor or purely symbolic element.

Lorca's Theatre of Poetry

Lorca's engagement with colour as a material and affective force is part of a sustained experimentation with his concept of a 'theatre of poetry' throughout his ten full-length plays. Perhaps due to Lorca's varied and complex stagecraft, these ten plays have traditionally been divided into different temporal or stylistic periods, for example his 'minor' plays (*El maleficio*, *Mariana Pineda*, *La zapatera*, and *Don Perlimplín*, according to Edwards) his 'surreal' or 'impossible' plays (*El público* [The Audience], *Así que pasen cinco años* (1931) [When Five Years Pass]), and his 'rural trilogy' (*Bodas de sangre* (1932) [Blood Weddings], *Yerma* (1934), and *La casa de Bernarda Alba* (1936) [The House of Bernarda Alba]), which is often seen as the culmination of his work. However, this categorisation fails to take into account the diachronic nature of Lorca's theatre, the importance he placed on *El público* and *Así que pasen* in terms of his theatre of poetry, and the fact that he intended the third part of his 'trilogy' to focus on the Biblical story of Sodom and Lot and to explore the theme of incest.[15] This grouping also complicates the status of *Doña Rosita la soltera o el lenguaje de las flores* (1935) [Doña Rosita the Spinster or the Language of Flowers] which interrupts the chronology of the 'trilogy' and was originally conceived in 1924, although it was not completed until 1935.[16] Rather than a separate, 'experimental' period, *El público* and *Así que pasen* form a crucial part of Lorca's opus, as in 1936 he stated that 'en estas comedias imposibles está mi verdadero propósito. Pero para demostrar una personalidad y tener derecho al respeto he dado otras cosas' [my true purpose lies in these impossible plays. But in order to show personality and respect

I have done other things].[17] These works are 'not a stepping stone to the rural trilogy', warns Wright.[18] Rather, this statement by Lorca suggests that these plays were the core of his work, and even problematises the status of some of his other works. This compartmentalisation has prevented us from exploring colour in its fullness and equivocation and offers an incomplete view of the richness and variety of Lorca's colour-work. Lorca's preoccupation with material colour is present in each of his plays in complementary and contrasting forms and, notwithstanding the distinctiveness of each work, there are also underlying trends which bring his theatrical corpus together as a whole. Rather than a series of distinct and divergent stylistic periods, each of Lorca's plays forms part of his theatre of poetry within which material colour plays a central role.

'Theatre of poetry' has been misunderstood by scholars such as Edwards as the use of verse in Lorca's theatre. However, Lorca clearly stated in 1935 that 'el verso no quiere decir poesía en el teatro' [verse does not mean poetry in the theatre].[19] For Lorca, poetry and theatre were not separate. He consistently referred to himself as 'el poeta' [the poet], including in the title page of *Bernarda Alba*, and *Yerma* and *Doña Rosita* are subtitled as '[un] poema trágico' [a tragic poem] and '[un] poema granadino' [a Granadan poem] respectively. He also referred to *El público* as 'un poema para silbarlo' [a poem to be booed at].[20] Rather than the use of verse in his plays, Lorca's theatre of poetry is the focus on the inner reality of everyday, ordinary people and the materialisation of poetic themes and symbols on stage, drawing on multi-modal and hybrid forms and styles. These ideas drive my discussion of colour as the material representation of mental states in *Bernarda Alba* in Chapter One, the somatic discourse of emotional suffering and the stabbing of the male body rendered through corporeal colour in Chapter Two, and the colours of sets, props, lighting, and costumes in Chapter Three. Throughout my study I demonstrate how Lorca's engagement with colour sheds light on these central ideas about theatre.

Lorca's theatre of poetry was an artistic rejection of the bourgeois, slice-of-life theatre and commercialism which dominated the Spanish stage in the early twentieth century. Edwards observes that theatre in Spain in the first two decades of the twentieth century 'presented a spectacle of almost unrelieved superficiality' and was dominated by 'dramatists who, on the whole, gave an undiscerning public what it wanted, and a public which would not tolerate serious or experimental plays'.[21] Lorca emphasises his anti-bourgeois, anti-traditionalist vision of theatre in the prologue to *La zapatera* when the Author laments the playwright's fear of his audience and the subsequent disappearance of 'poetry', in the form of surreal or unexpected transformations, from the stage.[22] Lorca reiterates these concerns in his lecture 'Charla sobre el teatro' [Talk about Theatre] in 1935, where he argued that theatre needed to move away from commercialism and audience demands: 'El teatro se debe imponer al público y no el público al teatro' [theatre should impose itself on the audience, rather than the audience imposing itself on theatre].[23] In a letter to his family in 1929 Lorca writes: 'todo lo que existe ahora en España está muerto. O se cambia el teatro de raíz o se acaba para siempre. No hay otra solución' [everything that exists right now in Spain is dead. Either we change theatre at its very roots or it ends forever. There's no other way].[24]

Theatre of poetry was a theatre for and about the everyday person, part of an attempt to 'devolver el teatro al pueblo' [to return theatre to the people].[25] This was also the driving force behind his work with travelling university theatre company La Barraca, which Lorca directed along with Eduardo Ugarte from 1931 until 1935.[26] With La Barraca, Lorca sought to bring popular, relatable performances of Golden Age Spanish theatre to the general public in more remote and rural areas of Spain. He wanted to make theatre accessible for an everyday audience, rather than only the middle-classes: 'Yo arrancaría de los teatros las plateas y los palcos y traería abajo el gallinero. En el teatro hay que dar entrada al público de alpargatas' [I would rip the stalls and box seats out of theatres and tear the Gods down. In theatre we should give admission to audience members who are living on a shoestring].[27] Despite Lorca's resistance to overt politicism, his concern with creating a popular theatre for all reveals a democratic drive and an active engagement with sociocultural change which is also reflected in his representation of disenfranchised groups in his poetry and his theatre, including his interest in Roma culture, as Wright observes.[28] Lorca suggested that there were two levels to his plays which took the diversity of his intended audience into account. First, there was '[el plano] vertiente al poeta que analiza y que hace que sus personajes se encuentren para producir la idea subterránea' [the poet's point of view, which is analytical and brings the characters together to reveal the ideas below the surface], a level which Lorca understood would only reach part of his audience, 'las clases cultas, universitarias' [the educated, university classes].[29] The 'idea subterránea' evokes Lorca's metaphor of 'theatre beneath the sand', which he uses in *El público* to describe a theatre which seeks the truth beneath the surface. Secondly, there was the emotive, popular dimension for 'el pueblo más pobre y más rudo' [the poorest and roughest audience members] which comprised '[un] plano natural, de la línea melódica, que toma el público sencillo para quien mi teatro físico es un gozo, un ejemplo y siempre una enseñanza' [the normal plane, the melodic line, which grips the simple audience for whom my physical theatre is a joy, an example, and always a lesson].[30] By balancing these two aspects of his theatre of poetry, Lorca was able to explore complex concepts without creating an erudite, exclusive form of theatre which could not be appreciated by the general public. This second, universal level was not intended to be didactic. As Andrew Anderson notes, Lorca 'is showing us how we are and how we live; never does he attempt to tell us how we *should* be or how we *should* live'.[31] Rather, the 'educational' aim of Lorca's theatre was to shed light on the contemporary issues of daily life in Spain through a striking portrayal of emotional suffering via his 'escuela de llanto y risa' [school of tears and laughter] and his creation of something that 'las masas pueden atrapar sin explicárselo, con sólo sentirlo' [the masses can understand without explanation, just by feeling it].[32] This theatre of everyday experiences and emotion relied on powerful 'human' characters:

> El teatro es la poesía que se levanta del libro y se hace humana. Y al hacerse humana, habla y grita, llora y se desespera. El teatro necesita que los personajes que aparezcan en la escena lleven un traje de poesía y al mismo tiempo que se les vean los huesos, la sangre. Han de ser tan humanos, tan horrorosamente trágicos y ligados a la vida y al día con una fuerza tal, que muestren sus traiciones, que se

aprecien sus olores y que salga a los labios toda la valentía de sus palabras llenas de amor o de ascos.[33]

[Theatre is poetry which steps out of the book and becomes human. And as it becomes human, it speaks and shouts, it cries and despairs. Theatre needs the characters that appear on stage to wear a costume of poetry and at the same time to let us see their bones, their blood. They have to be so human, so horrifyingly tragic and linked to life, to the moment, with such force, that their betrayals are revealed, we perceive their smells, and all of the courage of their words full of love or disgust can pour forth from their lips.]

These 'characters of bones-and-blood' stood in direct opposition to '[los] personajes huecos, vacíos totalmente' [the hollow, totally empty characters] of established, middle-brow theatre.[34] The ways in which Lorca captures the toxic effects of social norms and rigid gender roles on individuals offer a searing criticism of honour, marriage, and motherhood through the gut-wrenching suffering of his characters. Lorca's ability to capture the raw emotions of his characters and the effects of individual oppression has contributed to the longevity of his work.

The power of language in Lorca's plays and its emotional charge is also supported in the materialisation of the key symbols and themes of the language in the physical elements of his staging, in terms of costume, props, sets, and lighting. For example, in Act Three, Scene One of *Bodas de sangre*, the themes of death and fate are anthropomorphised in the figures of the Beggarwoman, the Moon, and the Woodcutters. Lorca stated that his favourite part of *Bodas de sangre* was this more surreal scene when the Moon and Death appear as characters and reality 'se quiebra y desaparece para dar paso a la fantasía poética' [breaks apart and disappears, giving way to poetic fantasy].[35] Despite critical backlash, Lorca tells us that he felt like 'un pez en agua' [a fish in water] creating this scene.[36] In *Doña Rosita* the central motif of the mutable rose is reflected in Rosita's name and costume and the structure of the play, and in *El público* the search for truth and the creation of a 'theatre beneath the sand' is represented by the X-ray prints and the folding screen which transforms the visual appearance of the characters. In *Bernarda Alba*, the central basis of my discussion in Chapter One, it is emotions that take plastic form as Lorca replicates the central conflict between Bernarda and her daughters and Bernarda's obsession with honour in the material whiteness of the house. Through the contrast of whiteness and colour, Lorca sets up a visual dialectic which is reflective of the characters' psychological states and is mutually supported by references to white and coloured objects in the dialogue. Part of this creation of physical poetry on the stage, or the representation of linguistic themes and ideas in material form, involves a high level of 'stylisation', which is how Lorca emphasises the visual elements of the staging to draw attention to the bones-and-blood of the stage and to move away from a mimetic spectating experience. For example, Andrew Anderson argues that the exaggerated visual aesthetic of *La zapatera* 'helps to undermine and destroy the conventional realistic theatrical illusion' and 'challenges spectators to use their mind and imagination, to accept the unrealistic or the fantastic'.[37] Likewise, this anti-mimetic, exaggerated effect is found in Lorca's *aleluya* aesthetic in *Don Perlimplín*.[38] Francis Fergusson suggests that 'an *aleluya* is something like a valentine [...] something heroic, overdone, absurd: an *extravagant* offering' which influences all the elements of the staging.[39] Michael Thompson argues that the overall effect of this 'startling' and 'unsettling' portrayal of ideas and feelings is one of defamiliarization which aims to 'blow apart [...] the "theatre of the bourgeoisie" and fill the stage with passion and magic' in ways that invigorated and moved the audience.[40]

Lorca's 'poetry' is both the representation of important images and themes in the dialogue and in the material staging, and the overarching idea that guides the play's aesthetic. Lorca weaves this central poetic image through all the different visual and verbal elements of the production, lifting the mutable rose or the *estampa* from the page and bringing them to life on the stage in three-dimensional form.[41] Many of Lorca's plays are defined by an overarching style or image that guides the transference of poetic themes and symbols to the three-dimensional stage and provides this internal poetic structure. Thompson describes this central image as a poetic 'core' or 'nucleus' surrounded by 'complex layers of associations [which] are built up by means of words, staging and movement' and which we should envision as 'a series of concentric circles' surrounding the poetic motif.[42] Likewise, Sumner M. Greenfield sees Lorca's theatre of poetry as 'a disciplined integration of an infinity of poetic elements [...] which are shaped and unified by a systematically conceived inner design'.[43] The subtitles are a crucial tool in terms of our understanding of this poetic core or inner design. Greenfield argues that Lorca's use of subtitles 'is the key, sometimes obvious, sometimes extremely subtle, to the artistic conception or the poetic substructure by which the dramatic action is given shape and is seconded or re-expressed'.[44] Sometimes the subtitles indicate the mood or genre of the play, without necessarily revealing the play's aesthetic influences and central motifs. However, the photographic documentary in *Bernarda Alba*, which forms part of my discussion of black-and-white contrasts in Chapter One, and the *estampa* in *Mariana Pineda*, the *aleluya* in *Don Perlimplín*, and the mutable rose in *Doña Rosita*, as I explore in Chapter Three, are critical for our understanding of Lorca's theatre of poetry in these works.

In this 'animation' of poetic themes, symbols, emotions, and two-dimensional images, Lorca drew on a vast range of aesthetic forms and influences across his plays and within each play. His work is multi-modal and hybrid, in the sense that it is inspired by different artistic media, and is influenced by both traditional and avant-garde sources. His style is always changing as he experiments with different methods of bringing poetry to the stage in material form and with creating an unsettling spectating experience. Whilst Edwards argues that Symbolism and Surrealism had the most impact on Lorca's work, Lorca's theatre also reflects the influences of *commedia dell'arte*, puppet theatre, classical and Greek tragedy, Golden Age theatre, 1920s and 1930s cinema, Expressionism, and Goya, Bosch, Cervantes and Shakespeare.[45] Paul McDermid argues that Lorca's fascination with bringing the two-dimensional to life in his theatre of poetry is reflected in his use of 'cuadros' to structure *Don Perlimplín*, *Así que pasen*, *El público*, *Bodas de sangre*, and *Yerma*. Whilst 'cuadro' can refer to a scene, it is also a 'painting', a 'frame', or a 'tableau'. McDermid suggests that throughout his theatre Lorca demonstrates 'a profound interest in the relationship between the fixed, still image — the print, the tableau, the photograph — and the unstationary, live representation of the theatre piece' which recurs in *Mariana Pineda*, *Don Perlimplín*, *El público*, *Así que pasen*, *Bodas de sangre*, *Yerma*, and *Bernarda Alba*.[46] There is also a real tension between tradition and the avant-garde throughout Lorca's works, as explored by Luis Fernández Cifuentes and by Dru Dougherty and María Francisca Vilches de Frutos.[47] As an individual, Lorca was a polymath and his opus consists of more than the poetry and full-length plays for which he is renowned and reflects the range of aesthetic influences in those works. His *obra completa* includes an unfinished opera; a film script; puppet plays; short plays; drawings; set and costume designs; the literary review *gallo*; lectures; recitals; and prose. On his death in 1936, Lorca left behind unfinished works, and his unedited juvenilia were published as recently as 1994.[48]

Lorca's time at the Residencia de Estudiantes in Madrid (1919–1928), which Leslie Stainton describes as 'an informal residential college where cultured young men could live and learn at leisure', was crucial in terms of these aesthetic influences.[49] During Lorca's stay at the Residencia he was exposed to visiting figures including Paul Valéry, Le Corbusier, Blaise Cendrars, Henri Bergson, Igor Stravinsky, and Maurice Ravel, and this is where he formed his famous friendships with Luis Buñuel and Salvador Dalí.[50] It was also in Madrid that Lorca met the director Gregorio Martínez Sierra, who would go on to stage Lorca's first play *El maleficio* in 1920. Lorca's correspondence reveals a wide circle of friends and acquaintances that included the composer Manuel de Falla, the art critique Sebastià Gasch, and the poets Rafael Alberti, Jorge Guillén, Gerardo Diego, and Luis Cernuda. Lorca, Alberti, Guillén, Diego, and Cernuda were part of the so-called 'Generation of '27', along with Pedro Salinas, Dámaso Alonso, Vicente Aleixandre, Manuel Altolaguirre, and Emilio Prados. Whilst C. Christopher Soufas has criticised the Spanish literary generation model for its exclusion of female writers, its elitism, and its reductive, pigeonholing nature, Lorca's inclusion as a member of the Generation of '27 does give us an idea of his status, at least as a poet, and of the influential circle of which he was part.[51] Lorca also maintained close working relationships with the director and founder of Club Anfistora, Pura Ucelay, the director Cipriano Rivas Cherif, actresses Margarita Xirgu and Lola Membrives, and the set designer and amateur actor Santiago Ontañón. As María Delgado tells us, the influence of Xirgu and her theatre company cannot be underestimated, especially in Latin America.[52] Xirgu went on to stage productions of *Mariana Pineda*, *Bodas de sangre*, *Yerma*, and *Bernarda Alba*.

French playwright and poet Jean Cocteau (1889–1963) is also an important contemporary as Cocteau's concept of 'poetry of the theatre' offers a useful parallel to Lorca's 'theatre of poetry'. We know that Lorca was familiar with Cocteau's work because he mentions him in his 1928 lecture 'Sketch de la nueva pintura' [Sketch of the New Painting], and Rivas Cherif, who worked closely with Lorca, staged Cocteau's play *Orphée* [Orpheus] in December 1928 with his experimental theatre company *El Caracol* [The Snail].[53] Cocteau and Lorca were both promoted in The Yellow Manifesto or the Catalan Anti-Art Manifesto, written by Dalí, Gasch, and Lluís Montanyà, which was published for the first time in Spanish translation in the literary review *gallo* which Lorca was involved with, also in 1928.[54] In his study of Lorca's and Cocteau's 'poetic language' Nelson Cerqueira draws our attention to the similarities of their ideas, particularly how their 'poetics of the theater' is 'not restricted to words' but incorporates all of the elements of the material staging and to the ways in which they create 'a new, startling reality on a transformed stage' which troubles the conventional division between audience and performance.[55] Cerqueira also sees their experiments with theatre and poetry as 'working along different paths to achieve the same goal: the rediscovery of poetic drama, a kind of magical realism [...] dancing between the real and surreal'.[56] Whilst Cerqueira attributes this effect to the characters' 'inability to face life as it is' and their consequent retreat into a world of fantasy, this aspect of theatre of poetry is more fruitfully interpreted as part of Lorca's and Cocteau's aims of unsettling and stimulating their audiences. Like Lorca, Cocteau is not advocating verse drama, which he saw as 'a misuse of the physical properties of the stage', as Laura Doyle Gates observes.[57] Rather, Cocteau 'wanted to overwhelm the spectator not with words but with image-filled, poetic architecture' in which metaphors were 'active, dynamic, dramatized' rather than merely spoken and were extended to all of the elements of the staging.[58] In the 1922 prologue to his ballet libretto *Les Mariés de la Tour Eiffel* [The Eiffel Tower Wedding Party], Cocteau explains the difference between his 'poetry *of* the theatre' and 'poetry *in* the theatre':

> L'action de ma pièce est imagée tandis que le texte ne l'est pas. J'essaie donc de substituer une 'poésie *du* théâtre' à la 'poésie *au* théâtre'. La poésie au théâtre est une dentelle délicate, impossible à voir de loin. La poésie du théâtre serait une grosse dentelle; une dentelle en cordages, un navire sur la mer. *Les Mariés de la Tour Eiffel* peuvent avoir l'aspect terrible d'une goutte de poésie au microscope. Les scènes s'emboîtent comme les mots d'un poème.[59]

> [The action of my play is not text but image. I'm trying to substitute 'poetry *of* the theatre' for 'poetry *in* the theatre'. Poetry in the theatre is a delicate lace, impossible to see at a distance. Poetry of the theatre is a thick lace; a rigging of lace, a ship on the sea. *The Eiffel Tower Wedding Party* has the power of the terrible appearance of a drop of poetry under a microscope. The scenes fit together like the words of a poem.]

The idea of a thick rigging of lace suggests that Cocteau intended his performances to draw attention to their theatrical nature. Annette Shandler-Levitt suggests that Cocteau 'wants us to see the workings of the theatre, to see how it functions, to be totally aware that we are seeing a theatrical production'.[60] Like Lorca's image of bones protruding from beneath the poetic costume, the 'rigging' of Cocteau's theatre will be evident to the spectator: bold and stylised rather than a subtle, delicate lace which offers the illusion of verisimilitude. Shandler-Levitt notes that the metaphor of poetry under the microscope is evocative of the exaggeration of the absurdity of reality.[61] This aim echoes Lorca's anti-mimesis and his fascination with incorporating music and dance into his plays, yet implies a distorting effect which we do not find in Lorca's theatre. Rather, Lorca's work acts as a mirror, reflecting the true nature of the audience, and explores people's inner realities beneath the masks of social appearances.

Another important difference between Cocteau's 'poetry of the theatre' and Lorca's 'theatre of poetry' is the role of the actors. Gates notes that in Cocteau's vision, 'the role of the actor increased until a veritable exchange of roles took place' and 'characters became objects and objects became characters'.[62] This was his 'décor qui bouge' or 'moving set' in which the characters function 'like different parts of a complex machine', an effect which is created by their visual appearance as archetypal figures, their movements, and 'the way in which other objects or stage situations control them'.[63] When Cocteau's ballet *Parade* premiered in 1917 the audience was 'shocked by the dehumanised, quasi-architectural or blatantly stereotyped "characters"'.[64] In contrast, Lorca's theatre of poetry is deeply rooted in the bones, blood, cries, and smells of what it means to be human. As Thompson argues, although many of Lorca's characters are 'associated with verbal and visual symbolic elements that define their function in the overall poetic structure' they 'simultaneously encapsulat[e] powerful evocations of human experience'.[65] The ways in which Lorca and Cocteau incorporate the linguistic and plastic elements of their theatre also differ. Rather than the mechanisation and dehumanisation which Cocteau explored, Lorca enhanced the associations between the linguistic and material elements of the staging by focusing on a key idea which he extended to all of the aspects of the performance and by using colour as a visual linking device to bring set, costume, props, and lighting together.

Chapter Outlines

My three chapters consider the role of colour in Lorca's theatre of poetry, focusing on the ways in which the linguistic and the material elements of his plays work together and on his exploration of the inner worlds of his characters and what lies beneath the surface. In Chapter One I explore how Lorca uses a white-colour dichotomy in terms of both dialogue and staging to explore the emotions and key concerns of his protagonists in *Bernarda Alba*. *Bernarda Alba* provides an important starting point for a re-consideration of colour in Lorca's theatre as part of his theatre of poetry in terms of his communication of the inner worlds of his characters, the creation of a holistic theatre experience in which the visual and the verbal elements mutually reflect each other, and the materialisation of poetic themes and symbols in the staging. Lorca centres the aesthetics of the play on Bernarda's obsession with whiteness and her loathing of colour as a visual corollary of her symbolic association of white with purity, and colour with sin and dishonour. He draws the audience into Bernarda's inner world by using the colour of the sets to represent her warped vision of colour and society, which is shaped by absence and sensory deprivation. Lorca highlights the disturbed nature of Bernarda's views on colour and society by offering Adela's chromatic desire as a disruptive, pleasurable counterpoint which is what lies beneath the façade of whiteness and respectability. The scarcity of colour and the dominance of whiteness in the play imbue colour with an eruptive and disruptive value for the audience when it does emerge, creating a greater affective impact and enhancing the theatrical possibilities of colour in Lorca's ideas of a theatre of poetry.

In Chapter Two I consider Lorca's aim of exposing the truth beneath the surface of his characters' daily lives as part of his theatre of poetry through a different lens: that of colour and corporeality. I begin by considering the trope of female bodily whiteness in *El maleficio*, *Mariana Pineda*, *Don Perlimplín*, and *Bodas de sangre* as a parallel to the façade of whiteness in the settings of *Bernarda Alba*. Like the superficial whiteness of Bernarda's world, the symbolic values of these white bodies give way to a more equivocal portrayal, especially in the contrast Lorca creates between the Bride's 'whiteness' and portrayals of her olive skin and bloodied clothes and hair in *Bodas de sangre*. A metaphorical discourse of bodily wounding in the dialogue of female characters, including the Bride and the Mother in *Bodas de sangre* and Yerma in *Yerma*, and the associated implicit colours of flesh, bruises, blushing, teeth, burns, sores, urine, rotting, and blood, offers insight into their inner emotional states. In contrast to the discourse of wounding in the female characters' dialogue, the suffering of the male characters in these plays is explored through a physical assault on the body and a 'literal' piercing of flesh. Whilst colour may appear to be a subsidiary focus in these portrayals, the motif of spilled blood and its implicit redness is central to this penetration of the male body and is invested with kinaesthetic as well as intersensory values. These bloody deaths shed light on the subjectivities of male characters and comprise an equally powerful critique of the effects of male gender roles. My discussion of the 'piercing' effect of the stabbing of the male body and the motif of blood leads me to consider the equally startling impact of anti-mimetic bodily colour and costumes in *El público* and in *Así que pasen*. The combined effect of these portrayals of bodily colour and inner truths in Lorca's theatre of poetry is a call for a more equivocal understanding of the body, a queering through material colour, and is a powerful critique of the effects of the social constructs of gender.

Chapter Three builds further on the role that colour plays in Lorca's exposure of the inner reality of his characters and the importance of implicit colour in his theatre of poetry. I explore how Lorca continues to 'make poetry flesh' through an analysis of object colour in his staging, in terms of props, sets, lighting, and costume. I consider how Rosita embodies the motif of the mutable rose in *Doña Rosita*, problematizing the role of the colours of her costumes in this visual and verbal alignment and considering the role of 'the language of flowers' indicated in the title in communicating Rosita's inner reality. My discussion of the corporeal and sensory dimension of Rosita's portrayal and the importance of material colour in her costume leads me to consider the role of the implicitly yellow quince motif in Act One of *Mariana Pineda* in terms of theatre of poetry and the ways in which Lorca reflects the central *estampa* aesthetic in the colours of the sets, the lighting, and Mariana's costumes. In *Don Perlimplín*, Lorca uses the green frock coat, the golden antlers, the red velvet cape, and the implicitly green emerald dagger to represent Perlimplín's transformation from a stock character to a protagonist of bones-and-blood in visual terms. Costume colour is also important in *La zapatera*, especially in Lorca's elevation of the Shoemaker's Wife from a stock character to a protagonist of 'bones-and-blood'. Throughout Lorca's theatre colour acts as an intermediary between the verbal and visual aspects of the works and empowers his experiments with bringing poetry from the page to the stage.

Notes to the Introduction

1. Throughout this study the dates of works indicate when they were written, as the publication and/or performance of many of Lorca's works was sometimes delayed significantly.
2. See Gwynne Edwards, *The Theatre Beneath the Sand* (London: Boyars, 1980).
3. Derek Harris, 'Green Death: An Analysis of the Symbolism of the Colour Green in Lorca's Poetry', in *Readings in Spanish and Portuguese Poetry for Geoffrey Connell*, ed. by Nicholas Round and D. Gareth Walters (Glasgow: University of Glasgow Department of Hispanic Studies, 1985), pp. 80–97 (p. 93).
4. Harris, p. 94.
5. 'Lorca', *In Our Time*, BBC Radio 4, 4 July 2019.
6. Robert Havard, 'The Symbolic Ambivalence of "Green" in García Lorca and Dylan Thomas', *Modern Language Review*, 67 (1972), 810–19.
7. Nelson R. Orringer, 'Absence of Color: Its Erotic Connotations in the *Diván del Tamarit*', *García Lorca Review*, 3.1–2 (1975), 57–66 (p. 63). 'Divan' is a type of Arabic verse form whilst 'Tamarit' refers to the Huerta del Tamarit in Granada, Lorca's uncle's country house.
8. Ryan Prout, 'Greenery Blues: Synaesthesia, Landscape and Lorca's Lassitude in Vermont', *Bulletin of Hispanic Studies*, 77.3 (2000), 393–411.
9. Prout, p. 407.
10. Emilio Peral Vega, *Pierrot/Lorca: White Carnival of Black Desire* (Woodbridge: Tamesis, 2015), p. 3 and p. 140. See also Sarah Wright's discussion of the clown and harlequin figures in *Así que pasen cino años* in *The Trickster Function in the Theatre of Federico García Lorca* (Woodbridge: Tamesis, 2000), pp. 92–94.
11. Whilst Lorca's poetry collection *Romancero gitano* has often been translated as *Gypsy Ballads*, 'Roma' is the politically correct term. For example, see Federico García Lorca, *Gypsy Ballads*, trans. by Robert Havard (Liverpool University Press: Liverpool, 1990) and Federico García Lorca, *Gypsy Ballads*, trans. by Jane Duran and Gloria García Lorca (Enitharmon Press: London, 2011).
12. María del Carmen Hernández Valcárcel, 'Federico García Lorca', in *La expresión sensorial en cinco poetas del 27* (Murcia: Universidad de Murcia, 1978), pp. 197–248 (p. 234).
13. Veronica Dean-Thacker and Pedro Guerrero Ruíz, *Federico García Lorca: El color de la poesía* (Murcia: Universidad de Murcia, 1998), p. 17.
14. See Paul Julian Smith, *The Theatre of García Lorca: Text, Performance, Psychoanalysis* (Cambridge: Cambridge University Press, 1998); Wright, *The Trickster Function*; and Paul McDermid, *Love, Desire and Identity in the Theatre of Federico García Lorca* (Woodbridge: Tamesis, 2007).
15. See Federico García Lorca, *Palabra de Lorca: Declaraciones y entrevistas completas* [Lorca's Word: Complete Declarations and Interviews], ed. by Rafael Inglada (Barcelona: Ediciones Malpaso, 2017), p. 129, p. 339, and p. 349.
16. In an interview in 1936, Lorca revealed that 'la concebí en el año 1924 [...] se me apareció terminada, única, imposible de reformar' [I thought up the play in 1924 [...] It came to me finished, unique, impossible to change], (*Prosa 1*, p. 731).
17. *Prosa 1*, p. 731.
18. 'Lorca', *In Our Time*, BBC Radio 4, 4 July 2019.
19. *Prosa 1*, p. 678.
20. *Prosa 1*, p. 630. Lorca's use of 'poeta' to refer to his role as dramatist is reflective of the Spanish Golden Age tradition of referring to the playwright as 'poeta' in contrast to the 'autor de comedias' [author of plays] who had more of a business manager role. This term also draws our attention to the subordination of authorial creation to commercial interests, as well as pointing to his concept of theatre of poetry.
21. Edwards, *Theatre Beneath the Sand*, p. 10.

22. Andrew Anderson observes how Lorca uses the prologue in *La zapatera* to draw attention to the theatrical nature of the piece and to stress that what we are seeing is not real life: 'Coming at the very beginning, the prologue is part of the play as a whole but not part of the main dramatic action: it is manifestly a framing device, used to introduce certain ideas and above all, given its intermediate and mediatory status, to emphasize strongly that all that is to follow is none other than theatre, fiction and make-believe', *García Lorca: La zapatera prodigiosa* (London: Grant and Cutler, 1991), p. 63. In her study, Wright explores the role of the prologue character as a trickster figure in *La zapatera*, puppet play *Retablillo de Don Cristóbal* [The Puppet Play of Don Cristóbal], and unfinished plays *Dragón* [Dragon] and *Comedia sin título* [Play without a Title]. She argues that the Author/Director/Poet 'is a trickster figure whose function is to open a dramatic dialogue with the audience, and [...] to lead them into the liminal space which is theatre'. The 'cape of stars' which the Author wears in the prologue of *La zapatera* invests him with the qualities of a magician, he is 'at once powerful creator of images and mere showman' and sets up 'the dichotomy between false illusion and magic power' which also pervades theatre, (*The Trickster Function*, p. 13 and p.17). When Lorca played the role of the Author in the premiere, he wore a long cape covered in stars which, along with the top hat, described in the same directions, that emits green light and a jet of water, enhances his magician-like appearance. In an interview in 1930, Lorca stated 'El prólogo lo digo yo... Esto es cosa mía... Debo compartir la zozobra del estreno como autor y como actor... Con una gran capa llena de estrellas...' [I deliver the prologue... That's mine... I should share the anxiety of the premiere as the author and an actor... With a long cape of stars...] (*Prosa 1*, p. 497).
23. *Prosa 1*, p. 429.
24. Federico García Lorca, *Prosa 2*, in *Obras Completas VII*, ed. by Miguel García-Posada (Madrid: Ediciones Akal, 2008), p. 1090.
25. *Prosa 1*, p. 575.
26. For a discussion of Lorca's work with La Barraca see Suzanne Wade Byrd, *García Lorca: "La Barraca" and the Spanish National Theater* (New York: Abrad Ediciones, 1975). Benjamín Palencia, Santiago Ontañón, and José Caballero designed the sets. Lorca would later work with Ontañón and Caballero on the designs for his own plays. Lorca was also an avid supporter of El Club Teatral Anfistora, originally El Club Teatral de Cultura, an experimental theatre group founded by Pura Ucelay, María Martínez Sierra, and María Rodrigo as part of a feminine cultural club Asociación de Cultura Cívica. When he was asked about the club's mission after their joint staging of *La zapatera* and *Don Perlimplín* in 1933, Lorca responded 'hacer arte. Pero arte al alcance de todo el mundo' [to make art. But art which is accessible for everybody]. *Prosa 1*, p. 530.
27. *Prosa 1*, p. 570.
28. 'Lorca', *In Our Time*, BBC Radio 4, 4 July 2019.
29. *Prosa 1*, p. 719.
30. *Prosa 1*, p. 719. Lorca described his play *Mariana Pineda* in similar terms in a 1927 interview, which suggests that these two 'levels' were an integral part of his theatre throughout his career: 'Hay en ella dos planos: uno amplio, sintético, por el que puede deslizarse con facilidad la atención de la gente. Al segundo — el doble fondo — solo llegará una parte del público', (*Prosa 1*, p. 487). [In *Mariana Pineda*] there are two levels: one which is broad, synthetic, which can easily capture people's attention. The second level — the false bottom — will only reach part of the audience.]
31. Anderson, *García Lorca: La zapatera prodigiosa*, p. 86.
32. *Prosa 1*, p. 428 and p. 595.
33. *Prosa 1*, p. 730
34. *Prosa 1*, p. 730.
35. *Prosa 1*, p. 535.
36. *Prosa 1*, p. 535. Reviewers writing for *ABC* criticised this scene, suggesting that 'el tercer acto es inferior a los otros por llevarse a la exageración el recurso del símbolo poético', [the third act is inferior to the others for its exaggerated use of the poetic symbol], 'Beatriz: *Bodas de sangre*', *ABC*, 9 March 1933, p. 43. However, Lorca defended his choice in an interview in October

1933: 'Algún burgués la acusaba de ser una obra fuera de la realidad. Yo podía decirle: "Usted, señor, se va a morir y saldrá con las manos cruzadas sobre el pecho en un ataúd. Y también estará fuera de la realidad. Ésa es la realidad"', [Some bourgeois man accused it of being a work outside of reality. I could say to him: "You, sir, are going to die and you will be carried out in a coffin with your arms crossed over your chest. And that too will be outside of reality. That is reality"'], (*Prosa 1*, p. 570). According to Lorca biographer Leslie Stainton, Lorca also 'resisted pressure from the play's director to eliminate the character of the Moon from the text' in at least one subsequent production, *Lorca: A Dream of Life* (New York: Farrar, Straus and Giroux, 1999), Kindle e, loc. 6051.

37. Anderson, *García Lorca: La zapatera prodigiosa*, pp. 101–02.

38. Paul McDermid defines the *aleluya* as 'a type of popular cartoon strip, principally enjoyed by, though not aimed at, children, and often sold at fairs or markets. Originating in the in the eighteenth century as paper prints of holy images, the *aleluya* developed into a cartoon strip, occasionally recounting the lives of saints, but more often depicting popular stories with a range of standard heroes. The figure of Don Perlimplín as a protagonist in these cartoons first emerged in the mid-nineteenth century', *Love, Desire and Identity in the Theatre of Federico García Lorca* (Woodbridge: Tamesis, 2007), pp. 69–70. See also Margarita Ucelay, 'Introducción', in Federico García Lorca, *Amor de Don Perlimplín con Belisa en su jardín*, ed. by Margarita Ucelay, 9th edn (Madrid: Ediciones Cátedra, 2010), pp. 9–232 (pp. 13–17).

39. Francis Fergusson, '*Don Perlimplín*: Lorca's Theatre-Poetry', *The Kenyon Review*, 17.3 (1955), 337–48 (p. 342).

40. Michael Thompson, 'Poetry that Gets up off the Page and Becomes Human: Poetic Coherence and Eccentricity in Lorca's Theatre', in *Fire, Blood and the Alphabet: One Hundred Years of Lorca*, ed. by Sebastian Doggart and Michael Thompson (Manchester: Manchester University Press, 2010), pp. 67–79 (p. 79).

41. The dictionary of the Real Academia Española defines an *estampa* as '[una] reproducción de un dibujo, pintura, fotografía, etc., trasladada al papel o a otra materia, por medio del tórculo o prensa, desde la lámina de metal o madera en que está grabada, o desde la piedra litográfica en que está dibujado [a reproduction of a drawing, painting, photograph, etc;, transferred onto paper or another material, via a press, from the sheet of metal or wood which it is etched on, of the lithograph stone it is drawn on].

42. Thompson, p. 70.

43. Sumner M. Greenfield, 'Lorca's Theatre: A Synthetic Re-examination', *Journal of Spanish Studies: Twentieth Century*, 5 (1977), 31–46 (p. 44).

44. Sumner M. Greenfield, 'The Problem of *Mariana Pineda*', *The Massachusetts Review*, 1.4 (1960), 751–63 (p. 753).

45. See Gwynne Edwards, *Dramatists in Perspective: Spanish Theatre in the Twentieth Century* (Cardiff: University of Wales Press, 1985).

46. McDermid, p. 74.

47. See Luis Fernández Cifuentes, *García Lorca en el teatro: La norma y la diferencia* [García Lorca in the Theatre: Norm and Difference] (Zaragoza: Universidad de Zaragoza, 1986) and Dru Dougherty and María Francisca Vilches de Frutos (eds), *El Teatro en España: Entre la tradición y la vanguardia, 1918–1939* [Theatre in Spain: Between Tradition and the Avant-Garde, 1918–1939] (Madrid: Consejo Superior de Investigaciones Científicas, Fundación Federico García Lorca, and Tabacalera, 1992). It was this blending of the folkloric and the avant-garde which led Lorca's close friends Buñuel and Dalí to view Lorca's work disparagingly, particularly his poetry collection *Romancero gitano*. Dalí described this collection as 'too local, too anecdotal, too tied up in the lyrical norms of the past'. Similarly, Buñuel suggested that *Romancero gitano* had 'the finesse and apparent modernity which any poetry needs nowadays [...] But between this and [...] the genuine, exquisite and great poets of today there is a deep gulf'. Cited in Ian Gibson, *Federico Garcia Lorca: A Life* (London: Faber and Faber, 1989), p. 216 and p. 220.

48. The unfinished work includes one complete Act of each of the plays *La destrucción de Sodoma* [The Destruction of Sodom], *Los sueños de mi prima Aurelia* [The Dreams of my Cousin Aurelia], and *Comedia sin título*, also known as *El sueño de la vida* [A Dream of Life].[48] We also have

fragments of the plays *Posada* [The Inn], *Diego Corrientes*, *Ampliación Fotográfica* [Photographic Enlargement], *Drama fotográfico* [Photographic Drama], *Rosa mudable* [Mutable Rose], *La bola negra* [The Black Ball], *Casa de maternidad* [House of Maternity], and *Dragón*. See Marie Laffranque, *Teatro inconcluso: Fragmentos y proyectos inacabados* [Unfinished Theatre: Incomplete Fragments and Projects] (Granada: Universidad de Granada, 1987). The two unwritten Acts of *Comedia sin título* were re-imagined by Alberto Conejero in 2018. See Federico García Lorca, *Comedia sin título, seguida de "El sueño de la vida" de Alberto Conejero* [Play without a Title, followed by 'A Dream of Life' by Alberto Conejero], ed. by Emilio Peral Vega (Madrid: Ediciones Cátedra, 2018). Lorca's 'juvenilia' included the plays *Cristo*, *Jehová* [Jehovah], *Místicas* [Mystics], *Sombras* [Shadows], and *La viudita que se quería casar* [The Little Widow Who Wanted to Wed]. See Wright, 'Theatre', in *A Companion to Federico García Lorca*, ed. by Federico Bonaddio (Woodbridge: Tamesis, 2010), pp. 39–62 (p. 41).

49. Stainton, loc. 1140. Lorca remained involved with the Residencia until his death in 1936. In June–July 2017 the Residencia held an exhibition about Lorca's time there entitled 'A Room of One's Own. Federico García Lorca in the Residencia de Estudiantes, 1919–1936', which was also displayed at the Federico García Lorca Centre in Granada in March–July 2018. The Community of Madrid celebrated the centenary of Lorca's arrival in 2019 with the Congreso Internacional Federico García Lorca: A Hundred Years in Madrid (1919–2019) from 18–23 February in collaboration with the Museo Reina Sofía. The conference encompassed Lorca's art and music as well as his theatre and poetry and key speakers included Lorca academics Emilio Peral Vega, María Francisca Vilches de Frutos, and Jonathan Mayhew. Peral Vega was heavily involved in the centenary celebrations, also taking part in a round table discussion on Lorca during the Madrid Libraries Fair on 10 June. See Emilio Peral Vega (ed.) *Federico García Lorca: 100 años en Madrid* (Madrid: Comunidad de Madrid and Consejería de Cultura, Turismo y Deportes, 2019).

50. Lorca's relationships with Dalí and Buñuel have been well-documented. See for example Manuel Delgado Morales and A. J. Proust, (eds), *Lorca, Buñuel, Dalí: Art and Theory* (London: Associated University Presses, 2001) and Gwynne Edwards, *Lorca, Buñuel, Dalí: Forbidden Pleasures and Connected Lives* (London: I. B. Tauris, 2009).

51. See C. Christopher Soufas Jr., *The Subject in Question: Early Contemporary Spanish Literature and Modernism* (Washington, D.C.: Catholic University of America Press, 2007), pp. 19–50.

52. 'Lorca', *In Our Time*, BBC Radio 4, 4 July 2019.

53. Prosa 1, p. 276 and Gibson, p. 209.

54. Gibson, p. 209. Gibson has also commented on the influence of *Orphée* on *El público* whilst Leslie Stainton suggests that *Así que pasen* is influenced by Cocteau's, Pirandello's, and Dalí's conceptions of time, Gibson, pp. 294–95, and Stainton, loc. 5385–5392.

55. Nelson Cerqueira, 'Poetic Language in the Plays of Lorca and Cocteau', *Chiricú*, 3.2 (1983), 20–38 (p. 21).

56. Cerqueira, p. 21.

57. Laura Doyle Gates, 'Jean Cocteau and 'la poésie du théâtre', *Romance Quarterly*, 35:4 (1988), 435–41 (p. 435).

58. Doyle Gates, p. 435.

59. Jean Cocteau, *Théâtre 1* (Paris: Grasset, 1957), p. 5. My emphasis.

60. Annette Shandler-Levitt, 'Jean Cocteau's Theatre: Idea and Enactment', *Theatre Journal*, 45.3 (1993), 363–72 (p. 364).

61. Shandler-Levitt, pp. 364–65.

62. Doyle Gates, pp. 435–36.

63. Doyle Gates, p. 438.

64. Doyle Gates, p. 437.

65. Thompson, p. 74.

❖

CHAPTER 1

Psychological Colour: Chromophobia and *La casa de Bernarda Alba*

In *Bernarda Alba*, Lorca uses material colour to reflect abstract emotions and key themes in visual form and to explore the inner realities and mental states of his characters in his 'theatre of poetry'. *Bernarda Alba* is often considered to be a starkly realistic play devoid of Lorca's usual imagery and lyricism. For example, Gwynne Edwards argues that in this play Lorca 'eliminated the poetic elements, notably the use of verse at given moments, which distinguish both [*Bodas de sangre* and *Yerma*]', thus 'mark[ing] a new direction in [his] theatre'.[1] However, the play is not a move away from Lorca's theatre of poetry but comprises an important exploration of the materialization of poetry on stage through colour. As Sumner M. Greenfield observes, the supposed realism of the play is 'interwoven with images, symbols, and stylizations which form the poetic restatement of the dramatic action'.[2] Colour is at the very heart of Lorca's conception of *Bernarda Alba* and is the sole focus of this chapter as it is the most explicit and sustained example of the importance of material colour in Lorca's theatre of poetry. The 'poetic core' of the play, which guides all elements of the staging and is interlaced through the dialogue, is inspired by a photographic documentary, as Lorca indicates in the character list. Although this aesthetic suggests a black-and-white colour scheme, which is reflected throughout the play in the contrast of the women's black costumes and the bold white set, it is whiteness that comprises the most dominant visual image. Whilst Lorca had explored the motif of whiteness to some extent in previous plays including *El maleficio*, *Mariana Pineda*, *Don Perlimplín*, and *Bodas de sangre*, as I will argue in Chapter Two, in *Bernarda Alba* white becomes not only the central motif of the play but also a powerful psychological and material force.

The dominance of material whiteness is emphasised in the stage directions at the beginning of each Act: the walls are described as '*blanquísima[s]*' (p. 308, Act One); '*blanca[s]*', (p. 342, Act Two); and '*blancas ligeramente azuladas*' (p. 378, Act Three) respectively.[3] The house begins as 'extremely white', using the superlative, then becomes merely 'white', then finally it is 'a lightly *blued* white' (my emphasis), which suggests both the lessening of the intensity of whiteness and the gradual intrusion of processes of colour. The importance of whiteness is also indicated in the title, as Bernarda's family name 'alba' means white, in poetic usage, from the Latin 'albus'. The title implies that the (white) house is a central concern of the work, perhaps even a protagonist with equal standing to Bernarda. Edwards suggests that the two central components of the play are the whiteness of the walls and the three increasingly interior locations.[4] The setting is stark and minimal, and the stage empty as the curtain rises. In contrast, there are occasional intrusions of hued colour in the play in both the dialogue and the material staging — such as Adela's red-and-green fan and her green dress, and the blue tint of the white walls in Act Three — which create a dialectic of whiteness and hued colour that captures the opposing forces of Bernarda and her family in physical form.

Much of the existing critical discussion of colour in *Bernarda Alba* focuses solely on the symbolic recuperations of whiteness rather than its psychological potency. In his reading of the play, Henryk Ziomek explores whiteness as indicative of sterility, of the numbing or suppression of emotions, and of purity.[5] Whilst Edwards's analysis is more fruitful, as it acknowledges the importance of material colour and the extension of the core poetic themes to other elements of the staging, he suggests that the white sets have a 'stark, simplified, symbolic character' that reflects the monotony of the women's lives, rather than seeing this whiteness as having any active, affective purpose.[6] Greenfield recognises the role of whiteness in Lorca's theatre of poetry in this play, yet he too fails to invest the material colour dynamic with any agency. Again, the walls are a passive surface, 'little more than a visual prop' for the scenic and poetic expression of the play and 'a symbol of the protagonist'.[7] Bernarda's symbolic imbrication of whiteness and honour, and of colour and dishonour, is an important starting point. However, Lorca also uses this ascetic whiteness to reflect Bernarda's disturbed and unstable state of mind. In turn, it is the affective power and vulnerable nature of whiteness that exacerbates Bernarda's paranoia, causing her to react to hued colour in ways that are indicative of a 'fear and loathing' of colour or 'chromophobia', which the artist David Batchelor explores in his study of the long history of the subordination of colour.[8] This extreme, abnormal state of whiteness incites anxiety in other characters, Adela for example, due to its connotations of imprisonment and death. In contrast, Adela's desperation for personal and sexual freedom is sparked by and reflected in her desire for colour, a chromatic desire which has Barthesian 'blissful' qualities due to its erotic, explosive values and the stimulating impact that these rare intrusions of visual colour have on the audience. Rather than purely symbolic phenomena or passive surfaces, both whiteness and hued colour are a powerful psychological force which have a marked effect on the characters and on the audience in Lorca's theatre of poetry.

Symbolic readings have shown us how Bernarda's privileging of white in *Bernarda Alba* is based on its associations of purity and innocence. In his study of 'white' people's representation of themselves in Western visual culture, Richard Dyer comments on the conflation of whiteness with 'purity, spirituality, transcendence, cleanliness, virtue, simplicity, chastity'.[9] I challenge this imbrication of symbolic and material portrayals of whiteness in my discussion of female bodily whiteness in Chapter Two. Dyer tells us that white as 'the colour of virtue' was 'by no means securely in place before the Renaissance, but since then it has become so commonplace as to be presented as inevitable, universal and natural'.[10] For Bernarda, white becomes the moral and aesthetic corollary of her obsession with the Spanish concept of honour and ideas of public reputation, as explored in the Spanish Golden Age honour play.[11] Edwards notes that whilst honour is an important theme in Lorca's other plays, especially *La zapatera*, *Bodas de sangre*, and *Yerma*, *Bernarda Alba* 'has honour in its sense of name, reputation and public image at the very centre of its tragic conflict'.[12] As part of his theatre of poetry, Lorca continually reflects the key themes of the play in the material staging, projecting Bernarda's fixation on honour and on the creation of a façade of social appearances onto the material whiteness of the house. In Act Three Bernarda tells Angustias that 'yo no me meto en los corazones, pero quiero buena fachada y armonía familiar' (p. 384) [I don't meddle inside hearts but I want a good façade and family harmony], which highlights her obsession with outward appearances and the central role of the house within this construct.[13] In the final scene of the play Bernarda's use of the imperfect subjunctive further demonstrates how the external façade of whiteness is valued above deeper reality: 'llevadla a su cuarto y vestirla *como si fuera* doncella' (Bernarda regarding Adela, p. 403, my emphasis) [take her to her room and dress her *as if she were* a virgin]. The emphasis on the outward appearance of Bernarda's household rather than the domestic reality within reflects the Spanish honour code. As Greenfield emphasises, 'if the dishonorable act does not become known abroad, it ceases to be dishonor'.[14]

The motif of whitewashing, which is both literal and figurative, enhances the ideas of concealment and outward appearances introduced by 'fachada'. The white façade belies the events inside the house; as Greenfield argues, it is a 'spotless coating of whitewash applied expressly to conceal whatever stains may lie in the substance beneath'.[15] It is a 'shell', an 'outer frame glistening virginally for all to see'.[16] María Delgado agrees, suggesting that 'Bernarda demands a whitewashing of all that is undesirable; her house an immaculate image of antiseptic sterility'.[17] Through the motif of cleansing, embodied in both the dramatic action and the dialogue, Lorca reveals both the importance and the strain of maintaining this clinical white façade and communicates the poetic concerns of the work through the actions of the characters. What Edwards sees as 'frenzied cleaning' is one of the first dramatic actions of the play — 'limpia bien todo. Si no ve relucientes las cosas me arrancará los pocos pelos que me quedan' (Poncia, p. 309) [clean everything properly, if she doesn't see things gleaming she'll pull out the few hairs I've got left] — and continues to be a central preoccupation throughout — 'tú empieza a blanquear el patio' (Bernarda, p. 326) [you — start whitewashing the patio].[18] For Bernarda, material cleanliness, decency, and social standing are inter-dependent: 'Ella, la más aseada; ella, la más decente; ella, la más alta' (Poncia, p. 310) [she, the cleanest and tidiest; she, the most decent; she, the most high and mighty]. Lorca's repeated use of the superlative with each adjective reveals Bernarda's extreme expectations of herself and others, and the level of cleanliness and whiteness she demands of her material environment.[19]

Bernarda's obsession with maintaining the white façade is shown to be a source of great mental and physical strain as Lorca explores the vulnerability of the front which she presents to the world and begins to burrow beneath the surface, exposing the growing tensions and burning desires within Bernarda's household through the material colours of the staging. In his 1925 essay 'A Coat of Whitewash: The Law of Ripolin', the architect Le Corbusier ironically reflects on the tyranny of the white surface and its 'moral' authority:

> Imagine the results of the Law of Ripolin. Every citizen is required to replace his hangings, his damasks, his wallpapers, his stencils, with a plain coat of white Ripolin. His home is made clean. There are no more dirty, dark corners. Everything is shown as it is [...] Once you have put Ripolin on your walls you will be master of yourself [...] If the house is all white, the outline of things stands out from it without any possibility of mistake; their volume shows clearly; their colour is distinct. The white of whitewash is absolute, everything stands out from it and is recorded absolutely, black on white, it is honest and dependable [...] Whitewash is extremely moral.[20]

Le Corbusier's essay probes the affective power of material whiteness in interior spaces and the medium of architecture. This brings to mind the dramatic significance of the physical white house in *Bernarda Alba*. He also reveals the power of whiteness as an unforgiving background or screen that will accentuate any dirt or stain. In *Bernarda Alba*, the material whiteness of the house becomes an unstable and exacting environment, demanding repeated actions of re-whitening which reflect Bernarda's fear of gossip and her paranoia in visual form. Poncia and the maid are continually trying, and failing, to keep the house as white as Bernarda desires. When Poncia complains that the glass is marked, the Maid replies that: 'Ni con el jabón ni con bayeta se le quitan' (p. 312) [I can't get [the marks] off even with soap and a cloth]. Greenfield suggests that the white façade is shown to be 'a superficial veneer of perfection,' a thin and delicate coating which is vulnerable to the staining qualities of life and colour.[21] Bernarda has chosen an exacting material environment as the external representation of her household's honour. However, Bernarda is unable to keep up with the demands of that white surface and instead the exacting whitescape exacerbates her paranoia and fixation on honour.

Lorca reveals whiteness to be a paradoxical force. White is both a tyrannical power which demands constant activity to maintain it and an extremely vulnerable surface, as any hint of hued colour will dirty it. Due to Bernarda's correlation of honour and whiteness, and of colour and dishonour, any instances of hued colour become charged with dramatic importance and psychological power due to the threat they pose to the whitescape. The association of colour with corruption is an historic one, which can be traced back to the *disegno* versus *colore* debate, the Aristotelian opposition between line and colour where colour is considered feminine, foreign, 'primitive', and ornamental.[22] Batchelor suggests that colour is either viewed as 'alien' and 'dangerous' or 'perceived merely as a secondary quality of experience, and thus unworthy of serious consideration'.[23] In his analysis of the work of French critic and colour theorist Charles Blanc, who published *The Grammar of Painting* in 1867, Batchelor notes that Blanc saw colour as constituting 'the mythic savage state' which mankind has lifted itself from; colour constitutes an Eve-like fall from grace. For Blanc, 'colour could not be ignored and dismissed [...] It had to be contained and subordinated'.[24] Batchelor suggests that this prejudice against and loathing of colour 'masks a fear': 'a fear of contamination and corruption by something that is unknown or unknowable' which manifests itself in the form of 'chromophobia'.[25] Bernarda's bodily, exaggerated reactions to intrusions of colour — such as Adela's red-and-green fan — speak of a complex psychological relationship with colour which exceeds purely symbolic readings. Bernarda's chromophobia is revealed when she is confronted by visual colour, such as her reaction to Adela's red-and-green fan in Act One:

> BERNARDA   [...] Niña, dame un abanico.
> ADELA   Tome usted. (*Le da un abanico redondo con flores rojas y verdes*)
> BERNARDA (*Arrojando el abanico al suelo*)   ¿Es éste el abanico que se da a una viuda? Dame uno negro y aprende a respetar el luto de tu padre. (p. 319)

> [BERNARDA   [...] Girl, give me the fan.
> ADELA   Here. (*She gives her a round fan with red and green flowers.*)
> BERNARDA (*Hurling the fan to the floor.*)   Is this the kind of fan you give a widow? Give me a black one and learn to respect the mourning period for your father.]

Although the rejection of a coloured fan during mourning could be seen as culturally appropriate, there are several factors which make this scene more equivocal and reflective of chromophobia. First, the violence of the gesture described in the stage directions belies Bernarda's measured verbal response. The use of the verb 'arrojar', to hurl, rather than something less violent like 'echar', reveals the extreme force of this reaction. Secondly, the fan is one of the rare examples of visual colour in the play, and one which is a central part of the dramatic action. Bernarda's chromophobia is revealed in similarly violent, bodily reactions throughout the play. For example, in Act One she scrubs the make-up from Angustias's face:

> ANGUSTIAS   Madre, déjeme usted salir.
> BERNARDA   ¿Salir? Después de que te hayas quitado esos polvos de la cara. ¡Suavona! ¡Yeyo! ¡Espejo de tus tías! (*Le quita violentamente con su pañuelo los polvos*) ¡Ahora vete! (p. 337)

> [ANGUSTIAS   Mother, let me go out.
> BERNARDA   Go out? After you have wiped that powder off your face. Wayward slut! Just like your aunts! (*She violently wipes the powder off her face with a handkerchief*) Now go!]

Here, Bernarda forcefully erases colour.[26] Bernarda's powerful physical reactions to colour, signs of her chromophobia, are even dominant when she is not on stage. In Act One Amelia warns Adela, who is wearing her green dress, '¡Si te ve nuestra madre te arrastra del pelo!' (p. 333) [If our mother sees you she'll drag you by your hair!].[27] Colour threatens Bernarda's authority and moral values, disrupting her controlling whitescape. Lorca uses this powerful rejection of colour to expose the inner turmoil and patent anxieties which lie beneath her dominance and tyranny.

Through his depiction of these chromophobic reactions and the abnormal nature of the whiteness, Lorca explores what lies beneath the façade and brings abstract emotions to the stage as part of his theatre of poetry. Emma Wilson's reading of material colour as 'the chromatic representation of a disturbance of the psychic subject' in Krzysztof Kieślowksi's 1993 film *Trois couleurs: Bleu* [Three Colours: Blue] suggests an approach for reading the whiteness of the setting and dialogue in *Bernarda Alba* as representative of Bernarda's inner world.[28] In *Bleu*, the protagonist Julie's trauma is revealed to us through blue light and classical orchestra and piano music. Wilson draws our attention particularly to the three swimming pool scenes as semiotic spaces which 'allow the viewer to question the imbrication of colour, trauma and denial'.[29] The idea of colour as a tool for portraying inner states in visual, ultra-linguistic terms is important for how colour and whiteness work in *Bernarda Alba* and also for our understanding of the highly visual nature of Lorca's colour-writing and his aim of bringing poetry from page to stage through a striking theatre of raw emotion. Despite the distinctiveness of these sources, the material colour scheme in *Bernarda Alba* can be seen as evocative of Bernarda's psychological state, as blue represents Julie's in *Bleu*. In her study, Wilson examines how the colour blue, particularly in the form of blue light, is used to convey Julie's grief and pain. Like Julie, Bernarda is suffering from a trauma which is reflected in colour. Yet blue in Kieślowksi's film is also used to communicate 'moments of near abstraction, interludes of sensory pleasure', and it disrupts Julie's disconnected state and brings her back to the world with a startling clash of blue light and music.[30] For example, when Julie is napping at the hospital she is woken by the music from her husband's and daughter's funeral. We see this scene through a filter of blue light. For Bernarda, however, the visual colour scheme represents a negative affective state and a sense of total disconnection because she fails to impose it and sustain it. *Bernarda Alba* does not portray a journey of healing and recovery like *Bleu*. Rather, it is the depiction of Bernarda's declining mental health which begins with the death of her husband and the confinement of her family for an eight-year mourning period at the beginning of the play, and ends in Adela's death after Bernarda's increasing oppression of her daughters fails and instead sparks an explosive, desperate desire for personal and sexual freedom. Bernarda's extreme values regarding honour and social appearances lead her to create a claustrophobic, unnatural environment that reflects her obsessive mental state in material form. Rather than 'a dehumanized human being', a 'puppet, Punch-like figure', and a 'one-dimensional character' as Edwards[31] and Virginia Higginbotham have suggested respectively, Bernarda's reactions to colour and whiteness in the play reveal her to be a complex character of bones-and-blood.[32] Within his theatre of poetry, Lorca communicates Bernarda's troubled inner landscape through the materiality of the staging and exposes the emotions and insecurities which lie beneath the glossy white façade.

Lorca also uses the material colours of the setting to communicate the frustration, desires, and suffering of Bernarda's daughters, especially passionate, young, and hopeful Adela who is the most significant counterpoint to Bernarda's tyranny. Whilst, for Bernarda, hued colour is the cause of fear and paranoia, white can also spark negative affective states and anxiety, revealing the equivocal power of whiteness and hued colour. It is only through death that Adela is reclaimed by whiteness, a death which she foresees but cannot escape: 'He visto la muerte debajo de estos techos' (p. 397) [I have seen death under this roof]. Dyer's exploration of the symbolic links between whiteness and death and the horror whiteness can provoke has implications for our understanding of how whiteness sparks anxiety in Adela.[33] Dyer suggests that 'to be really, absolutely white is to be nothing [...] to be nothing is to be dead'.[34] Dyer's idea of whiteness as a void is especially significant when we consider whiteness in *Bernarda Alba*, due to the shared root of 'blanco' and 'blank' in Castilian. In Act One, Adela reveals her fear of being absorbed into the whiteness of the house:

> ADELA (*Rompiendo a llorar con ira*) ¡No, no me acostumbraré! Yo no quiero estar encerrada. No quiero que se me pongan las carnes como a vosotras. ¡No quiero perder mi blancura en estas habitaciones! ¡Mañana me pondré mi vestido verde y me echaré a pasear por la calle! ¡Yo quiero salir! (p. 335)

> [ADELA: (*Bursting into tears of rage*) No, no I won't get used to it! I don't want to be locked up. I don't want my flesh to become like yours. I don't want to lose my whiteness in these rooms! Tomorrow I'll put on my green dress and I'll go for a walk down the street! I want to go out!]

Adela's reference to 'blancura' here creates a paradox because it indicates a contrast between her whiteness, on the one hand, and the skin of her sisters and the whiteness of the house on the other. Adela suggests that her sisters have already been absorbed by the white house and that they have become blank and sterile; they have lost their physicality and become literally hue white like the walls. Edwards comments on the 'faded quality' of the play's perpetual gloom, dull 'like the skin of the characters themselves [...] like one of those old pre-colour photographs'.[35] In contrast, Adela's skin is still luminous and vital. Her skin has a 'lustre' which conflicts with both 'the dull and uniform whiteness of the room' and the 'sallowness' of her sisters' skin.[36] These multiple evocations of material whiteness are indicative of the complex and labile values of colour in Lorca's theatre of poetry. Both Greenfield and Ziomek see a tension between sterility and fertility in these different forms of material whiteness. Ziomek argues that white is an important material reflection in Lorca's development of the 'abnegación emocional' [emotional self-sacrifice] of the Alba women which is juxtaposed with the 'significado sexual' [sexual meaning] of the stallion, the lamb, and Angustias's pearl engagement ring.[37] Greenfield suggests that these more natural images of whiteness — the huge white stallion and the sperm-like allusions to sea foam in María Josefa's speech in Act Three — represent more specifically 'an elemental masculine force' which threatens Bernarda's authority.[38] For Ziomek, Greenfield, and Edwards it is the antiseptic whiteness of negation and death which dominates. Greenfield notes that 'the whiteness of the house, the white of sterility,' ultimately triumphs 'over the white foam of life and productivity'.[39] Edwards agrees, observing that 'all that is creative is overwhelmed' by the blankness of the whitescape with its connotations of death and barrenness.[40] This house is the representation of what Batchelor, in his description of an artist's ascetic white house, calls a white which 'is not created by bleach but that itself is bleach [...]

This white was aggressively white. It did its work on everything around it and nothing escaped'.[41] Adela's fear of being absorbed by the whitescape turns out to be well-founded. Whilst Adela has enjoyed the passions of a physical relationship, the creative force of her body is negated by her suicide. A state of whiteness which is so extreme that either death or madness constitutes the only 'escape' is the ultimate proof that Bernarda has created a warped world within her walls.

Throughout the play Lorca creates an overwhelming sense of claustrophobia and imprisonment and extends the sensory deprivation of the whitescape and the core poetic image of whiteness to the lighting, or lack of light, moments of silence, and the intonation and patterns of the characters' speech.[42] Edwards suggests that *Bernarda Alba* is defined by a 'terrible sense of enclosure' from the beginning of the play, arguing that 'the room with its thick walls, its oppressive silence, and its depressing and inescapable uniformity of colour' is the 'physical symbol' of the many ways in which the characters are constrained, an oppressive environment which is also emphasised by the searing heat and by the sounds outside the house such as the tolling of bells.[43] In Act One, Bernarda tells her daughters that during their eight years of mourning 'no ha de entrar en esta casa el viento de la calle' [not a breath of air should enter the house from the street], demanding that they pretend that 'hemos tapiado con ladrillos puertas y ventanas' (p. 320) [we have bricked up the doors and windows]. Some of these instances are metaphorical, such as Bernarda's immurement of her family and her threat of chaining her daughters: 'tengo cinco cadenas para vosotras' (p. 366) [I have five chains for you]. However, the daughters' movements are also physically limited to the house and grounds, the windows are barred, and during the wake María Josefa is locked in her room and gagged by the Maid: 'me ha costado mucho trabajo sujetarla [...] Tuve durante el duelo que taparle varias veces la boca con un costal vacío' (p. 321) [it was a real struggle to restrain her [...] I had to stuff an empty sack in her mouth several times during the wake]. The sense of imprisonment is compounded by cries for release throughout Act One: '¡Yo quiero salir!' (Adela, p. 335) [I want to go out!], 'Madre, déjeme usted salir' (Angustias, p. 337) [Mother, let me go out], '¡Déjame salir, Bernarda!' (María Josefa, p. 339) [Let me out, Bernarda!]. This is not a house or a home, it is a domestic prison. In his 1986 article 'The Austere Abode', C. B. Morris argues that Bernarda's 'casa' is a perversion of the saccharine 'hogar' extolled in the Granada press of the early 1900s.[44] He notes that the house is referred to by the characters through a range of negative metaphors, such as, 'infierno' [hell] (Angustias, p. 343), 'convento' [convent], 'casa de guerra' [house of war] (Poncia, p. 355 and p. 392), and 'presidio' [prison] (Adela, p. 401).[45] In conversation with friend Carlos Morla Lynch in 1936, Lorca described the home on which the play was based as 'un infierno mudo y frio en ese sol africano, sepultura de gente viva bajo la férula inflexible de cancerbero oscuro' ['a mute, cold hell beneath that African sun, a tomb of living people under the inflexible rule of a dark Cerberus].[46]

This is a hell where the sun cannot reach. In Act One, Magdalena laments: 'sé que yo no me voy a casar. Prefiero llevar sacos al molino. Todo menos estar sentada días y días dentro de esta sala oscura' (p. 320) [I know I'm not going to get married.

I would rather haul sacks at the mill. Anything rather than sitting here day after day in this dark room]. The gloom of Bernarda's house and the interplay between light and darkness mimics Bernarda's black-and-white thinking: there are no grey areas. There is also a lack of shadow in the play, reminiscent of the white room in the final scene of *Bodas de sangre*: '*No habrá ni un gris, ni una sombra, ni siquiera lo preciso para la perspectiva*' (p. 402) [there will not be a single grey or shadow, not even what is needed for perspective].[47] This image is echoed in Act Three of *Bernarda Alba*: '*El decorado ha de ser de una perfecta simplicidad*' (p. 378) [the decor must be perfectly simple]. Whilst light would have emphasised the whiteness of the walls, Lorca has chosen to set the house in a pervasive gloom, adding to the sensory deprivation of the characters that is shared with the audience. As Edwards notes, when light and colour do break through, they are momentary and emphasise the women's imprisonment:

> These splashes of light and colour, conjur[e] up a different kind of world. [...] The effect of the light that suddenly floods in as a door is opened and is then gone again is, like those other splashes of colour, not only to suggest a different world outside the house, but, by so doing, to heighten the impression of the total isolation of Bernarda's household from that world.[48]

These brief surges of light and colour highlight the extreme environment of Bernarda's house by providing a marked contrast between the gloom and relentless whiteness of the house and the bright and vibrant world outside. The absence of stage directions regarding lighting is highly unusual and contrasts with Lorca's other plays such as *Mariana Pineda*, which I discuss in Chapter Three, where coloured light is a central device. By excluding colour from the lighting, Lorca extends the monotony and uniformity of material colour in the play to other aspects of the staging, using the pervasive gloom to reflect the characters' inner despair in physical form as part of his theatre of poetry. In Act Two there is a rare instance when light breaks through: '*Todas oyen en un silencio traspasado por el sol*' (p. 357) [they all listen in a silence pierced by sunlight].[49] This scene captures the suffering of the women as they remain trapped in the whitescape and excluded from the world of light and colour outside. This glimpse of the outside world only causes them to imagine a life they cannot have: '*Martirio queda sentada en la silla baja con la cabeza entre las manos*' (p. 358) [Martirio sits in the low chair with her head in her hands]. As the characters suffer and wither in the ascetic house the play grows gradually darker until Act Three, which is set at night. Lighting is referenced in the stage directions in the final act but only to indicate a lack — '*Las puertas, iluminadas por la luz de los interiores, dan un tenue fulgor a la escena. En el centro, una mesa con un quinqué*' (p. 378) [the doorways, illuminated by the light from the inside rooms, give the scene a soft glow. In the centre, a table with an oil lamp] — and grows still scarcer when Poncia and the Maid leave the room, taking the lamp — '*La escena queda casi a oscuras*' (p. 394) [the scene is left in almost total darkness]. Rather than merely symbolic connotations — darkness representing the characters' movement 'towards their tragic fate' as Edwards argues, for example — the effect adds to the sense of increasing claustrophobia and reinforces the idea of the house as a domestic prison.[50] What becomes clear from the sequestering of the household and the extreme white–colour dichotomy is that the material setting is the sensory and visual representation of a deeply troubled psyche.

As well as reflecting the restrictive environment of the white house in the lighting, Lorca extends this occlusion of colour to the suppression of speech in the play. White is not just a representation of psychological values in *Bernarda Alba*; it is also an important material force and takes on acoustic values, forming part of Lorca's appeal to the audience's senses and of his move towards a more interactive and demanding theatrical practice in his theatre of poetry. In his probing of white in modern French poetry and art, Eric Robertson finds what he calls a 'conflation of visual and auditory sensation' and a paralleling of whiteness and silence.[51] For example, Robertson sees Stéphane Mallarmé's poem 'Un coup de dés jamais n'abolira le hasard' (1897) [A Roll of the Dice Will Never Abolish Chance] as blending visual and auditory values in the references to music in the preface and also in 'the intersensory analogy that Mallarmé establishes between colour and auditory effects — in this case white and crystalline silence'.[52] The auditory possibilities of whiteness are also a key part of Robertson's exploration of the paintings of Simon Hantaï, whose method of folding and tying his canvases resists the paint in certain places and produces leaf-like white patterns on a bold, coloured background. Significantly, Hantaï sees these patches of unpainted canvas as the central element of his work, gaps which he refers to as 'retinal silences'.[53] Moments of silence in *Bernarda Alba* can also be seen as an auditory extension of the visual values of whiteness, which in turn act as a visual silence due to its values of absence and vacancy and its resistance to hued colour. *Bernarda Alba* is framed with a void of silence: there is a '*gran silencio umbroso*' (p. 308) [a great brooding silence] which complements the extremely white setting as the play opens, and 'silence' is the first word which Bernarda speaks — '*(A la Criada)* ¡Silencio!' (p. 314) [(*To the Maid*) Silence!] — and her last as the curtain falls — '¡Silencio, silencio he dicho! ¡Silencio!' (p. 404) [Silence, silence I said! Silence!]. Silence becomes part of the white claustrophobia of the house, continually re-instated in both stage directions and, ironically, dialogue, as Lorca extends the core image of whiteness to all aspects of the staging. Lorca's use of pauses acts as a staccato of silence, piercing the dialogue, such as when Martirio tries to tell Amelia about Adela's affair with Pepe in Act Two:

> Martirio   Amelia.
> Amelia *(En la puerta)*   ¿Qué?
> *(Pausa)*
> Martirio   Nada.
> *(Pausa)*
> Amelia   ¿Por qué me llamaste?
> *(Pausa)*
> Martirio   Se me escapó. Fue sin darme cuenta.
> *(Pausa)*
> Amelia   Acuéstate un poco. (pp. 360–61)

[MARTIRIO   Amelia.
AMELIA *(In the doorway)*   Yes?
(Pause)
MARTIRIO   Nothing.
(Pause)
AMELIA   Why did you call me?
(Pause)
MARTIRIO   It just slipped out.
(Pause)
AMELIA   Get some rest.]

Lorca's use of silence in this scene is a prime example of the economy of language in the play as a whole. Morris praises the 'tightness and restraint' of the dialogue in *Bernarda Alba*, suggesting that the play also 'impresses by what it does not say'.[54] Silence is as central to the action of the play as the characters' speech, as it is indicative of their inability to connect and communicate and conveys the complex relationships between them. As Edwards notes, Bernarda's tyranny 'becomes inevitably her daughters' tyranny of each other', which in turn communicates 'the power of passion to set individuals against each other' and their 'increasing isolation' even from one another despite their shared plight.[55] The scene in Act Two in which the theft of Pepe's photo is discovered is a particularly significant example of the interplay between actual silence, indicated in the stage directions, and the act of silencing in the dialogue. The scene oscillates between Bernarda's demands for answers — '¿Cuál de vosotras? (*Silencio*) ¡Contestarme! (*Silencio*),' (Bernarda to her daughters, p. 362) ['Which of you was it? (*Silence*) Answer me! (*Silence*)] — and calls for silence — '¡Silencio!', '¡Silencio digo!' (pp. 365–66) [Silence! Silence I said!].[56] Through his use of silence throughout the play, Lorca encapsulates the visual silencing of hued colour in the suppression or absence of speech.

The dominance of whiteness is not merely found in empty space or pockets of silence which resist speech; it is also captured in the tone of the dialogue itself. In *Le degré zero de l'écriture* (1953) [Writing Degree Zero], Roland Barthes develops his concept of 'white writing', a spare, stripped-down discourse, suggesting an interrelation between white, silence, and writing that has parallels with the links between the monochrome set and the spare dialogue in *Bernarda Alba*. Barthes views Albert Camus's novel *L'Étranger* (1942) [The Outsider] as offering an alternative way of 'disengaging literary language' by 'creating a white writing, freed from all bondage to a pre-ordained state of language'.[57] This 'écriture blanche' [white writing] represents a 'new neutral writing' and a 'silence of form' which 'deliberately forgoes any elegance or ornament'.[58] Barthes suggests that 'white writing' 'achieves a style of absence which is almost an ideal absence of style; writing is then reduced to a sort of negative mood in which the social or mythical characters of a language are abolished in favour of a neutral and inert state of form'.[59] Something approaching this ascetic, minimalist 'white writing' can be seen in *Bernarda Alba*, where the stark whitescape is reflected in silence and pared-down dialogue. As Edwards observes, the dialogue is 'stripped of needless clutter as are the sets themselves'.[60] Bernarda's constant negation, use of imperatives, demands for silence, and the brevity of sentence and line length create an abrupt and aggressive discourse centred on absence and denial. When Poncia suggests donating some of Bernarda's dead husband's clothes, Bernarda exclaims 'Nada. ¡Ni un botón! ¡Ni el pañuelo con que le hemos tapado la cara!' (p. 327). ['Nothing. Not even a button! Not even the cloth which we used to cover his face!']. Likewise, her imperatives are often negative: 'Magdalena, no llores', (p. 314) [Magdalena, don't cry] and 'no procures descubrirlas, no le preguntes y, desde luego, que no te vea llorar jamás,' (to Angustias, p. 385) [don't try to find things out, don't ask him about it, and, of course, never let him see you cry]. Through silence, absence, and negation, Lorca evokes the whitescape in the 'white' writing of the play.

Writer Annie Ernaux's practice of 'écriture plate', or 'flat writing', which Frédéric-Yves Jeannet has called 'clinique', 'blanche', and 'minérale' [clinical, white, and mineral], complements and expands on Barthes's idea of 'white writing'.[61] Eylem Aksoy Alp explicitly makes the connection between Barthes's 'white writing' and Ernaux's 'flat writing' in her 2015 article, suggesting that both styles are 'fragmentaire[s], asyndétique[s], coupante[s], lapidaire[s]' [fragmentary, asyndetic, sharp, lapidary].[62] According to Warren Motte, Ernaux's writing is 'an example of minimalist writing in which emotions, poetics, and subjectivity are intentionally and vehemently excluded in favor of a more neutral and factual style'.[63] In her 1983 novel *La Place* [The Place], in which she narrates the life of her late father, Ernaux writes:

> I have no right to adopt an artistic approach, or attempt to produce something 'moving' or 'gripping' [...] No lyrical reminiscences, no triumphant displays of irony. This neutral way of writing came to me naturally. It was the same style I used when I wrote home telling my parents the latest news.[64]

Ernaux aims for an objective, 'neutral' writing style which 'actively attempts to reject any sort of poetic, emotional, or otherwise subjectively construed interventions'.[65] This idea of 'écriture plate' offers a way of exploring what Morris suggests is an oral 'flatness' in the dialogue of *Bernarda Alba* that mirrors 'the visual flatness of the play'.[66] Bernarda's direct, unadorned, and negative dialogue is complemented by what Edwards sees as the 'leaden and lifeless' dialogue of Magdalena and Martirio, which captures the characters' inner despair in verbal form, such as Martirio's statement: 'yo hago las cosas sin fe, pero como un reloj' in Act One (p. 327) [I do things without faith but like clockwork].[67] By reflecting the dull monotony of the white walls in the lighting, the moments of silence, and the dialogue of the play, Lorca encapsulates the core poetic image of whiteness throughout multiple aspects of the staging as part of his theatre of poetry. The combined effect is the creation of a domestic dystopia of whiteness; this is a disturbing and negative idea of home that is indicative of Bernarda's extreme views and the precarity of her state of mind. This 'casa' far exceeds the traditional, whitewashed Andalusian house in its antiseptic, ascetic nature, a deviation which both John Corbin and Herbert Ramsden have underlined.[68]

However, instances of visual and verbal colour continually remind the audience that Bernarda's unblemished whitescape is an illusion which is reflected in the weakening of the whitescape in the stage directions as the walls become 'lightly blued'. Whilst Bernarda demands a 'buena fachada', her failure to consider what she cannot control — 'lo que [cada uno] piensa por dentro' (p. 384) [what everyone thinks on the inside] — means that her white façade is a false front and a sham, as the very nature of a 'façade' implies. As Poncia warns Bernarda, 'ni tú ni nadie puede vigilar por el interior de los pechos' (p. 390) [neither you nor anybody else can police the inside of people's hearts]. Even the name 'alba' belies the possibility of absolute whiteness, as the flowers of the 'white' alba rose are actually pinkish-white. The audience is being shown Bernarda's visual world yet her chromophobia means that she becomes blind to some of the intrusions of colour: 'Ahora estás ciega' (Poncia, p. 367) [now you are blind]. Morris suggests this is a wilful denial of the truth, the sign of an 'ostrich mentality'.[69] It is only at the beginning of the play when the stage is empty of actors that the setting is extremely white. The sequestering of Bernarda's household is equally illusory, indicated by the use of the figurative 'pretend' when Bernarda speaks of bricking up the walls and windows. As Morris observes, the very presence of the audience shows Bernarda's 'quarantine' to be a failure from the beginning as Lorca 'takes us inside [the house] and proves how misplaced her trust in walls is by removing one of them: the one between her and the reader or spectator'.[70] Pure, isolated whiteness would mean nothingness: a house without inhabitants, a play without plot, text, characters, or audience. Adela's death does not mean she had been reclaimed by the whitescape, as Bernarda perceives. Rather, she has made her creative mark upon it. Even in death, Adela's more pallid body will not be white; her body will show lividness, the 'bluish' discoloration of the corpse, and the marks on her neck made by the rope.

The blackness indicated by the black-and-white photographic documentary image also subverts the authority of the whitescape from the very beginning of the play.[71] The vitality of the characters and the action of the play pushes back against the whitescape, challenging its static, unbroken monotony. Whilst the play begins with an empty stage and the walls as 'blanquísima', this extreme whiteness is immediately challenged by the arrival of the black-clad characters. As Delgado has noted, the women dressed in black contrast with the white walls, 'like black stains on a landscape primed for visibility'.[72] Greenfield agrees, arguing that '[white] is then, in all its obviousness, a spotless coating of whitewash applied expressly to conceal whatever stains may lie in the substance beneath. The stains in this case are the seven black-robed women who reside within the house'.[73] The women contrast physically with the whitescape in both their costume and their corporeal colour. As Dyer points out, even 'white' people are not hue white.[74] The play is replete with black-on-white contrasts.[75] For example, in the final Act the white stallion is contrasted with the night sky — '¡Blanco! Doble de grande, llenando todo lo oscuro' (Adela, p. 387) [White! Twice as big, filling the darkness] — and the black shawls are juxtaposed with white nightgowns. The nightgowns themselves contrast with the black clothing of the previous acts, as Simon Haworth observes in his review of Jennifer Sealey's 2017 production for the Manchester Royal Exchange.[76] There are specks of black in the dialogue throughout the play: the markings of the hyena, the leopard, and the 'hormiguita' [little ant] in María Josefa's song in Act Three (pp. 394–95) and the fleas which 'pepper' Adela's legs in Act One: 'unas cuantas pulgas que me han acribillado las piernas' (p. 333) [some fleas that have dotted my legs with bites].[77] These instances of blackness are like ink marks against the blankness of the whitescape, an inherently creative force. Black is thus shown to be a process, particularly in the form of dyeing. In Act One, Martirio suggests spitefully that Adela dye her iconic green dress black: 'Lo que puedes hacer es teñirlo de negro' (p. 333) [what you can do is dye it black]. Whilst the women must wear black following mourning customs, the dyeing of clothes shows the transition to blackness as a process of staining and saturation like the black ink or printed text gradually filling the white page. The very concept of black-and-white photography suggests that blackness will continually intrude on the whitescape from the beginning of the play. However, the action of the play itself also stains the white background in the form of blood, spittle, marks, footprints, and make-up. Bernarda's idea of pure whiteness is an impossible goal and a hollow facade, which is further emphasised by acts of cleaning that ironically lead to more staining: 'sangre en las manos tengo de fregarlo todo' (the Maid to Poncia, p. 310) [I've got blood on my hands from scrubbing everything]. The act of scouring the material house and its contents to reveal whiteness in turn abrades the 'white' skin to expose colour, the creative potential of the body staining the sterile whitescape.

Due to the occlusion of colour, when it does appear in visual form — the red-and-green fan and Adela's green dress in Act One, and the blue tint of the walls which has appeared in Act Three — it has a powerful effect on the audience that is intensified by Bernarda's reactions. The effect Lorca creates through this juxtaposition on the material stage is one of *jouissance* or 'bliss' which Barthes describes as an eruptive and galvanising force. Bliss is disquieting and challenges at a subjective level. In *Le plaisir du texte* (1973) [The Pleasure of the Text] Barthes suggests that bliss 'unsettles [the reader's] historical, cultural, psychological assumptions, the consistency of his tastes, values, memories, brings to a crisis his relation with language'.[78] In his discussion of artist Cy Twombly, Barthes extends his idea of bliss specifically to material colour, suggesting that even the briefest appearance of colour has a 'lacerating' effect as it materializes 'like an apparition' which disappears in the blink of an eye.[79] Barthes's reading of bliss in both a visual and verbal context has important ramifications for *Bernarda Alba*: colour can be particularly impactful in its scarcity, and colour is continually in motion, appearing fleetingly. The idea of colour bliss offers insight into Bernarda's character, particularly in her extreme reactions to colour which reveal how colour is a threat to her sense of self. It also allows us to consider how the attempted repression of colour creates moments of chromatic eruption which startle both the protagonist and the audience as part of Lorca's rejection of a mimetic, passive spectating experience. Lorca invests colour with a disruptive quality from the beginning when he warns the audience that the play is a photographic documentary, therefore subverting expectations when he introduces colour. Representations of colour are thus significant due to the chromophobia, anxiety, and the desire for colour that they spark and reflect and because of their impossibility. For example, the red-and-green fan in Act One immediately follows the image of the two hundred women dressed in black who contrast with the extremely white walls. The use of visual colour at this point in the play as part of the dramatic action has a particularly unsettling effect, as it disrupts the white-and-black colour scheme that had just been so forcefully introduced. The scarcity of colour in *Bernarda Alba* means that it becomes imbued with a stimulating, disconcerting quality every time it appears on stage in contrast to the stark and ascetic blankness of the whitescape.

The characters of María Josefa and Adela are the most important in terms of this colourful challenge to Bernarda's white tyranny. In her first appearance in Act One, María Josefa is described as 'ataviada con flores en la cabeza y en el pecho' (p. 338) [adorned with flowers on her head and chest]. Although Lorca does not stipulate that the flowers are coloured, they have often been shown as such in stage productions, perhaps due to María Josefa's association with verbal colour and rebellion. In the same act, María Josefa breaches the colour taboo, bringing colour to the whitescape as the Maid describes her as wearing 'anillos' and 'pendientes de amatistas' (p. 321) [rings and amethyst earrings]. Like Adela's green dress, María Josefa's jewels and her verbal colour — 'leopardo' (p. 394), 'hyena' (p. 394), 'coral' (p. 395), 'chocolate' (p. 396), 'trigo' (p. 396), 'ranas' (p. 396) [leopard, hyena, coral, chocolate, wheat, and frogs] — disrupt the whitescape and suggest an alternative world. Her madness and eccentricity and the fantasy world captured in her dialogue only serve to emphasise the startling appearance of visual colour.[80] María Josefa also challenges the authority of the sterile white house by providing an alternative, fertile vision of whiteness:

> Está todo muy oscuro. Como tengo el pelo blanco crees que no puedo tener crías, y sí, crías y crías y crías. Este niño tendrá el pelo blanco y tendrá otro niño, y éste otro, y todos con el pelo de nieve, seremos como las olas, una y otra y otra. Luego nos sentaremos todos, y todos tendremos el cabello blanco y seremos espuma. ¿Por qué aquí no hay espuma? Aquí no hay más que mantos de luto [...] Yo quiero casas, pero casas abiertas. (p. 396)

> [Everything is very dark. Because I have white hair you think I can't have children, and I can, children and children and children. This child will have white hair and will have another child, and that one will have another, all with snow-white hair, we will be like the waves, one after another after another. Then we will all sit down together, and we will all have white hair and we will be foam. Why is there no foam? There isn't anything here except mourning shawls [...] I want houses, but open ones.]

Her white hair, the white hair of her imaginary child, the white lamb, and the white foam in her dialogue are all linked with her desire for marriage and physical freedom, all denied by the clinical whitescape. This is the fertile whiteness of the natural world which Ziomek highlights, the white foam evocative of sperm, which is emphasised by the similarity of the words 'espuma' [foam] and 'esperma' [sperm] in Castilian. This alternative, vital whiteness undercuts the authority of the white house, revealing its disturbing and unnatural state. This is emphasised in both María Josefa's appearances, in Act One and Act Three. In Act One she parallels white and black objects with her desire for marriage and the seashore:

> Bernarda, ¿dónde está mi mantilla? Nada de lo que tengo quiero que sea para vosotras, ni mis anillos, ni mi traje negro de moaré, porque ninguna de vosotras se va a casar. ¡Ninguna! ¡Bernarda, dame mi gargantilla de perlas! [...] Me escapé porque me quiero casar, porque quiero casarme con un varón hermoso de la orilla del mar, ya que aquí los hombres huyen de las mujeres. (p. 338)

> [Bernarda, where is my *mantilla*? I don't want any of you to have anything of mine, not my rings, nor my black moire dress, because none of you are going to get married. None of you! Bernarda, give me my pearl choker! [...] I escaped because I want to get married, because I want to marry a beautiful young man from the seashore, because here men run away from women.]

The 'mantilla', a traditional Spanish head covering associated with Catholicism, which is often made of black or white lace, the black moire dress, and the pearl choker are all images of black and white associated with fertility and marriage.[81] Her black dress contrasts with the black mourning dresses and shawls of the other women because 'moire' fabric is silk which is pressure-treated to create a rippled, watery effect. María Josefa's chromatic desire is strongly associated with water, her seascapes a striking contrast to the heat and thirst of the sterile white house.

However, Adela is a much more powerful counterpoint, as she has greater stage presence and presents a more obvious challenge to Bernarda's authority in visual form. When colour intrudes in the play, it is also often associated with Adela: the coloured fan which she gives to Bernarda, the bluing of the walls, and the green dress, in terms of visual colour, and 'sandías' (p. 333), 'fuego' (p. 352), 'cuatro mil bengalas amarillas' (p. 352), 'sangre' (p. 353), 'maroma' (p. 374), and 'león' (p. 401) in her dialogue [watermelons, fire, four thousand yellow flares, blood, rope, and lion]. Adela's colour-presence offers an alternative kind of expression as a creative, transgressive force that refuses to be 'contained' in whiteness. The bluing of the walls, which has troubled critics — Vicente Cabrera sees this bluing as symbolic of sexual staining and dishonour; Edwards and Greenfield suggest that the blue tint represents moonlight, and Edwards also sees it as a premonition of death — can also be seen as a creative presence which seeks to transgress the whiteness and demonstrates how the action of a play dirties the white walls.[82] Rather than emblematic of sin — a reading which is problematised by blue's privileged values as meliorative and beatific in Western iconography and academic colour scholarship[83] — Edwards sees the bluing of the walls as showing that change has occurred and that the whitescape is no longer absolute.[84] Adela's views on colour are essentially the reverse of Bernarda's: her anxiety is sparked by whiteness and she desires colour. In Act Two when Adela expresses her fear of the whitescape, of losing her 'blancura', her chromatic desire is also revealed: '¡Mañana me pondré mi vestido verde y me echaré a pasear por la calle! (p. 335) [Tomorrow I will put on my green dress and go for a walk down the street!]. The importance of the green dress — one of the rare examples of bold, hued colour in the play — is twofold. First, it has an effect of colour bliss on the audience due to the scarcity of hued colour throughout the play and acts as a vibrant contrast to the dominance of material whiteness.

What Edwards calls the 'freshness and vitality' of Adela's green dress also stands in stark contrast to the mourning garments of the other women.[85] Secondly, the green dress represents Adela's physical desire for sexual and personal freedom and the threat she poses to Bernarda's authority in material form. Morris sees the dress as Adela's 'standard in her private campaign for personal liberty' and as representative of her 'youthful insouciance and her mental resistance' in contrast to the other characters.[86] The vibrant and subversive nature of Adela's green dress is the visual reflection of the burning desire which consumes her. For example, when Poncia warns Adela not to pursue Pepe and bring dishonour into the house in Act Two, Adela replies:

> Es inútil tu consejo. Ya es tarde. No por encima de ti, que eres una criada: por encima de mi madre saltaría para apagarme este fuego que tengo levantado por piernas y boca ¿Qué puedes decir de mí? ¿Que me encierro en mi cuarto y no abro la puerta? ¿Que no duermo? ¡Soy más lista que tú! Mira a ver si puedes agarrar la liebre en tus manos. (p. 352)[87]

> [Your advice is useless. It's too late. Not over you, you're a maid: I would leap over my mother to quench this fire rising through my legs and mouth. What can you say about me? That I shut myself in my room and don't open the door? That I don't sleep? I am cleverer than you! See if you can catch the hare in your hands].[88]

Through this juxtaposition of material greenness and images of fire, Lorca appeals to and represents the *blissful* body. In *The Pleasure of the Text* Barthes suggests that bliss as a disruptive and ecstatic state of affective impact is also centred on the sensual body and can be seen as an orgasmic force due to its explosive capacity. Barthes speaks of a 'body of bliss consisting solely of erotic relations' that is spurred by 'the fires of language (those living fires, intermittent lights, wandering features strewn in the text like seeds)'.[89] Barthes's reading of the blissful impact of the text in terms of the body in literature captures the power of colour bliss to spark and reflect desire. The powerful image of Adela's chromatic desire as a burning, a 'fuego', suggests that Adela is being consumed not just by the 'fires of language', but by fires of visual colour and desire. Bernarda's attempts to control and subjugate colour only increase the urgency and intensity of this desire. As Edwards observes, Bernarda's obsession with honour and whiteness 'blind[s] [her] to the reality of her daughters' needs yet simultaneously sharpen[s] them'.[90] This growing chromatic pressure is complemented by references to storms in the dialogue and by the white stallion kicking the walls in Act Three. For example, Bernarda tells her daughters 'yo veía la tormenta venir, pero no creía que estallara tan pronto' (p. 366) [I saw the storm coming but I didn't expect it to hit so soon] whilst Poncia warns the maid 'hay una tormenta en cada cuarto. El día que estallen nos barrerán a todas' (p. 392) [there is a storm brewing in each bedroom. The day it hits it will sweep us all away]. Lorca's use of 'estallar', 'to explode', in both of these examples emphasises the violence and suddenness of this impending climax. Kathleen Dolan suggests that each Act in this play surges like a wave, 'each one building towards its own climax' and forming 'part of a whole which appears to move in a horizontal line toward a single, conclusive catastrophe'.[91] Adela's chromatic desire is presented as an unstoppable force, building in intensity towards a moment of eruptive, orgasmic colour bliss. The bluing of the walls is the material representation of this impending climax as chromatic desire becomes such a powerful force that the white house is permanently changed.

Lorca also uses the characters' dialogue to capture the key dialectic between hued colour and whiteness in the play at an oral as well as visual level. Rather than entirely 'white' or 'flat', much of the dialogue in *Bernarda Alba* can be seen as 'sharp' or 'colourful'. As well as 'flat' writing, Ernaux has explored the idea of 'l'écriture comme un couteau' or 'knife-writing'. Jeannet has praised Ernaux's 'phrases sans métaphores, sans *effets*, leurs silex affûtés qui tranchent dans le vif, écorchent' [sentences without metaphors, without *effects*, sharpened flints that cut into the flesh, that flay].[92] Ernaux's later discussion of her writing practice acknowledges a dialogue of sharpness and flatness in her work, describing her 'imaginaire des mots' [imaginary of words] as centred on 'la pierre et le couteau' [the stone and the knife] and offering a more complex view of the relationship between subjectivity and objectivity.[93] She adds that 'ces lettres auxquelles je fais allusion étaient toujours concises, à la limite du dépouillement, sans effets de style, sans humour' [these letters to which I allude were always concise, at the limit of asceticism, without stylistic effects, without humor], emphasising her focus on concise and unembellished narrative which creates affect through its very starkness.[94] The idea of 'writing like a knife' captures the dynamic between flatness and sharpness in *Bernarda Alba*: the leadenness of Magdalena's and Martirio's dialogue and the blunt, violent, cutting essence of Bernarda's voice. The ways Lorca captures the sharpness of Bernarda's speech and gestures undermine the minimalism of 'white writing', emphasises her conflicted and complex mental state and offers ways of exploring how the core poetic theme of whiteness is reflected within modes of speech. Whilst Bernarda's dialogue is pared down and minimalist, it is also passionate and, literally, loud. The economy of her discourse does not imply the elimination of emotional language and expressive punctuation that 'white' and 'flat' writing aim for. Rather, Edwards notes that Bernarda 'uses her stick to reinforce her words, her words are themselves like blows'[95] whilst Morris suggests that the protagonists 'transform words into weapons'.[96] During the wake in Act One, one of the neighbours accuses Bernarda of having a 'lengua de cuchillo' (p. 316) [knife tongue]. Significantly, Lorca avoids the use of 'como' that would create a simile here, instead creating a stronger image through metaphor; Bernarda's tongue is not like a knife, it is a knife.

The passion and violence of Bernarda's speech also reveals the pervasive 'colour' of the play's dialogue as a whole, especially in the discourse of María Josefa, Poncia, Adela, and Martirio. The 'colour' of the dialogue of *Bernarda Alba* can be interpreted on several levels: as referring to verbal colour and to speech which is metaphorically 'colourful', in the sense that it is passionate, metaphorical, colloquial, or vulgar. Poncia is an important character in this respect, not solely in her verbal colour, which is centred on material, quotidian peasant life — 'chorizos' (p. 309), 'garbanzos' (p. 309), 'pan' (p. 311), 'uvas' (p. 311), 'tierra' (p. 311), 'lagarto machacado' (p. 311), 'lagartija' (p. 342), 'fuego' (p. 344), 'colorines' (p. 348), 'lentejuelas' (p. 356), 'ojos verdes' (p. 356), 'trigo' (p. 356), 'veneno' (p. 393), 'sangre' (p. 393) [chorizo, chickpeas, bread, grapes, earth, squashed lizard, little lizard, fire, sequins, green eyes, wheat, goldfinches, poison, and blood] — but also in what Edwards suggests is her 'normal, humorous, earthly and loquacious' dialogue which is 'colourful' in the metaphorical sense. Edwards argues that the varied, flexible nature of Poncia's dialogue — which is more inhibited when she is with Bernarda — stands in contrast to that of the other characters, which 'reflects their obsessions in its repeated patterns'.[97] However, Adela's, Martirio's, and even Bernarda's language can be seen as equally 'colourful'. The passion, violence, and 'colour' of Adela's dialogue — 'mirando sus ojos me parece que bebo su sangre lentamente' (p. 353) [looking into his eyes I feel like I am slowly drinking his blood], 'he ido como arrastrada por una maroma' (p. 374) [I have been dragged here as if by a rope] — is ultimately matched by Martirio in the final act. Martirio's apathy has given way to an unbearable jealousy, as shown by the change in her speech. Her 'flat' dialogue gradually becomes one of violence and 'colour', especially her exchanges with Adela in Act Three: 'Déjame que el pecho se me rompa como una granada de amargura' (p. 398) [let my chest explode like a pomegranate of bitterness] and 'hubiera volcado un río de sangre sobre su cabeza' (p. 402) [I would have poured a river of blood over her head]. These powerful images of the explosive, staining capacity of colour offer Martirio a means of expressing her anger and emotional pain in terms of bodily wounding and violence, a theme which is central to my discussion of *Bodas de sangre* and *Yerma* in Chapter Two. Martirio's verbal colour images reflect what Edwards suggests is the 'unmitigated savagery' and 'cruelty' of the characters in the play, in which they are reduced to an animal-like ferocity as indicated by María Josefa's description of Bernarda as a leopard and Martirio as a hyena.[98] As María Josefa observes, the daughters are women 'rabiando por la boda, haciéndose polvo el corazón' (p. 339) [battling fiercely for a wedding, turning their hearts to dust].[99] Poncia also refers to Martirio as a 'pozo de veneno' (p. 393) [a well of poison] which Morris sees as reflective of her 'dark thoughts' and 'disturbed psychology' and which also has chromatic implications of greenness.[100] Martirio's verbal colour captures the threat which her simmering rage and desperation poses to the material whitescape; when the pressures of the play finally reach their climax the white walls will not be left unharmed.

The 'colour' of Bernarda's discourse is the most unexpected and reflects the inner workings of her conflicted psyche. It creates a contradiction between the way she speaks and what she says, and undercuts the dominant monotone of the whitescape. Despite the white 'façade' Bernarda presents, her discourse reveals certain similarities with the other characters and suggests that she too suffers from an anxiety sparked by the material demands of the whitescape and perhaps a desire for an alternative. Verbal colour creeps into Bernarda's dialogue — 'limonada' (p. 315), 'hierbas' (p. 366 and p. 390), 'sangre' (p. 368) [lemonade, grass, blood] — and Edwards has emphasised the linguistic similarity between Adela and Bernarda: 'of all the daughters' dialogue, it is Adela's that, in its force and vigour, is closest to

Bernarda's'.[101] Unexpectedly, the verbal colour in Bernarda's language and gesture contradicts the stipulations of 'white' and 'flat' writing. Her discourse is full of exclamations, interrogatives, insults, and shouting, supported by the noise of her cane. For example, when the daughters fight after the theft of Pepe's photograph, Bernarda responds:

> BERNARDA (*Golpeando con el bastón en el suelo*)   ¡No os hagáis ilusiones de que vais a poder conmigo! ¡Hasta que salga de esta casa con los pies adelante mandaré en lo mío y en lo vuestro!' (p. 338)

> [BERNARDA (*Banging her cane on the floor*)   Don't get the idea that you can mess with me! Until I leave this house feet first, I will be in charge of my business and of yours!]

In contrast, Barthes suggests that white writing 'takes place in the midst of all those exclamations and judgements without becoming involved in any of them; it consists precisely of their absence'.[102] Not only is Bernarda's dialogue full of Barthesian 'exclamations and judgements', but the play also has an oral and popular nature, what Morris calls its 'pervasively colloquial texture'.[103] Bernarda's 'colourful' language belies a more complicated relationship with colour, or at least reveals the strain and unnaturalness of her quest for chromatic extremes, a slippage exposed in her very speech. In his 2014 study *The Luminous and the Grey*, Batchelor looks back on the ideas explored in *Chromophobia*. He argues retrospectively that 'it is only texts that might be called chromophobic or chromophilic, not people' and recognises that 'our relationship with colour is best described as ambivalent: most of us are both drawn to *and* repelled from colour'.[104] It is only in media such as film, literature, and art where 'we can step outside colour'; in real life 'we can't choose to be or not to be in colour' as the failure of Bernarda's whitescape has revealed.[105] Batchelor's comments on the equivocation surrounding our feelings towards colour offer scope for understanding the conflation of chromophobia and the desire for colour in *Bernarda Alba* as these chromatic states are revealed to be overlapping rather than mutually exclusive. The 'colour' of the dialogue reveals the precarious authority of Bernarda's whitescape and her deeply conflicted state of mind, but also enhances the complexity of her portrayal and her role as a fully developed character of bones-and-blood.

Far from being a passive symbol, colour in *Bernarda Alba* has the power to penetrate and affect the psyche, offering the audience a glimpse into the minds of the protagonists and capturing the reality of life inside the white cube in physical form. Bernarda's violent reactions to colour reveal her chromophobia and the mental strain of maintaining her sterile white environment, a material whiteness which she conflates with morality and honour. The white walls reflect and exacerbate Bernarda's conflicted mental state as Lorca creates a claustrophobic, white dystopia which exposes her warped view of the world and her deteriorating mental state and which sparks horror and anxiety in the other characters. Hued colour becomes an aggressive, orgasmic force due to its scarcity, unsettling and moving the audience and Bernarda, when it does appear, and communicating and triggering Adela's erotic desire which is imbricated with her chromatic desire. The complex visual interplay between colour and whiteness is perpetuated at a textual level as the unadorned whitescape is reflected in the pared-down dialogue and the 'colour' of Bernarda's discourse which undercuts the dominance of whiteness and reveals her conflicted state of mind and the complex overlapping nature of our feelings towards colour. Indeed, the dominance of the whitescape is frequently subverted and challenged by the core aesthetic image of the photographic documentary and by these explosive intrusions of hued colour. Through this equivocal representation of hued colour and whiteness, Lorca offers us a glimpse of the characters' private inner worlds and the intense suffering which lurks beneath the white façade. Rather than an abandonment of theatre of poetry, *Bernarda Alba* embodies these concerns, capturing complex and labile emotional states in the material colours of the staging and creating one of his most powerful examples of a wounding, instinctive, and pervasive poetry on the material stage.

Notes to Chapter 1

1. Gwynne Edwards, *Theatre Beneath the Sand* (London: Boyars, 1980), p. 265.
2. Sumner M. Greenfield, 'Poetry and Stagecraft in *La casa de Bernarda Alba*', *Hispania*, 38.4 (1955), 456–61 (p. 456).
3. Hereafter all parenthetical references to this play are to Federico García Lorca, *La casa de Bernarda Alba*, in *Obra completa IV*, ed. by Miguel García-Posada (Madrid: Ediciones Akal, 2008 [1936]).
4. Gwynne Edwards, 'Productions of *La Casa de Bernarda Alba*', *Anales De La Literatura Española Contemporánea*, 25:3 (2000), pp. 699–728 (p. 703).
5. See Henryk Ziomek, 'El simbolismo del blanco en *La casa de Bernarda Alba* y en *La dama del alba*' [The Symbolism of White in *The House of Bernarda Alba* and in *The Lady of the Dawn*], *Symposium*, 24.1 (1970), 81–85 (pp. 82–83).
6. Edwards, *Theatre Beneath the Sand*, p. 266.
7. Greenfield, 'Poetry and Stagecraft', p. 457.
8. David Batchelor, *Chromophobia* (London: Reaktion Books, 2000), p. 22.
9. Richard Dyer, *White: Essays on Race and Culture* (Oxford: Routledge, 1997), p. 72. See also John Gage, *Colour and Meaning: Art Science and Symbolism* (London: Thames and Hudson, 1999), p. 70.
10. Dyer, pp. 72–73.
11. Francisco Aguilar Piñal defines the Spanish concept of honour as 'un complejo sentimiento de dignidad familiar ante la sociedad, cuyo peso recae sobre la conducta sexual femenina' [a complex feeling of family dignity in wider society, the weight of which rests on the sexual behaviour of women], 'La honra en el teatro de García Lorca' [Honour in the Theatre of García Lorca], *Revista de literatura*, 48.96 (1986), 447–54 (p. 448). Malveena McKendrick classifies the Spanish 'Golden Age' as the sixteenth and seventeenth centuries. She notes that Spanish theatre 'clearly distinguishes [the Spanish idea of honour] from classical and medieval attitudes to honour, that is, an almost exclusive emphasis on honour as social reputation as distinct from honour as public virtue or personal integrity', 'Honour/Vengeance in the Spanish Comedia: A Case of Mimetic Transference?' *The Modern Language Review*, 79.2 (1984), 313–35 (p. 318). Bernarda's understanding of honour is based on these Early Modern ideas of public image, social reputation, and outward appearance, which still held sway in Lorca's time. See also Peter L. Podol, 'The Evolution of the Honor Theme in Modern Spanish Drama', *Hispanic Review*, 40.1 (1972), 53–72.
12. Edwards, *Theatre Beneath the Sand*, p. 238.
13. All translations are my own unless otherwise stated.
14. Greenfield, 'Poetry and Stagecraft', p. 461.
15. Greenfield, 'Poetry and Stagecraft', p. 461 and Maria M Delgado, *Federico García Lorca* (Oxford:

Routledge, 2008), p. 106. In their 1964 production (Teatro Goya, Madrid), director Juan Antonio Bardem and set designer Antonio Saura capture this clinical whiteness, presenting a 'glistening, antiseptic décor devoid of folkloric hangings or adornments'. Delgado, *Federico García Lorca*, p. 110.

16. Greenfield, 'Poetry and Stagecraft', p. 457.

17. Delgado, *Federico García Lorca*, p. 106.

18. Edwards, *Theatre Beneath the Sand*, p. 243.

19. We also see this obsessive cleaning of white surfaces in *Yerma*. The Fourth Washerwoman's statement that 'cuanto más relumbra la vivienda, más arde por dentro' (p. 450) [the more the house shines, the more it burns inside] is equally applicable to the jealousy, hatred, desire, and paranoia fermenting behind the thick white walls in *Bernarda Alba*.

20. Le Corbusier, 'The Decorative Art of Today', in *Essential Le Corbusier: L'Esprit Nouveau Articles*, trans. by James I. Dunnett (Oxford: Architectural Press, 1998), pp. 185–92 (p. 186, p. 190 and p. 192). Le Corbusier was a contemporary of Lorca, and Lorca attended his lecture at the Residencia de Estudiantes in 1928. See *Prosa 1*, p. 283. Ripolin is a brand of white paint.

21. Greenfield, 'Poetry and Stagecraft', p. 457.

22. See also Chapter Seven of John Gage *Color and Culture: Practice and Meaning from Antiquity to Abstraction* (London: Thames and Hudson, 1993) in which Gage, an art historian, charts the resurgence and development of the *disegno–colore* debate in Italian Renaissance thought.

23. Batchelor, *Chromophobia*, p. 23.

24. Batchelor, *Chromophobia*, p. 23.

25. Batchelor, *Chromophobia*, p. 22.

26. In Jenny Sealey's 2017 production with Graeae at the Manchester Royal Exchange, the viciousness of this scene is emphasised further. Alfred Hickling observes that: 'not content with wiping away the offensive makeup from her daughter's face, [Bernarda] seizes the lipstick and smears it across her [daughter's] cheeks and forehead as if to ensure the humiliation is writ large', 'The House of Bernarda Alba review — Hunter is a domestic dictator in anti-fascist classic', *The Guardian*, 8 February 2017 <https://www.theguardian.com/stage/2017/feb/08/the-house-of-bernarda-alba-review-kathryn-hunter-royal-exchange-manchester> [accessed 20 February 2022].

27. The image of being dragged is particularly important as both Adela, in this play, and the Bride, in *Bodas de sangre*, describe their desire as being beyond their control, as if they are being dragged against their will. I discuss the Bride's discourse of somatic wounding in the following chapter.

28. Emma Wilson, '*Three Colours: Blue*: Kieślowski, Colour and the Postmodern Subject', *Screen*, 39.4 (1998), 349–62 (p. 350).

29. Wilson, '*Three Colours: Blue*', p. 355.

30. Wilson, '*Three Colours: Blue*', p. 355.

31. Edwards, *Theatre Beneath the Sand*, p. 239 and p. 269.

32. Higginbotham argues that 'because her behaviour is so predictable, Bernarda resembles the villain of a puppet farce, whose body jerks into stiff but automatic poses. Like a marionette whose wooden face is carved into a grimace, she insults the villagers, threatens her daughters with petty violence, and keeps her aged, demented mother under lock and key', *The Comic Spirit of Federico García Lorca* (Austin: University of Texas Press, 1976), p.113.

33. See Dyer's analysis of the 'certain nameless terror' of the monstrous white whale in Herman Melville's *Moby Dick* (1851) and the cult of the exsanguinated, cadaverous white body in popular culture, such as the portrayal of vampires and zombies. Dyer, pp. 210–13.

34. Dyer, p. 79 and p. 81.

35. Edwards, *Theatre Beneath the Sand*, p. 276.

36. Edwards, *Theatre Beneath the Sand*, p. 249. In playwright David Hare's translation, he suggests that the sisters' skin is yellow or sallow in comparison to Adela's. 'I won't spend my whole life, I won't watch my skin — I won't watch it turn yellow till it's the colour of yours — let my body become like yours', *The House of Bernarda Alba* (London: Faber and Faber, 2005), loc. 489, Kindle edition.

37. Ziomek, p. 83.

38. Greenfield, 'Poetry and Stagecraft', p. 458.
39. Greenfield, 'Poetry and Stagecraft', p. 461.
40. Edwards, *Theatre Beneath the Sand*, p. 243.
41. Batchelor, p. 10.
42. The link between whiteness and sensory deprivation is a known one, as captured in the interrogation technique of 'white torture' which is 'torture based on the use of sensory deprivation techniques' according to Pau Pérez-Sales. He adds that the designs of these cells 'precluded any human contact and the environment was comprised entirely of white tones, with minimal stimulus' and also 'formed the basis for the design of maximum security experimental prisons'. Studies by Donald Hebb and his students at McGill University in the 1950s found white torture to produce immediate effects, leading to hallucinations and psychosis in two days and causing long-lasting after-effects, even 'permanent mental damage'. Pau Pérez-Sales, *Psychological Torture: Definition, Evaluation and Measurement* (London: Routledge, 2017), p. 8.
43. Edwards, *Theatre Beneath the Sand*, p. 240 and p. 243. For the spectator, the disorienting effects of Bernarda's disturbed vision of whiteness and the madness sparked by it in others are intensified through acoustic and visual stage effects which disrupt the viewing experience. Some of the effects which Lorca uses are easier to assess than others — such as the boom of the stallion kicking the wall in Sealey's production which 'successfully makes many audience members jump'. Simon Haworth, 'The House of Bernarda Alba, the Royal Exchange', *Manchester Review*, 3 February 2017 <http://www.themanchesterreview.co.uk/?p=7196> [accessed 20 Feb 2022]. Sound effects are central to *Bernarda Alba,* what Delgado calls 'the auditory texture' of the play which is 'constantly cutting into the silence', disrupting the insularity of the whitescape. Delgado, *Federico García Lorca*, p. 106.
44. C. B. Morris, 'The "Austere Abode": Lorca's *La casa de Bernarda Alba*', *Anales de la Literatura Española Contemporánea*, 11.1–2 (1986), 129–41 (p. 131).
45. See Morris, 'Austere Abode', pp. 132–33. To these terms Morris adds 'mortuary' and 'madhouse', whilst Delgado suggests 'fortress' and 'coffin', and the theatre critic Michael Billington sees the house as 'a prison courtyard, a nunnery and an asylum'. See Delgado, *Federico García Lorca*, p. 107, and Gwynne Edwards, 'Productions of *La casa de Bernarda Alba*', p. 721.
46. Lorca cited in Herbert Ramsden, 'Introduction', in Federico García Lorca, *La casa de Bernarda Alba* (Manchester: Manchester University Press, 1983), pp. vii–lix (pp. xxxii–xxxiii).
47. Federico García Lorca, *Bodas de sangre* in *Obra completa III*, ed. by Miguel García-Posada (Madrid: Ediciones Akal, 2008).
48. Edwards, *Theatre Beneath the Sand*, p. 276.
49. Lorca's use of 'traspasar' here calls to mind Mavor's reading of the lingering impact of the punctum, which I explore in my discussion of bodily colour and emotional 'bruising' in *Bodas de sangre* and *Yerma* in Chapter Two and in *Doña Rosita* in Chapter Three.
50. Edwards, *Theatre Beneath the Sand*, p. 240. Heavy doors and iron grilles or window bars, continuing the achromatic motif of imprisonment, are found in Margarita Xirgu's, Phillips's, Nuria Espert's, and Polly Teale's productions. In their stagings, Bardem and Saura increase the height of windows and doors, to suggest that 'no hay salida ni escape' [there is no exit or escape], Bardem cited in Edwards, 'Productions', p. 707. Delgado comments on Teale's use of a large double door, smaller openings, locks, and grilles and the 'imposing portal of bolted prison-like doors with grilles and slats that filtered in light from the outside world', Delgado, *Federico García Lorca*, p. 112. Roni Toren's set design for Gadi Roll's 2008 production (Belgrade Theatre, Coventry) takes the parallel even further, transposing the set from a house to a high-security prison with metal walls.
51. Eric Robertson, ' "Le blanc souci de notre toile": Writing White in Modern French Poetry and Art', *French Studies*, 71.3 (2017), 319–32 (p. 323).
52. Robertson, p. 323.
53. Cited in Robertson, p. 328.
54. C. B. Morris, *García Lorca: La casa de Bernarda Alba* (London: Grant and Cutler, 1980), p. 117.
55. Edwards, *Theatre Beneath the Sand*, pp. 251–52.
56. In Bardem's production, the interplay between sparing dialogue and minimalist setting is

particularly highlighted. Bernarda, played by Cándida Losada, is carefully controlled with a 'sobriedad de gestos' [soberness of gesture] and 'raises her voice only when her control is threatened,' a portrayal which differs from Lorca's text and reinforces the visual monotony of the play. Edwards, 'Productions', p. 711. Sealey's production offers an especially novel portrayal of this white claustrophobic silence as the Graeae theatre company use D/deaf and disabled actors and a combination of sign language, captioning, interpreting, and audio description. 'The silent space she creates for her character is as telling and as simmering as a louder one. It's a kind of literal embodiment of the quiet that Bernarda often demands, her suicide being the ultimate kind of silence' (Haworth, *Manchester Review*). Alfred Hickling notes that 'when [Bernarda] has the final word, it is not a word at all, but a terse repetition of the BSL gesture commanding silence' (Hickling, *The Guardian*, 8 February 2017).

57. Roland Barthes, *Writing Degree Zero*, trans. by Annette Lavers and Colin Smith (London: Cape, 1967), pp. 81–82.

58. Barthes, *Writing Degree Zero*, pp. 82–84.

59. Barthes, *Writing Degree Zero*, p. 77.

60. Edwards, *Theatre Beneath the Sand*, p. 268.

61. Annie Ernaux and Frédéric-Yves Jeannet, *L'écriture comme un couteau: Entretien avec Frédéric-Yves Jeannet* [Writing Like a Knife: Interview with Frédéric-Yves Jeannet] (Paris: Stock, 2003), Kindle edition, loc. 307 and loc. 842–47.

62. Eylem Aksoy Alp, 'De l'écriture blanche d'Albert Camus à l'écriture plate d'Annie Ernaux', [From the white writing of Albert Camus to the flat writing of Annie Ernaux], *Frankofoni*, 27 (2015), pp. 189–202, (p. 199).

63. Cited in Jennifer Anderson Bliss, 'Writing as Flat as a Photograph: Subjectivity in Annie Ernaux's *La Place*', *Lit: Literature, Interpretation and Theory*, 24.2 (2013), 164–83 (p. 164).

64. Annie Ernaux, *A Man's Place*, trans. by Tanya Leslie (New York: Four Walls Eight Windows, 1992), p. 13.

65. Anderson Bliss, p. 164.

66. Morris, *García Lorca: La casa de Bernarda Alba*, p. 105.

67. Edwards, *Theatre Beneath the Sand*, p. 270. In Bardem's production, he replaces the singing at the wake with atonal recitation to further emphasise this monotone speech. Juan Antonio Bardem, 'Notas de dirección' [Director's Notes], in Federico García Lorca, *La casa de Bernarda Alba* (Barcelona: Ayma, 1964), p. 52.

68. See John Corbin, 'Lorca's "Casa"', *The Modern Language Review*, 95:3 (2000), pp. 712–27, (p. 712) and Herbert Ramsden, 'Introduction' to Federico García Lorca, *La casa de Bernarda Alba* (Manchester and New York: University of Manchester, 1983), pp. vii–lix, (p. xlix). Lorca actually saw Andalusia as full of colour: 'el amarillo de Cádiz [...] el rosa de Sevilla [...] el verde de Granada' [The yellow of Cadiz [...] the pink of Seville [...] the green of Granada], Federico García Lorca, *Prosa, 1, Obras completas VI* ed. by Miguel García-Posada, (Madrid: Ediciones Akal, 2008), p. 528.

69. Morris, *García Lorca: La casa de Bernarda Alba*, p. 77.

70. Morris, 'Austere Abode', p. 138.

71. For a discussion of the influence of photography on the play see C. Christopher Soufas Jr, 'Dialectics of Vision: Pictorial vs. Photographic Representations in Lorca's *La casa de Bernarda Alba*', *Ojancano*, 5 (1991), 52–66, and *Audience and Authority in the Modernist Theater of Federico García Lorca* (Tuscaloosa, AL: University of Alabama Press, 1996), pp. 130–38.

72. Delgado, *Federico García Lorca*, p. 106.

73. Greenfield, 'Poetry and Stagecraft', p. 457.

74. Dyer, p. 42.

75. The contrast between black and white is a central preoccupation in productions of the play. For example, in Calixto Bieito's more abstract 1998 production with scenographer Alfons Flores (Teatro María Guerrero, Madrid) the set was, according to Delgado, 'a white vertical panel against which the black clad performers moved like eerie shadows'. She adds that Robin Phillips's 1973 production with the set designer Daphne Dare (Greenwich Theatre, London) also sought to emphasise the element of blackness in the play, creating a set which used 'the black

walls of the theatre as a contrast to one white wall and floor', (*Federico García Lorca*, p. 114). In Bardem's production, the black clothing is especially emphasised, with the women dressed in 'long black mourning garments, buttoned at the neck and reaching down to their black shoes'. Edwards, 'Productions', p. 707. Also, rather than the combination of white petticoats and black shawl that Bernarda wears in the final act, Bardem dresses her entirely in black: 'Bernarda va de negro siempre. Es lo negro' [Bernarda always wears black. She *is* the colour black], (Edwards, 'Productions', p. 708). According to Edwards, the effect was one of 'seven black beetles trapped in a jar' (Edwards, 'Productions', pp. 707–08).

76. Haworth, *Manchester Review.*

77. Thank you to the University of Bristol 'The Theatre of Federico García Lorca' final year undergraduate students for their valuable thoughts on these specks of blackness in my December 2017 guest seminar.

78. Roland Barthes, *The Pleasure of the Text*, trans. by Richard Miller (New York: Hill and Wang, 1975), p. 14.

79. Roland Barthes, 'Cy Twombly: Works on Paper', in *The Responsibility of Forms: Critical Essays on Music, Art and Representation*, trans. by Richard Howard (Berkeley: University of California Press, 1985), pp. 157–76 (p. 166).

80. In Sealey's production, María Josefa's 'colourfulness' is strongly emphasised: 'Paddy Glynn's María is all feather boas, excessive make-up and layered chintzy colours, bringing a rebellious dose of glamour to the forcibly sober dress and controlled deportment of the household' (Haworth, *Manchester Review*).

81. Whiteness is also implicit in the lace and white-on-white embroidery of Angustias's marriage trousseau. See Roberta Ann Quance's discussion of embroidery, female roles, and unfulfilled desires in *La casa de Bernarda Alba* in 'Los arquetipos de Venus y la Virgen: Un tema bordado' [The Archetypes of Venus and the Virgin: An Embroidered Theme], in the exhibition catalogue *Jardin deshecho: Lorca y al amor* [Damaged Garden: Lorca and Love], ed. by Christopher Maurer (Granada: Centro Federico García Lorca, 2019), pp. 88–105 (pp. 99–102),<https://www.centrofedericogarcialorca.es/es/publicaciones/catalogo-de-exposicion/17/jardin-deshecho-lorca-amor> [accessed 20 February 2022].

82. See Vincente Cabrera, '"Poetic Structure in Lorca's *La casa de Bernarda Alba*", *Hispania*, 61:3 (1978), pp. 466–71, (p. 466); Greenfield, *Poetry and Stagecraft*, p. 456, and Edwards, *Theatre Beneath the Sand*, p. 268.

83. See Michel Pastoureau, *Blue: The History of a Colour* trans. by Markus I. Cruse (Princeton, NJ: Princeton University Press, 2001) Chapter Four 'The Favorite Colour' in which he discusses the popularity of blue from the eighteenth to twentieth century. Pastoureau notes that 'at the same time that blue became the most common color in twentieth-century Western dress, it also became the favorite color. The preference for blue, which was more intellectual or symbolic than physical in its motivations, had ancient roots. We saw earlier how, in the thirteenth century, blue began to compete with red as the color of aristocracy and royalty [...] blue became a dignified and moral color', p. 169.

84. Edwards, *Theatre Beneath the* Sand, p. 268.

85. Edwards, *Theatre Beneath the* Sand, p. 249.

86. Morris, *García Lorca: La casa de Bernarda Alba*, p. 49.

87. Images of burning are also an important part of my discussion of the Bride's discourse of bodily colour in *Bodas de sangre* in Chapter Two.

88. The symbol of the hare has been associated with women and sexuality in Spanish Golden Age theatre. For example, in Lope de Vega's *Fuenteovejuna* (1612) 'hare' is used with these connotations by the Commander regarding Laurencia, and as an insult by Laurencia to the men of the Council. See Teresa Kirschner 'Typology of Staging in Lope de Vega's Theater' in *The Golden Age Comedia: Text, Theory, and Performance* ed. by Charles Ganelin and Howard Mancing, pp. 358–71: 'Juan-Eduardo Cirlot links the hare to lust and to fertility and considers it a symbol with an inseparable feminine character, and Raymond Barbera demonstrates that the hare, from medieval times, alluded graphically to the feminine sexual organ. Also, as I have shown elsewhere, Lope always uses the image of the hunt to refer to the sexual act' (p. 369).

89. Barthes, *The Pleasure of the Text*, pp. 16–17.
90. Edwards, *Theatre Beneath the Sand*, p. 238.
91. Kathleen Dolan, 'Time, Irony and Negation in Lorca's Last Three Plays', *Hispania*, 63.3 (1980), 514–22 (p. 521).
92. Ernaux and Jeannet, *L'écriture comme un couteau*, loc. 90. Original emphasis.
93. Ernaux and Jeannet, *L'écriture comme un couteau*, loc. 857.
94. Ernaux and Jeannet, *L'écriture comme un couteau*, loc. 332.
95. Edwards, *Theatre Beneath the Sand*, p. 268.
96. Morris, *García Lorca: La casa de Bernarda Alba*, p. 107.
97. Edwards, *Theatre Beneath the Sand*, p. 271.
98. Edwards, *Theatre Beneath the Sand*, p. 261 and p. 263.
99. Whilst 'rabiar' means a desperate longing or suffering for something, it also implies an uncontrollable violence and anger, like a rabid animal. These connotations are an important aspect of my discussion of the Shoemaker's Wife's 'rabid green dress' as the visual representation of her burning rage in *La zapatera prodigiosa* in Chapter Three.
100. Morris, *García Lorca: La casa de Bernarda Alba*, p. 54. Michel Pastoureau has commented on the link between poison and the colour green: 'the term *vedastre* appeared in Middle French about the mid-fourteenth century to describe the colour of a poison.' Michel Pastoureau, *Green: The History of a Colour*, trans. by Jody Gladding (Princeton, NJ: Princeton University Press, 2014), p. 229. According to Pastoureau, Napoleon Bonaparte was literally poisoned by green; he was exposed to arsenic-based Schweinfurt green paint. Poison is a recurring motif throughout the play: 'el veneno de sus lenguas' (Bernarda describing the villagers, p. 319) [the poison of their tongues], 'siempre se bebe el agua con el miedo de que esté envenenada', (Bernarda, p. 319) [I always drink water with the fear that it may be poisoned], 'Me hacéis al final de mi vida beber el veneno más amargo que una madre puede resistir' (Bernarda, p. 363) [at the end of my life you make me drink the bitterest poison that a mother can bear].
101. Edwards, *Theatre Beneath the Sand*, p. 270.
102. Barthes, *Writing Degree Zero*, p. 83.
103. Morris, *García Lorca: La casa de Bernarda Alba*, p. 110. Morris highlights the addition of pronouns such as 'me llegué a ver' (Adela, p. 322) and 'me estoy en mi sitio' (Poncia, p. 390) and the addition or removal of definite articles as in 'la Magdalena' (Poncia, p. 308), 'es buen hombre' (Martirio, p. 332), and 'tengo mal cuerpo,' (Adela, p. 349), (*García Lorca: La casa de Bernarda Alba*, p. 111). '(Me) I went to see', '(Me) I am in my place', 'Our Magdalena', 'He's (a) good man', '(My) body is bad.'
104. David Batchelor, *The Luminous and the Grey* (London: Reaktion Books, 2014), p. 13.
105. Batchelor, *The Luminous and the Grey*, p. 13.

CHAPTER 2

❖

Bodily Colour:
Making Poetry Flesh

The role of material colour in communicating character subjectivity and sparking complex mental states in *Bernarda Alba* has wider ramifications for Lorca's creation of a theatre of poetry through colour across this theatre. Building on these ideas of the materialisation of abstract themes and emotions, the pursuit of the 'truth' of the protagonists' inner worlds, and the unsettling and invigoration of the audience, I now consider the importance of material colour offered by representations of the body in *El maleficio*, *Mariana Pineda*, *Don Perlimplín*, *El público*, *Así que pasen*, *Bodas de sangre*, and *Yerma*. I explore Lorca's engagement with female bodily whiteness, the expression of female psychological suffering in colourful somatic terms, and the piercing of the male body with its evocation of redness as part of Lorca's quest to 'make poetry human', to create characters of bones-and-blood, and to move towards a more fluid representation of gender.

White Women and Emotional Bruising

White is not merely an important material and psychological force in *Bernarda Alba*; it is also part of how Lorca depicts the female body throughout his theatre, particularly in *El maleficio*, *Mariana Pineda*, *Don Perlimplín*, and *Bodas de sangre*. At one level, Lorca's portrayal of the white female body focuses on three key aspects: the virginal (the Bride), the dying (the Butterfly and Mariana), and the erotic (Belisa). The correlation of femininity and whiteness is a perennial Western trope, particularly the associations between white, beauty, and characteristics such as grace, modesty, and kindness. The 'shining beauty and goodness of the heroine' is a core tenet of fairy tales and myth, as explored by Marina Warner in *From the Beast to the Blonde* (1994). Warner notes that the Old English usage of 'fair' as a synonym of beautiful segued into 'unblemished' by the thirteenth century and 'light in colour' by the sixteenth century, condensing these values.[1] Richard Dyer also suggests that virginity and morality were thought to manifest themselves physically in whiteness: 'the cult of virginity expressed an idea of unsullied femininity [...] which was held to be visible in a woman's appearance', a parallel which is reminiscent of the strong relationship between the cleanliness of the white house and morality and honour in *Bernarda Alba* as explored in Chapter One.[2] This conflation of the symbolic values of virginity with the Bride's body in *Bodas de sangre* is indicative of what Dyer, in his study of whiteness in Western culture, calls 'the slippage between white as hue, skin and symbol'.[3] Whilst the Bride's skin is not literally white, Lorca uses her clothing and the repeated description of her as 'blanca' to reflect the central poetic themes of purity and honour in the staging and the dialogue of the play in ways which are mutually enhancing. The visual whiteness of her orange-blossom crown, petticoats, and bodice in the stage directions is coupled with verbal references to whiteness and to virginity in the wedding morning song: 'la blanca novia' (p. 357) [the white bride], 'blanca doncella' (p. 361) [the white maiden], and 'blanca niña' (p. 362) [the white girl].[4] The Bride's purity and corporeal whiteness are further intertwined in the final scene when she defends her virginity by claiming that 'ningún hombre se haya mirado en la blancura de mis pechos' (p. 409) [no man has seen himself [reflected] in the whiteness of my breasts]. The symbolic values of purity are transferred to her body; the whiteness of her breasts is evidence of her sexual untouchedness. Like the white walls in *Bernarda Alba*, pure and unmarked material whiteness in *Bodas de sangre* is indicative of honour and the absence of sin.

White as absence — in particular, the absence of blood — is also reminiscent of death and the initial pallor of the corpse. In *El maleficio* and *Mariana Pineda*, Lorca uses the associations between whiteness and death to communicate the physical decline of the Butterfly and of Mariana in material and symbolic terms. Throughout *El maleficio* the Butterfly's body is fading, leaving the material world: 'la Muerte me dio dos alas blancas' (p. 82) [Death gave me two white wings]. The Butterfly's fairy-tale fairness is emphasised by the multiple references to the material whiteness of her body, and by the syntax of 'la blanca durmiente' (p. 81) [sleeping white one] which echoes 'la bella durmiente' [sleeping beauty]. This second image foreshadows a deathly sleep in which the white body remains perfectly preserved, like Sleeping Beauty or Snow White. The Butterfly's white wings are described in tactile terms as both 'blanquísima seda' (p. 71) [whitest silk] and 'blancas como el armiño' (p. 74) [as white as ermine]. From her first appearance, the Butterfly's body achieves the literal hue whiteness which cannot normally be encapsulated in human skin and stands in stark contrast to the shiny black bodies of the other beetle characters.[5] Whilst the dying Butterfly is white from the beginning of the play in *El maleficio*, in *Mariana Pineda* we find Mariana's physical depletion depicted in the gradual fading of her body and her costume, indicative of colour as a process. In his 2007 study, Paul McDermid probes the symbolic ramifications of Mariana's corporeal fading in this play and suggests that her increasing whiteness signals 'a movement from the substantial to the ethereal' which is indicative of the 'absence of the physical' and 'the white of the void', reminding us how the material and the symbolic are inextricably linked.[6] Whilst Mariana's skin is not literally white, as with the Bride in *Bodas de sangre*, Lorca uses the characters' dialogue to refer repeatedly to her growing paleness, which is then supported further by her white costume in Act Three. Throughout the play Mariana's costume changes from '*malva claro*' (Act One, p. 106) [pale mauve] to '*amarillo claro, un amarillo de libro viejo*' (Act Two, p. 143) [pale yellow, an old-book yellow] to '*un espléndido traje blanco*' (Act

Three, p. 185) [a splendid white costume]. The move from mauve to yellow to white in Mariana's clothing also mimics the healing of a bruise. The old-book yellow also has olfactory values. I explore the significance of her costumes in relation to the central poetic images of the play in Chapter Three. Angustias's and Clavela's descriptions of Mariana in the first Act are an early indication of her corporeal fading, a process which has already begun when the play begins: 'Se le ha puesto la sonrisa casi blanca, como vieja flor abierta en un encaje', (p. 103) [her smile has turned almost white, like an ageing lacework flower] and 'aquellos colores de flor de granado desaparecieron de su cara', (p. 125) [those pomegranate-flower colours have disappeared from her face].[7] The transformative verb 'ponerse' emphasises the ongoing process of this whitening or bleaching, whilst the two floral metaphors remind us of other processes in which hued colour and vitality are gradually depleted.[8] By Act Three, Mariana's living body has become shrouded like a corpse in her white clothes: 'Ella me parece amortajada cuando cruza el coro bajo con esa ropa tan blanca', (p. 201) [she looked like she was in a shroud when she crossed the choir in such white clothing]. Lorca's use of the superlative *'palidísima'* (p. 185) [extremely pale] to describe Mariana's white body in the final act is suggestive of a transformation which has reached its final stage. Whilst the material whiteness of the Butterfly and Mariana is indicative of death, it is also reminiscent of the 'sublime pallor' of the dying tubercular heroine in nineteenth-century literature and what Dyer describes as 'the beauty of white death as well as the romantic longing for it'.[9] These romanticised depictions of white female beauty and the theme of exsanguination offer a striking contrast to the representation of the male body which I explore later in this chapter. The more abject representation of white and death which we find in *Bernarda Alba* — white as terrifying and pathological — is absent in these portrayals. Rather, white is a meliorative force with positive aesthetic values of beauty, as opposed to the visual representation of, and cause of, mental trauma in *Bernarda Alba*.

Lorca's portrayal of Belisa in *Don Perlimplín* reveals another facet of white female beauty: the erotic and the sensual. Sarah Wright sees Belisa as a depiction of surface femininity, a masquerade which may not reveal anything beneath.[10] McDermid builds on this interpretation, suggesting that the whiteness of Belisa's body is indicative of a spiritual lack; she is an 'empty shell', a purely carnal form which will be transformed by Perlimplín's 'self-sacrifice'.[11] There are potential symbolic readings of Belisa's white body, but the sensory and the material can be seen as equally central to her 'whiteness'. Whilst the exotic 'foreign' female body or woman of colour is the most common erotic trope, Warner also draws our attention to the motif of the sensual blonde woman in Western literary and visual culture, particularly in representations of the goddess of love in Homer and in Botticelli's *The Birth of Venus* (c. 1486).[12] These erotic values of Western feminine whiteness are already present in Lorca's earlier plays and remind us of the inherent overlap between these representations: the tactile values of the Butterfly's white ermine and silk body are markedly sensual, as is the portrayal of Mariana's white neck in *Mariana Pineda*, which Pedrosa desires and covets, reminding us that there is also a material and sensual aspect to their 'white' bodies. In *Don Perlimplín*, the erotic white body becomes the central site of female beauty in the play, particularly in the display of Belisa's body; she is often semi-nude or has bare arms. In the prologue Belisa is described as 'blanca' (p. 266) [white] and compared to lilies and white sugar by her mother:

> Es una azucena. ¿Ve usted su cara? (*Bajando la voz.*) ¡Pues si la viese por dentro!... Como de azúcar... Pero... perdón. No he de ponderar estas cosas a persona tan moderna y competentísima como usted... (p. 269)

> [She's a lily. Do you see her face? (*Lowering her voice.*) Well if you could see her on the inside!... Like sugar...But.... forgive me. I don't have to marvel at these things to someone as modern and capable as you.]

The repeated image of white sugar appeals to our haptic and gustatory senses, blending the visual values of colour with the non-visual senses of touch and taste.[13] The fact that the Mother lowers her voice also suggests that 'inside' is a sexual reference, enhancing the eroticism of the scene. This sensual portrayal of whiteness is particularly evident in the bathing scene in the song in Act Three:

> Por las orillas del río
> se está la noche mojando [...]
> Y en los pechos de Belisa
> se mueren de amor los ramos [...]
> La noche canta desnuda
> sobre los puentes de marzo [...]
> Belisa lava su cuerpo
> con agua salobre y nardos [...]
> La noche de anís y plata
> relumbra por los tejados [...]
> Plata de arroyos y espejos
> y anís de tus muslos blancos. (pp. 297–98)[14]

> [By the shores of the river
> the night is growing damp [...]
> And on Belisa's breasts
> the branches die of love [...]
> The night sings naked
> over the March bridges [...]
> Belisa washes her body
> in salt water and lilies [...]
> Night of aniseed and silver
> shines on the rooftops [...]
> Silver of river and mirrors
> and the aniseed of your white thighs.]

In Belisa's song, the night itself is anthropomorphised and eroticised; it is damp and naked, aniseed-scented (or white like aniseed flowers) and shining silver. Belisa refers to her own body in the third person as if she were a voyeur, describing her breasts and her washing of her body in salt water and tuberose flowers, both of which are implicitly associated with white.[15] These sensually-charged motifs of whiteness are continued in the image of white, aniseed thighs (referring both to her lover and herself when the 'voices' repeat the refrain), an area of the white body whose proximity to the sexual organs is usually hidden by clothing. The voluptuous portrayal of female whiteness offers a counter-image to the white body as virginal and self-contained, depicting a different kind of white bodily beauty centred on the sensual and erotic rather than on traditional symbolic assumptions of 'whiteness'.

Lorca's multi-faceted portrayal of female bodily whiteness reveals that there is no static depiction of colour, even a single colour, in Lorca's work. In his theatre of poetry he is constantly experimenting and engaging with the equivocal affective and material possibilities of the chromatic. Whilst there are important symbolic aspects to these portrayals, Lorca also problematizes these 'white' and often overlapping representations of femininity. First, portrayals of the body as hue white mask the reality of 'whiteness' as a skin colour. As Dyer notes: 'White people are neither literally nor symbolically white. We are not the colour of snow or bleached linen, nor are we uniquely virtuous and pure'.[16] Rather, 'whiteness' is a social construct, and an ascriptive and privileged racial category. It both 'creates a category of maybe, sometime whites, peoples who may be let in to whiteness under particular historical circumstances' and 'incites the notion that some whites are whiter than others'.[17] The description of Belisa's body as white sugar reminds us of the colonial and imperial freight of such renderings of 'whiteness' in its evocations of Black slavery.[18] Secondly, these women are Hispanic and thus likely to have darker colouring. For example, the wedding-morning song in Act Two of *Bodas de sangre* paradoxically reveals the Bride's brownness as she is described as 'morena' and 'morenita' (p. 357) [dark haired and olive skinned].[19] Furthermore, in the final scene, the Beggarwoman describes how the Bride is covered in blood, her hair and black dress sticky with congealing redness even as she refers to the 'whiteness' of her breasts:

> Flores rotas los ojos, y sus dientes
> dos puñados de nieve endurecida.
> Los dos cayeron, y la novia vuelve
> teñida en sangre falda y caballera.
> Cubiertos con dos mantos ellos vienen
> sobre los hombros de los mozos altos.
> Así fue, nada más. Era lo justo.
> Sobre la flor de oro, sucia arena. (p. 407)

> [Their eyes broken flowers, and their teeth
> two fistfuls of hardened snow.
> The two fell, and the bride returns
> her skirts and hair dyed with blood.
> Covered in two blankets they come
> over the shoulders of the tall boys.
> That's how it was, nothing more. It was as it should have been.
> On the golden flower, dirty sand.]

Lorca's use of the verb 'teñir', 'to dye', also implies not only colour as a process but a permanent change in colouring which represents the poetic theme of the staining of honour in the dialogue in physical form, like the blue tinted walls in *Bernarda Alba*. The Bride has now become a sullied form of the 'golden flower' which she is described as in the wedding-morning song. Whilst the redness would not be as apparent against her dark hair and black wedding dress, we still get a sense of staining and of viscosity.[20] This is a brown female body 'dyed' with blood, representing a strong contrast with the symbolic portrayals of whiteness.[21] To restrict Lorca's engagement with race to the wedding night in *Don Perlimplín*[22] and to his representation of Black and Roma protagonists in his poetry is to elide the repeated emphasis on 'whiteness' in his theatre and to propagate what Dyer sees as 'the invisibility of whiteness as a racial position in white discourse'.[23] As Sara Ahmed notes, 'whiteness is only invisible for those who inhabit it or those that get so used to its inhabitance that they learn not to see it'.[24] Lorca's representations of 'white' women are more complex than they first appear and 'whiteness' is only one aspect of their portrayal. The 'slippage' that Dyer identifies between symbolic and material readings of whiteness in his discussion of Western visual culture is one possible reading of these plays, yet Lorca is also employing bodily colour in other, more intricate ways. As we shall see, Lorca's exploration of female bodily whiteness gives way to a more equivocal portrayal which turns away from socially inscribed bodily surfaces to the truth that lies within.

Lorca's exploration of the colouration of the female body is not limited to symbolic values of purity, innocence, and beauty but also forms part of his expression of character subjectivity in his creation of an emotive, 'human' theatre of poetry. Skin colour is just one element of corporeal colour yet enjoys the most critical focus due to the conflation of skin colour and the social and cultural implications of race. In his 2003 study of human skin in Western culture, Steven Connor draws our attention to the chromatic potential of the body beyond ideas of racial colour. Associations between the body and non-racial colour date back to Hippocrates's (460–370 BC) humoral theory in which the four elements of the earth corresponded to the bodily fluids of black bile, phlegm, blood, and yellow bile. Connor notes that due to how skin colour and bodily fluids are affected by disease, corporeal colour is often seen in medical or pathological terms. He cites examples such as chlorosis or green-sickness, yellow fever, scarlet fever, purpura, jaundice, Black Death, cholera (Greek *chole*, yellow or black bile), candidiasis or fungal infections (Latin *candidus*, white), leukaemia (Greek *leukos*, white), melanoma (Greek *mavro*, black), and cyanosis or blue-jaundice (Greek *kyanos*, dark blue). Likewise, there are other dominant evocations of bodily colour in Lorca's work which have important ramifications for the subtle ways in which he employs colour in his theatre of poetry, especially in his use of implicit colour, where colour is associated with an object rather than expressed through colour words, and in the communication of the emotional suffering of his female protagonists.[25] White is not the only aspect of Lorca's portrayal of the Bride's bodily colour; she is also described in brown terms, and other bodily colours — such as red, yellow, and black — are imprinted upon her either literally (blood), or figuratively in her dialogue (through images of bruising, burns, sores, ulcers, and rotting). The Bride's powerful description of her emotional pain in bodily terms fills the text with corporeal colours that metaphorically stain and mark her 'white' body. The colours which these images induce are also deeply rooted in her experience of bodily pain, suggesting that verbal colour, colour instances in the dialogue, offers a glimpse of her inner experience. C. B. Morris suggests that the Bride 'can explain her feelings only in images and sensations', creating an allegorical discourse of her conflicted state of mind.[26] This discourse is part of Lorca's concern with creating a theatre of poetry which explores the pain of daily life and furthers my discussion of colour as a means of communicating complex character subjectivities in *Bernarda Alba* in Chapter One. Many critics have viewed Lorca's protagonists as universal 'everyman' characters, particularly in *Bodas de sangre* where all the characters except Leonardo have generic names and where many of the protagonists are defined by their social relations to each other, roles centred on marriage and procreation ('father', 'mother', 'bride', 'groom', 'wife', 'mother-in-law'). For example, Paul Julian Smith argues that it 'would seem vain to offer personalised psychological readings of characters who within the play itself are denoted only according to their familial function'.[27] However, a reading of any of Lorca's protagonists as generic ciphers undercuts their depth and the affective impact of these portrayals, particularly as he aims to expose the hidden pain of ordinary, everyday existence. The protagonists' suffering may be timeless and universal, but they are still complex emotional individuals in their own right, as shown by Lorca's portrayal of their internal realities. The Bride is not a two-dimensional character but one who expresses complex and competing desires and whose suffering is figuratively imprinted on her body in highly chromatic and intersensory ways.

One of the most potent examples of the Bride's expression of her emotional pain in bodily terms is in Act Three, Scene Two, in the final moments of the play:

NOVIA   Yo era una mujer quemada, llena de llagas por dentro y por fuera, y tu hijo era un poquito de agua de la que yo esperaba hijos, tierra, salud; pero el otro era un río oscuro, lleno de ramas, que acercaba a mí el rumor de sus juncos y su cantar entre dientes. Y yo corría con tu hijo que era como un niñito de agua fría y el otro me mandaba cientos de pájaros que me impedían el andar y que dejaban escarcha sobre mis heridas de pobre mujer marchita, de muchacha acariciada por el fuego. Yo no quería, ¡óyelo bien!; yo no quería. ¡Tu hijo era mi fin y yo no lo he engañado, pero el brazo del otro me arrastró como un golpe de mar, como la cabezada de un mulo, y me hubiera arrastrado siempre, siempre, siempre, aunque hubiera sido vieja y todos los hijos de tu hijo me hubiesen agarrado de los cabellos! (pp. 409–10)

[BRIDE   I was a burnt woman, full of sores inside and out, and your son was a little bit of water with which I hoped for children, land, and health; but the other one was a dark river, full of branches, which brought me the murmur of his reeds and the song between his teeth. And I ran with your son, who was a little child of cold water, and the other one sent hundreds of birds that blocked my path and left frost on my wounds of a poor withered woman, my wounds of a young woman caressed by fire. And I did not want to! Listen! I did not want to. Your son was my destiny and I have not deceived

him, but the arm of the other one dragged me like a booming wave, like
the butt of a mule, and he would have dragged me forever, forever, forever,
even if I were old and all of your son's children had held me down by my
hair!]

The Bride portrays her suffering body in terms of the effects of burns, sores,
ulcers, drowning, and being dragged, adding to the motif of rotting in Act Two,
Scene One: 'tengo el pecho podrido de aguantar' (p. 355) [my chest is rotten from
endurance]. Depictions of fire and burning — 'burnt' and 'caressed by fire' — create
powerful images of a body blackened by soot and flames and reddened by burns.
This is not merely physical desire for the Bride but the searing pain of dishonour
and grief. Paradoxically, Lorca's use of 'acariciar' suggests an initial tenderness,
such as a lover's caress, which has ultimately burnt her in an intricate blending of
pleasure and pain. Her relationships with both men involve a search for relief from
this burning: 'a little bit of water' (Groom) and 'frost' (Leonardo) respectively. Her
body is 'full of sores inside and out', evoking ulcers, which are white, red, and even
yellow. The Bride's suffering is also conveyed in terms of bodily struggle against
the currents of the 'dark river' and the 'hundreds of birds' which block her path,
and 'a booming wave'. The repeated metaphor of being dragged, including by her
hair, creates mental images of violent bodily injury. The violence and colour of
the Bride's discourse is emphasised further through images which metaphorically
pierce her body, creating a figurative counterpart to the stabbing of the male body
that I explore later in this chapter. The Bride's search for punishment has become
conflated with the need for her body to mirror her emotional pain, a powerful
portrayal of the suffering female body which has a lingering affective impact on the
audience. She demands death twice in the final Act of the play. First, in Act Three,
Scene One when she has eloped with Leonardo, she combines the motif of burning
with references to shooting and to shards of glass:

> Y si no quieres matarme
> como a víbora pequeña
> pon en mis manos de novia
> el cañón de la escopeta.
> Ay, qué lamento, qué fuego
> me sube por la cabeza!
> Qué vidrios se me clavan en la lengua! (p. 397)

> [If you don't want to kill me
> like a small viper
> put in my bride's hands
> the barrel of a shotgun
> Oh what regret, what fire
> rises through my head!
> What shards of glass pierce my tongue!]

The metaphor of glass piercing her tongue is particularly powerful both as an image
of extreme pain and as an assault on the organ of speech and taste.[28] The shards of
glass are an extension of the knife motif which is threaded throughout the play and
which keeps the vulnerability of the body centre stage. Secondly, the Bride asks her

mother-in-law to kill her at the end of the play after Leonardo and the Groom have stabbed each other to death: 'pero no con las manos; con garfios de alambre, con una hoz, y con fuerza, hasta que se rompa en mis huesos' (p. 409) [but not with your hands; with wire hooks, with a sickle, and with all your strength, until it breaks my bones]. The figurative piercing of the body continues in these images, breaching the body's surface and exposing the implicit colour underneath in ways evocative of the journeying through the body. These images suggest an intensely chromatic 'output' of suffering which is written upon the female body.

The violence and colour of the Bride's discourse is reflected in the dialogue of the Mother. Morris sees the Mother as a 'disturbing character', suggesting that Lorca 'depicts scars left on her mind by grief' as she 'keep[s] alive the hatreds of the past'.[29] Speech is the sole expression of a simmering rage which she cannot act upon due to the restrictions of her gender and of 'civilised' society. In Act One, Scene One, the depth of her fermenting hatred towards the Félix clan — Leonardo's family and the opposing side of the blood feud which resulted in the deaths of her husband and her elder son — is already clear. She tells the Groom, her remaining son, that she cannot move to his new property with the Bride as the Félix family might try to bury their relatives in the graveyard where her husband and son are buried:

> No. Yo no puedo dejar aquí solos a tu padre y a tu hermano. Tengo que ir todas las mañanas, y si me voy es fácil que muera uno de los Félix, uno de la familia de los matadores, y lo entierren al lado. ¡Y eso sí que no! ¡Ca! ¡Eso sí que no! Porque con las uñas los desentierro y yo sola los machaco contra la tapia. (p. 314)

> No. I can't leave your father and your brother here alone. I have to go every morning, and if I move away it's too easy for one of the Félixes to die, one of that family of killers, and be buried alongside them. No! Never! Because with my nails I would dig them back up and I alone would crush them against the wall.

This is a particularly disturbing, violent image in which the sacred rite of burial and respect for the dead body are both overturned. In the same scene, she tells her neighbour that: 'Pero oigo eso de Félix y es lo mismo *(entre dientes)* Félix que llenárseme de cieno la boca *(escupe)*, y tengo que escupir, tengo que escupir por no matar (p. 320) [But when I hear the name "Félix" it is the same *(between gritted teeth)* "Félix" which fills my mouth with slime *(spits)* and I have to spit, I have to spit so I do not kill]].[30] The vitriol of this image is emphasised by the stage directions, where the actress speaks through gritted teeth and spits on the floor. The haptic quality of mud is central to both of these images; it is stuck under the fingernails of the imagined gravedigger and it fills the Mother's mouth and browns her spit. Much of the Mother's dialogue involves containing her violent impulses: she spits 'por no matar' in the first scene and, in the final scene, she pretends not to recognise the Bride 'para no clavarla mis dientes en el cuello' (p. 409) [so I do not sink my teeth into her neck], a cannibalistic image of white teeth and the red blood of the torn jugular. Despite the Mother's animosity towards the Bride, they are paradoxically linked by their embodied emotional pain. There is a significant parallel found in 'tengo el pecho podrido de aguantar' (the Bride) [my chest is rotten from endurance]

and 'tengo en el pecho un grito siempre' (the Mother, p. 367) [I have an eternal cry
in my chest], especially in the mirroring of 'tengo' and 'pecho'. Throughout *Bodas
de sangre* Lorca uses corporeal colour and metaphors of violence against the body
to capture the agonizing suffering of the Bride and the Mother. This is a pain that
goes very deep: 'me duele hasta la punta de las venas' (the Mother, p. 367) [it hurts
to the very tips of my veins]. It is a turmoil left unresolved as the men lie dead but
the women live on to cry alone inside their dark houses, isolated even from each
other, like Bernarda's daughters in *Bernarda Alba*.[31] The play ends with the Mother's
reference to 'la oscura raíz del grito' (p. 413) [the dark root of a scream] which will
torment these women forever, trapped by a fate worse than death.[32]

The terrible, unrelenting pain of the Bride's and the Mother's discourse and
Lorca's aim of expressing the desperate reality of his human characters continue in
Yerma. Like the Bride's and the Mother's suffering, the pain of Yerma's childlessness
penetrates on a deep bodily level; it is in her flesh and her bones. She tells her
husband Juan that 'lo que sufro lo guardo pegado a mis carnes' (p. 488) [I keep my
suffering close to my flesh] and he responds that the bitterness he complains of is
entrenched 'en los huesos' (p. 492) [in my bones]. Like the Bride, Yerma resorts to
images of ulcers to communicate the agony of her childlessness when she tells the
Old Woman: 'has puesto el dedo en la llaga más honda que tienen mis carnes' (p.
474) [you have put your finger in the deepest sore in my flesh]. Yerma's dialogue
and expression of pain are rooted in the somatic and what Smith calls the 'speaking
of and in the woman's body', a reading that also sheds light on the Bride's and the
Mother's discourse.[33] However, Yerma's speech does not solely draw on images
of bodily wounding as the expression of her suffering. Rather, the source of her
pain, her childlessness, is woven through the dialogue through the motifs of blood
(redness) and milk (whiteness), part of what Smith refers to as Lorca's 'frequent
appeal to lyrical and often liquid imagery drawn from the natural or organic worlds
(to streams and clouds, to blood and milk)'.[34] These motifs draw attention to the
central role of Lorca's implicit colour and object colour in his theatre of poetry,
which I explore in my discussion of object colour in Chapter Three. Blood and
milk conjure up redness and whiteness and those substances invest colour with
viscose or fluid properties; the visual qualities of colour become intertwined
with its 'texture' and 'density', and colour and object become permanently fused.
Connor captures these tactile properties in his definition of implicit object colour:

> Colour [...] mingles with an object or substance, imparting its tincture to it,
> and receiving back the object's impress. The coloured object — gold, milk, sky,
> blood — gives rise to what we might call an object-colour, a colour with its
> own phantasmal form, texture and density.[35]

The use of implicit colours in *Yerma* and *Bodas de sangre* highlights the material and
intersensory nature of Lorca's colour-work and captures the pain of Yerma's denied
maternity in its cruel repetition of maternal colour. Unlike the spilled male blood
which pervades Lorca's theatre, these representations of whiteness and redness are
positive, creative chromatic forces that Yerma's body is denied. Whilst Yerma has
been read as an intersexual type by Smith and as the masculine counterpart to her

effeminate husband by McDermid, *Yerma* is deeply rooted in what it means to be a woman and is centred on the primal and painful forces of maternity.[36] Through his exploration of these implicitly-coloured bodily fluids, Lorca conveys the depth of the suffering hidden beneath and caused by Yerma's flesh in terms of the internal colours of the body, capturing a uniquely feminine portrayal of pain.

Blood is the first key motif that captures Yerma's suffering in chromatic form. The emotional pain metaphorically written on Yerma's flesh and bones stands in contrast to the blood and the bodily suffering created by pregnancy, childbirth, and nursing, which are to be embraced:

> YERMA   ¡Bah! Yo he visto a mi hermana dar de mamar a su niño con el pecho lleno de grietas y le producía un gran dolor, pero era un dolor fresco, bueno, necesario para la salud [...] Tener un hijo no es tener un ramo de rosas. Hemos de sufrir para verlos crecer. Yo pienso que se nos va la mitad de nuestra sangre. Pero esto es bueno, sano, hermoso. (p. 427)

> YERMA   Rubbish! I've seen my sister breastfeed her baby with a chapped breast and it was very painful, but it was a fresh, good, healthy pain [...] Having a child isn't a bed of roses. We have to suffer to see them grow. I think they take half of our blood. But it is good, healthy, beautiful.

There is a sacrificial tone to this offering of 'half our blood' but, in the natural context of childbirth, Yerma reads the redness of ulcerated breasts and blood as desirable and 'healthy', revealing her desperate desire for motherhood at any cost in Lorca's de-idealised vision of maternity. This is the blood of birth rather than death and a pain of which Yerma is unafraid, in contrast to other women in the play who have sought Dolores's help. Yerma wants a child to bloom inside her 'aunque tenga mil espinas' (p. 484) [even if it has a thousand thorns] and will do almost anything to conceive: 'aunque me mande clavarme agujas en el sitio más débil de mis ojos' (p. 433) [even if you tell me to stick needles in the softest part of my eyes]. However, blood can also be a constraining force and the antithesis of maternity. In Act Two, Scene Two she cries: 'Ay qué dolor de sangre prisionera me está clavando avispas en la nuca!' (p. 461) [Oh, what pain of imprisoning blood is stabbing my neck with wasps!]. Her reference to 'sangre prisionera' reveals that, for Yerma, blood has a different meaning to that of motherhood and childbirth. Instead, it represents the agony of her hope and her continuing menstrual cycle. Blood becomes part of the pervasive feeling of imprisonment which Andrew Anderson traces throughout the play, represented by allusions to tomb-like houses, walls, rocks, wells, and the phantom of her would-be child sat on her chest.[37] This is all indicative of what McDermid sees as the 'limits of [Yerma's] female body, and the gender located and culturally constructed upon it'; Yerma's body is trapped by 'the prison of gender'.[38] The painful image of wasp stings compounds the pain of her failed maternity. As Anderson observes, these are not ordinary stings; through Yerma's 'heightened' language, the marks of these black-and-yellow creatures are 'likened in turn to a nail being driven into the nape of her neck'.[39] This psychological torture enacted on the body only ends with Juan's murder and the certainty that her menstrual blood will come every month: 'Voy a descansar sin despertarme sobresaltada, para ver si la sangre me anuncia otra sangre nueva' (p. 494) [I am going to rest without starting awake to see if my monthly blood has come yet again]. Doubt is worse than the certainty of childlessness.

These images of blood and motherhood in *Yerma* are accompanied by the white motif of breastmilk, which also cruelly emphasises Yerma's lack. The repeated references to breastmilk are all found in Yerma's dialogue: 'estos dos manantiales que tengo de leche tibia' (p. 461) [those two springs I have of warm milk], 'ese arroyo de leche tibia [...] se les llene la cara y el pecho de gotas blancas' (p. 473) [this stream of warm milk [...] which speckles their face and chest with white drops], 'arroyos de leche tibia juegan y mojan la cara de las estrellas tranquilas' (p. 484) [streams of warm milk play and dampen their face with calm stars].[40] These images of milk are vital and pulsing, flowing in 'springs' and 'streams'. In both of the latter images there are references to faces speckled with milk, the bodily colour of one person marking the body of another. However, this fertile bodily whiteness is contrasted with Yerma's ongoing inability to conceive and her 'pechos de arena' (p. 452) [breasts of sand] and her outpouring of grief in Act Two, Scene Two:

> YERMA
> [...] Estos dos manantiales que yo tengo
> de leche tibia, son en la espesura
> de mi carne, dos pulsos de caballo,
> que hacen latir la rama de mi angustia.
> ¡Ay pechos ciegos bajo mi vestido!
> ¡Ay palomas sin ojos ni blancura! (p. 461)

> [YERMA
> [...] Those two springs I have
> of warm milk, are the thickness
> of my flesh, two horse pulses
> which make the branch of my anguish beat.
> Oh, blind breasts beneath my dress!
> Oh, doves without eyes or whiteness!]

Yerma describes her breasts as 'blind' and lacking the visual 'whiteness' of fertility represented by the milk, an image which contrasts bodily colour, creation, and motion with her colourless, dry sterility.[41] There is also a powerful rhythm of these images of milk; they 'pulse' and 'beat' with the strength of a horse's heart. However, Yerma will never experience this nourishing, maternal whiteness. Like the conflict of sterile and fertile evocations of whiteness which Sumner M. Greenfield and Henryk Ziomek identify in *Bernarda Alba*, Anderson argues that the frequent allusions to implicit whiteness in *Yerma* — for example, sheep, lambs, wool, doves, sheets, light, milk, jasmine, frost, snow, and the moon — create a dialectic of natural, creative forms of whiteness that stands in stark contrast with 'blankness [...] the negative side of *blancura*' represented by the ascetic white house and Yerma herself: '¡Ay qué blanca, la triste casada!' (p. 486) [Oh how white the sad wife is!].[42] Instead of blooming with life, Yerma's body becomes increasingly arid, her flesh withering and her childless body described by a dusty, neutral palette: 'el vientre seco y la color quebrada' (p. 486) [A dry abdomen, drained of colour]. 'Quebrado' in the sense of colouring can mean drained with fatigue yet, more literally, we can read her colour as 'broken'; Yerma's body is unable to achieve the red and white of motherhood. This dryness and pervasive lack is indicated from the beginning by the play's title, although Yerma is not explicitly named until Act Two, Scene Two, sealing a fate which was instigated by her baptism, as Anderson suggests.[43] Yerma is only referred to by 'name' once within the play — leading Simon Stone in his controversial 2016 adaptation to rename the female lead 'Her' — and her name is inferred from the title. It has been argued that 'yerma' is not a proper name but an insult or an indication that her sense of personhood has been obliterated by her condition of childlessness. For example, Edwards observes that ' "Yerma" is not a real name but an adjective to describe barren, desert-like land and which the villagers have cruelly applied to Yerma — "the barren one" — on account of her failure to produce a child'.[44] The agricultural image of childlessness suggested by 'yerma' recurs in Lorca's use of 'marchita', which refers to the withering of vegetation. This wilting permeates the final scene of *Yerma*: the fertility prayer and ritual, Yerma's argument with the Old Woman, and Yerma's final fatal encounter with Juan. Yerma's first line after she murders her husband is an acknowledgement of this state: 'marchita, marchita, pero segura' (p. 494) [withered, withered, but sure]. We also see this use of 'marchita' in *Bodas de sangre* and *Así que pasen* to describe the Bride and the Young Man respectively. Unlike the events of *Bodas de sangre*, this suffering is not the result of action. As Anderson observes, 'there is no blame, it just is', a punishment which is 'unfair, unjust, undeserved' as Yerma has willingly conformed and 'bought into the system' yet she has still not conceived.[45] Like Rosita's spiritual death in *Doña Rosita* and the dark scream which the women in *Bodas de sangre* are left with, Yerma's fate is worse than death.

Whilst I discuss the literal piercing of the male body later in the chapter as having the sharp, shocking effect of 'the punctum', the emotional reaction to the small photographic detail which Roland Barthes describes in *La chambre claire: Note sur la photographie* (1980) [Camera Lucida: Reflections on Photography], these colourful portrayals of feminine inner pain have a different effect. Lorca uses these depictions of female suffering to express complex inner states, to burrow beneath the surface, and to create human, visceral characters of bones-and-blood in his theatre of poetry. The true power of this discourse of corporeal colour and wounding lies in its effect on the audience. In her study of the affective impact of the filmic image, Carol Mavor extends the piercing impact of Barthes' punctum to ideas of emotional 'bruising' and a residual impact, a reading which has clear chromatic ramifications due to its corresponding image of blackness and blueness. Although Barthes is speaking in psychological and aesthetic terms — for him the punctum is a mental rather than bodily impact — Mavor blurs the boundaries between the affective pricking of the mind and the piercing of the body, considering bruising as an injury that is 'neither outside or inside'.[46] This is the residual impact of the punctum; the sharp shock gives way to a lingering pain which stands in contrast to the explosive, disruptive values of colour bliss. After the initial sharpness 'a tenderness remains, though we may have forgotten how the bruise got there' and we are left with 'that Barthesian black-and-blue feeling of that which has been'.[47] It is this wounding effect which we find in the speech of the Bride, the Mother, and Yerma. Unlike the male characters, which die a literal death, the women linger, and their agony and grief remains with us. Lorca's portrayal of the raw pain of these women through a discourse of sores, ulcers, burns, blood, lacerations, and withering, is the essence of the power and longevity of his craft. We are haunted by these words and mental images far beyond any temporal restraints of text or performance; their pain permeates the text. Any successful production of these plays must capture this quintessential Lorquian 'bruising' impact. Charles Spencer, reviewing the 2006 production of *Yerma* at the Arcola Theatre for *The Telegraph*, admits 'there are moments of raw hurt here that I found almost too painful to watch'.[48] Simon Stone's controversial 2016 adaptation of *Yerma* at the Young Vic, which is only very loosely based on the original work, also captures this agonising depiction of the pain of childlessness. Ben Lawrence, again writing for *The Telegraph*, suggests that 'you end up feeling numb with pity'.[49] This is not the brief, piercing impact inspired by a visual detail. Rather, it is something that hurts us deep inside and which remains long after that moment of encounter has passed. As Yerma tells us, 'es mucho mejor llorar por un hombre vivo que nos apuñala, que llorar por este fantasma sentado año tras año encima de mi corazón' (p. 474) [It's much better to cry for the living man who stabs us, than to cry for this ghost sat year after year on my heart].

Pierced Male Bodies and Spilled Blood

Lorca's exploration of colour and the male body offers a more 'physical' counterpart to the emotional wounding of the female body and is centred on acts of puncturing and stabbing, creating colour through the 'literal' piercing of the body and the spilling of male blood. Within his exploration of male corporeality, Lorca continues to experiment with a human theatre of bones-and-blood which both contrasts with and complements his depiction of female pain and bodily colour. The stabbing of the male body is a pervasive motif which we find in the fatal knife duel between Leonardo and the Groom in *Bodas de sangre*; the execution of the Young Man by the three Fates or card players in *Así que pasen*; Perlimplín's suicide by dagger in *Don Perlimplín*; and the murder of the First Man and the torture of the Red Nude in *El público*. Robert Lima sees this series of violent deaths as 'frequently resulting from an entry of a knife into human flesh'.[50] However, whilst the knife motif has enjoyed the most critical attention, particularly in *Bodas de sangre*, the range of sharp objects in these plays is markedly varied. References throughout the plays include 'bisturí', 'lanceta', 'jeringuilla', 'pica', 'tijeritas', 'aguja', 'hacha', 'espada', 'tiro' and 'flecha', in addition to 'puñal', 'cuchillo' and 'navaja' [scalpel, lancet, syringe, pike/lance, scissors, needle, axe, sword, gunshot, arrow, dagger, knife, knife/razor]. Even the ubiquitous knife blade in *Bodas de sangre* is described in increasingly creative forms by the characters: 'la luna deja un cuchillo abandonado en el aire' (p. 390) [the moon leaves a knife abandoned in the air], 'el aire va llegando duro, con doble filo' (p. 392) [the air hardens, like a double blade].[51] The relationship between the sharp object and male flesh can be read as a dynamic between the inanimate object and the human body, a relationship which produces corporeal colour through the spilling of male blood. These omnipresent metaphors foreshadow the piercing of the male body, and keep the vulnerability of male flesh at the forefront of our minds even when the male characters are 'stabbed' offstage. Whilst the female body is a surface upon which emotions are metaphorically inscribed, Lorca's exploration of the male body is centred on what lies beneath the canvas-like skin, complementing Connor's interpretation of human skin in Western culture as 'a screen which lets out colour from within, especially, of course, the colour and the coursings of the blood'.[52] This 'screen' of skin is a surface layer which conceals, and then reveals, the crimson of blood underneath as it is spilled and represented in different stages of dryness and viscosity. Considering the male body as a site of internal as well as external colour and as a vessel for bodily fluids reminds us of the vigorous rather than passive and decorative possibilities of colour. It also highlights the importance of the blood motif as part of Lorca's work with implicit colour, particularly in the spilling of male blood in *Bodas de sangre* and *Así que pasen*. In these two plays Lorca probes the sensory and mobile capacities of material redness (blood) and the draining of the male body. In *Don Perlimplín* and *El público*, more disturbing portrayals of the body and the male psyche begin to emerge, both in Perlimplín's self-stabbing and fractured personality and in the sadistic treatment of the First Man by the Director and of the Red Nude by the Nurse. Through his exploration of the internal colours of the male body Lorca seeks to expose what is below the surface and to create equally powerful male counterparts to his portrayals of female suffering, calling into question the damaging effects of both male and female gender roles.

The body as a screen for redness is central to the blood discourse of *Bodas de sangre*. This is also the play in which Lorca gives the most sustained attention to the dynamic between male flesh and the knife motif, leading Lima to suggest that the knife becomes a 'sinister protagonist', a menace which is continually reaffirmed by the Mother's obsession with and fear of 'todo lo que puede cortar el cuerpo de un hombre' (p. 311) [everything that can cut a man's body].[53] The blade has an ominous recurring presence in the dialogue as both 'cuchillo' and 'navaja' and is even central to the baby's lullaby, metaphorically present in the 'puñal de plata' (p. 323) [silver dagger] which pierces the horse's eye. The knife incites fear and power even in its diminutive forms as 'el cuchillo más pequeño' (p. 311) [the smallest knife] and 'un cuchillito que apenas cabe en la mano' (p. 412) [a little knife barely as big as your hand]. This repertoire of piercing tools makes blood a central image in *Bodas de sangre*, as indicated by the very title. Blood has multiple competing connotations in the play, such as the hereditary blood line, the blood feud between two families, the 'elemental instinctive force of life' and erotic passion, and the loss of virginity, as Reed Anderson observes.[54] Lima also sees blood in the play as indicative of honour, passion, temperament, vitality, fertility, fate, and the libation made to the earth.[55] In *Bodas de sangre*, redness is often a mobile, liquid force which is described in terms of flowing and spilling as the punctured male body is drained of its vital life-force. Unlike the motifs of blood and milk in *Yerma*, these bodily colours are not part of a creative cycle but are indicative of processes of exsanguination and death. Leonardo and the Groom become 'dos cántaros vacíos [...] dos arroyos secos'

(p. 388) [two empty pitchers [...] two dry streams], creating a chthonic counterpart to the 'arroyos' of breast milk in *Yerma* and of silver in Belisa's bathing scene in *Don Perlimplín*. Lorca also describes the men as 'dos hombres duros con los labios amarillos' (p. 312) [two stiff men with yellow lips], a rare engagement with explicit bodily colour in the play which captures the rigor mortis of their bodies and the morbid colours of death. The mobile, violent images of redness add to the tension of the play as we wait for the spilling of blood, which now seems inevitable, and are present throughout the dialogue. For example, in the lullaby in Act One, Scene Two we are told that 'la sangre corría más fuerte que el agua' (p. 323) [blood flowed faster than water]. These fluid evocations of redness often take on eruptive values, such as the Moon's and the Second Woodcutter's references to blood as 'esta fuente de chorro estremecido' (p. 392) [this trembling jet-like fountain of blood] and 'el chorro' (p. 396) [jet] respectively in Act Three, Scene One. This is a pulsing and rapid flow of blood which is prone to spurt from the male body in violent ways. Lorca's use of 'trembling' also enhances the kinaesthetic properties of this image. Bodily redness throughout the play is a powerful and eruptive force which keeps the suffering and vulnerability of male body at the forefront of the audience's mind and emphasises the deep anxieties of the characters and the tension building towards the inevitable violence of the final Act.

Lorca's exploration of blood in *Bodas de sangre* is also steeped in the sensory, like the haptic qualities of the images of blood and milk in *Yerma*. As spent blood congeals, it becomes more viscous, creating images of a sticky, darkening redness. However, these representations of blood are not limited to the tactile; there are several disturbing references to the gustatory qualities of blood. In Act Two, Scene Two, the Mother describes herself as licking her elder son's blood from her hands:

> PADRE   Lo que yo quisiera es que fuera cosa de un día. Que en seguida tuviera
> dos o tres hombres.
>
> MADRE   Pero no es así. Se tarda mucho. Por eso es tan terrible ver la sangre de
> uno derramada por el suelo. Una fuente que corre un minuto y a nosotros
> nos ha costado años. Cuando yo llegué a ver mi hijo, estaba tumbado en
> mitad de la calle. Me mojé las manos de sangre y me las lamí con la lengua.
> Porque era mía. Tú no sabes lo que es eso. En una custodia de cristal y
> topacios pondría yo la tierra empapada por ella. (p. 368)

> [FATHER   I wish it only took a day. That straight away there were two or three
> men.
>
> MOTHER   But it's not like that. It takes a long time. That's why it's so terrible
> to see a man's blood spilled over the floor. A fountain which runs for one
> minute but has taken us years. When I reached my son, he was lying in the
> middle of the street. I dipped my hands in his blood and licked them with
> my tongue. Because it was mine. You don't know what that means. I would
> put the earth soaked with it in a holy vessel of crystal and topaz.]

Again, blood is a gushing and flowing force spilled quickly and violently. Here Lorca also combines the haptic, gustatory, olfactory, and even auditory values of this redness with a maternal possessiveness, creating a ferocious and primal portrayal of motherhood. This scene reflects the almost uncontrollable instincts that drive the characters in this play and reminds us of the colouring of maternity in *Yerma*. These multi-sensory evocations of bodily colour continue in Act Three, Scene One, when the Second Woodcutter and the Moon anticipate the spilling of the lovers' blood as their escape is foiled by the blue light of the moon. The Second Woodcutter suggests that their spilled blood will be imbibed by the earth — 'sangre que ve la luz se la bebe la tierra' (p. 387) [blood which sees the light is drunk by the earth] — a gustatory act echoed in the Moon's repeated reference to its bloodied cheeks: 'esta noche tendrán mis mejillas roja sangre' (p. 390), [tonight there will be red blood on my cheeks], 'para que esta noche tengan mis mejillas dulce sangre' (p. 391) [so that tonight there is sweet blood on my cheeks].[56] The sinister nature of the Moon character is accentuated by the cruelty of its dialogue and these disturbing images of it drinking blood and revelling in death. The Moon also appeals to the haptic and auditory qualities of blood: 'que la sangre me ponga entre los dedos su delicado silbo' (p. 392) [let the blood leave a delicate whistle between my fingers]. The 'delicate whistle' of blood against its fingers captures both the noise and the texture of its colour-sensation.

These portrayals of material redness capture the explosive and fluid force of colour and Lorca's appeal to the senses, both part of his aim of creating an active, visceral theatre of poetry. However, these punctured bodies are actually absent from the stage and the spilling of male blood remains largely verbal. Instead the male body becomes a 'lost object' which is 'at the centre of García Lorca's practice of tragedy', as Smith suggests.[57] Whilst we see their blood — Leonardo and the Groom's blood on the Bride's hair and clothing, in *Bodas de sangre*, and Perlimplín's blood and the dagger in his chest, in *Don Perlimplín* — the 'actual' stabbing of the male body is withheld from the stage, with the exception of the Red Nude in *El público*. In turn, the death of the Young Man in *Así que pasen* is bloodless; he is killed when the First Player shoots an illuminated heart projected onto the wall. The withholding of the visual stabbing of the men is not out of respect for audience sensibilities, as Lorca is not afraid of subverting our expectations and shocking us with visual details. Rather, the focus of his theatre of poetry is a metaphorical exploration of surfaces and an engagement with human emotion and grief, rather than literal bodily pain. In *Bodas de sangre* it is not the act of stabbing that is important but rather the deep-rooted grief it sparks in the female characters, enhancing the powerful dialogue and corporeal wounding of the Mother and the Bride. The men are dead by Act Three, Scene One. Indeed, the men die between the two scenes, represented only by cries off stage and by the events which the Beggarwoman relates to the two young women at the begging of Act Three, Scene Two. The final scene belongs only to the grieving women as the Bride goes to the Mother to ask for death. It is also in this final scene where redness finally becomes flesh as the Bride returns soaked in blood; the material redness of these male deaths is staged only on *her* body. However, the evocations of blood in the dialogue build up to this moment through their repetition and the foreboding they create. As Morris observes 'there is no escape from mentions and pictures of blood in this play; and the shedding of it is reported or predicted in a succession of gory echoes'.[58] He adds that due to the pervasiveness of these blood images, at times we forget the lack of visual redness: 'we have been so conditioned by constant visions of blood spilt and prophesies of blood to be spilt that it may come as a surprise to learn that the red yarn [in Act Three, Scene Two] is the first time that Lorca actually puts the colour before our eyes instead of before our imagination'.[59] It is only in the final scene where blood becomes visual as the Bride returns with her hair and skirt soaked in that of her lovers. Throughout *Bodas de sangre* the implicit redness of blood is a pervasive mental image that continually reinstates the central poetic motif and forms part of Lorca's exploration of an instinctive and immersive theatre of poetry, imprinting both male and female suffering on the body through verbal and visual colour.

The eruptive and sensory capacity of spilled male blood and its chromatic output are also important in the final scene of *Así que pasen*. As we wait for the Players or Fates to finish their game of chance with the Young Man, their dialogue is full of forceful images of blood which foreshadow the Young Man's impending death. The jet-like movement of blood which we find in *Bodas de sangre* is echoed in the Players' discussion of the pallid Young Man and of a past victim:

> JUGADOR 1.° (*Al 2°*)   No aprenderás nunca a conocer a tus clientes. ¿A éste? La vida se le escapa en dos chorros por sus pupilas, que mojan la comisura de sus labios y le tiñen de coral la pechera del frac.
> JUGADOR 2.°   Sí. Pero acuérdate del niño que en Suecia jugó con nosotros casi agonizante, y por poco si nos deja ciegos a los tres con el chorro de sangre que nos echó. (pp. 264–65)

> [FIRST PLAYER (to SECOND)   You will never learn to know your clients. Him? His life is escaping in two jets through his pupils, moistening the opening of his lips and staining the front of his dinner jacket coral.
> SECOND PLAYER   Yes. But remember the boy who played with us in Sweden who was close to death, and still nearly blinded the three of us with that gush of blood that spurted out.]

Like *Bodas de sangre*, we see blood represented as a 'chorro' or 'gush'. This spurt of blood is particularly violent as it nearly blinds the three Players — 'poco si nos deja ciegos' — and creates an image of their faces bloodied by the redness of the dying boy. The 'two jets' of 'life' gushing out of the other victim's pupils also conjure a disturbing image of blindness. The moistness and coral colour suggest that this life-force is also a reference to blood. Lorca's use of 'teñir' [to dye] captures the power of this liquid to change the colours of bodies and objects, creating a new colour as the red blood turns pink against the white shirt front and reminding us of the reference to dyeing Adela's iconic green dress black in *Bernarda Alba* and of the Bride soaked in blood in *Bodas de sangre*. The reference to 'blood' moistening lips also evokes the gustatory value of redness, which is intensified by First Player's reference to the playing cards which 'beben rica sangre' (p. 264) [drink rich/tasty blood]. As in *Bodas de sangre*, male blood is tasted and is described in comestible terms, here 'rica' rather than 'dulce' [sweet]. However, these powerful images of redness are not made visual in the Young Man's rare on-stage death. Rather, this is a highly stylised and surreal scene:

En este momento, en los anaqueles de la biblioteca aparece un gran as de coeur iluminado. El Jugador I. ° saca una pistola y dispara sin ruido con una flecha. El as desaparece, y el joven se lleva las manos al corazón. (p. 270)

[In that moment, a large, illuminated ace of hearts appears on the library shelves. The First Player draws a pistol and soundlessly shoots it with an arrow. The ace disappears, and the Young Man clutches his chest.]

Despite the verbal references to blood in this scene, the Young Man dies a bloodless death. This is a striking scene in which the ghostly Players are dressed in black suits and long white capes, which Farris Anderson sees as indicative of a 'deathly pallor'.[60] However, the theatrical and unusual nature of the scene is less potent than the raw grief and pervasive threat of the knife in *Bodas de sangre*, leaving us surprised rather than moved by this anti-mimetic portrayal of death. Rather than an outpouring of redness this is a detached and quasi-cinematic vision of death which avoids the literal piercing of the male body through the proxy of the illuminated, theatrical heart.

Lorca's portrayal of bodily colour in *Así que pasen* is more deeply rooted in the white, moribund male body which does not produce redness in visual form because it has already been drained of its life force and colour. This whiteness is more effective in Lorca's vision of a theatre of poetry because the verbal references are reinforced in the materiality of the staging and in the Young Man's bodily movements. The pallor of the Young Man's body and his bloodless death are indicative of a process of exsanguination and the bleaching of colour which is dominant from the beginning of the play. Wright argues that *Así que pasen* can be read as 'a sort of "frozen progression"' of photographs in which we move from one 'essentially dead image' to the next.[61] Indeed, Wright suggests that *Así que pasen* could be a fully-developed version of one of Lorca's unfinished 'photographic' plays in which he suggests 'la escena ha de estar impregnada de ese terrible silencio de las fotos de muertos y ese gris difuminado de los fondos' [the scene must be impregnated with that terrible silence of photos of the dead and that grey which blurs the backgrounds].[62] If we read the play as not only a series of static photographic images but also as a series of 'photos of the dead', the body, particularly the Young Man's body, takes on new meanings. Unlike the romanticised depictions and ethereal beauty of the white bodies of the Butterfly and Mariana discussed earlier in this chapter, the Young Man's whiteness is part of a more abject, eerie representation which substitutes the positive haptic values of silk and ermine with wax, ice, and withered leaves. The Young Man's physical appearance, with his bloodless, white waxen cheeks and hands, frozen teeth, and withered lips, evokes the dead body: 'esas mejillas de cera' (p. 175) [those cheeks of wax], 'una mano de cera cortada' (p. 212) [a severed wax hand], 'mi otro novio tenía los dientes helados; me besaba, y sus labios se le cubrían de pequeñas hojas marchitas. Eran unos labios secos', (p. 200) [my other boyfriend had frozen teeth; he kissed me and his lips were covered with little withered leaves. They were dry lips]. In the final scene of the play, this bleaching of bodily colour and vitality is complete. The outfit which the servants have laid out for the Young Man — a mo[u]rning suit and leather shoes 'que tienen cinta de seda negra' (p. 262) [which have black silk ribbons] — is funereal, a 'prelude to his own spiritual and physical death' as Edwards observes.[63] In terms of the Young Man's physical appearance, Lorca tells us that the character '*da muestras de una gran desesperanza y un desfallecimiento físico*' (p. 260) [shows signs of deep despair and physical exhaustion]. Instead of using 'desmayar', from the Old French 'esmaiier', Lorca chooses 'desfallecer', from 'fallecer', which has shifted semantically from 'to deceive or trick' in Latin to 'to die' in Castilian. Here, Lorca uses the richness of Spanish language to align the sapping of the Young Man's physical strength with a temporary state of 'death' or a 'pre-death', foreshadowing his actual demise. Like the fainting, white-clad Rosita at the end of *Doña Rosita* and the pallid Mariana in her shroud-like white dress in *Mariana Pineda*, Lorca imprints the Young Man's body with the physical and chromatic signs of his movement towards death.

The motifs of the stabbed male body and the spilling of bodily colour in *Don Perlimplín* and *El público* have a more disquieting effect than the discourse of bodily wounding in *Bodas de sangre* and the corporeal fading of the Young Man in *Así que pasen*. Both *Don Perlimplín* and *El público* reflect in different ways an assault on the male body which is indicative of disturbed mental states and comprises a translation of the psyche into evocations of material colour, as I explored in my analysis of *Bernarda Alba* in Chapter One. Whilst José Badenes has interpreted Perlimplín's suicide in *Don Perlimplín* as representative of a Christological bodily sacrifice which draws on the *auto sacramental* tradition, there is also a range of evidence that supports John Lyon's reading of Perlimplín as a complex, ever-changing character with a wide range of motivations, including revenge.[64] This complex characterisation is also reflected in Lorca's exploration of male bodily colour in the play, both in his blurring of 'male' and 'female' forms of bodily wounding and in his portrayal of Perlimplín's death, which is both the suicide of one side of his personality (Don Perlimplín, the husband) and the murder of the other side (Belisa's mystery admirer, the young man in the red cloak). At the end of Scene One, Perlimplín troubles the distinction between the portrayals of emotional (female) wounding and the stabbing of the (male) body we have seen so far when he describes the pain of Belisa's inaccessibility. His dialogue invokes the blades and quasi-surgical tools we see in the puncturing of the male body in *Bodas de sangre* and *El público*, and later in this play, yet is a metaphorical attack on the male body:

> Amor, amor,
> que estoy herido
> Herido de amor huido;
> herido,
> muerto de amor.
> Decid a todos que ha sido
> el ruiseñor.
> Bisturí de cuatro filos,
> garganta rota y olvido.
> Cógeme la mano, amor,
> que vengo muy mal herido,
> herido de amor huido
> ¡herido!,

¡muerto de amor!
CORTINA (p. 286)

[Love, love,
I am wounded.
Wounded by fleeing love;
wounded,
dead from love.
Tell everybody that it was
the nightingale.
Four-bladed scalpel,
broken throat and oblivion.
Take my hand, love,
I come badly wounded,
wounded by fleeing love;
wounded!
dead from love!
CURTAIN]

The focus on wounding is rhythmic in its repetition, emphasised by the falling curtain as the Act ends. The violent image of the quadruple scalpel blade and his earlier description of feeling love 'como un hondo corte de lanceta en mi garganta' (p. 277) [like a deep lancet cut in my throat] is suggestive of a violent, bloody assault on the throat which reminds us of Mariana's off-stage death by garrotte in *Mariana Pineda*. Belisa perpetuates these images when she threatens to kill Perlimplín to protect her 'lover': 'Marcolfa, bájame la espada del comedor que voy a atravesar la garganta de mi marido' (p. 301) [Marcolfa, get me the sword from the dining room, I am going run my husband through the throat]. The throat, a facet of white female beauty and death in *Mariana Pineda,* becomes a space of male vulnerability in *Don Perlimplín* and is under attack by traditionally masculine surgical and military tools — the scalpel, the lancet, the sword. These powerful images of the severing of Perlimplín's throat — the site of breathing, eating, drinking, and speech — imply a severing of the head from the body and of the psyche from the soma. They capture his emotional pain in equally powerful ways to the colourful bodily wounding in the discourse of the Mother and the Bride and Yerma in *Bodas de sangre* and *Yerma* respectively and extend the piercing of the male body by sharp instruments to the psychological realm.

This metaphorical piercing of Perlimplín's body and spilling of male redness is complemented by his 'actual' stabbing with the emerald dagger in the final scene. The green dagger is the only weapon in the play which takes material form on stage. It is also one of the agents of his transformation from caricature to protagonist of bones-and-blood as I discuss in Chapter Three. Although Perlimplín's stabbing takes place offstage, we see his bloodstained chest and the protruding dagger when he returns, the vibrant jewel colour merging with the tactile qualities of the red velvet cloak and spilled blood:

PERLIMPLÍN. (*Descubriéndose.*)   Tu marido acaba de matarme con este puñal de esmeraldas. (*Enseña el puñal clavado en el pecho.*) [...] Me ha matado... con este ramo ardiente de piedras preciosas.

[PERLIMPLÍN. *(Removing his cloak.)*   Your husband has just killed me with this
emerald dagger. *(He reveals the knife protruding from his chest.)* [...] He has
killed me... with this burning bouquet of precious stones.]

Lorca does not withhold the resulting bodily redness of the dagger but rather keeps
the act offstage in order to demonstrate the extent of Perlimplín's belief in the
illusion he has created. This allows Perlimplín to remain in his role as the admirer
in the red velvet cape even when he is mortally wounded, opening the cape to show
the dagger in his chest as part of his grand reveal. In his own troubled narrative,
Perlimplín is not the victim, but rather the attacker: '*Your husband* has just killed
me' (my emphasis). Perlimplín's insistence on maintaining the two different roles
in this scene captures the extent to which his psyche has become fractured as he
splits himself into two men who are simultaneously killed by the puncturing green
dagger. Perlimplín becomes detached from the ultimate stabbing of his own body,
developing a male alter-ego whom he associates with his unfulfilled visions of
masculinity yet simultaneously feels the need to destroy. In one sense, we can see
Perlimplín as the victim of traditional expectations of masculinity and of the social
pressures which brought a teenage girl and an old bachelor together in an unsuitable
marriage. However, Perlimplín is also a man pursuing a cruel and seemingly gleeful
revenge: "¡[...] don Perlimplín no tiene honor y quiere divertirse!' (p. 296) [Sir
Perlimplín has no honour and wants to have fun!]. Regardless of the cause, this is
an unsettling assault on the male body which represents a disturbed and divided
psyche. Perlimplín's conflicted inner world is translated into the piercing of his
body and the spilling of his blood as his madcap, theatrical scheme — which Belisa
never comprehends — is taken to the ultimate limit.

Whilst male bodily colour in *Don Perlimplín* results from self-inflicted injuries, in
El público bodily wounding and its chromatic output are centred on acts of violence
towards others, which is represented in the dialogue between the Director and
the First Man and their multiple identities in the play and by the quasi-surgical
mistreatment of the Red Nude in Scene Four. Whilst there are few physical
demonstrations of violence in the play, Kay García argues that the characters'
dialogue and the stripping away of costumes creates an 'atmosphere [which] is
charged with an overwhelming and shocking violence, principally because of the
reference to off-stage occurrences and the constant threat of physical assault'.[65] What
Wright identifies as a pervasive trend of 'sexual violence and ambivalence towards
the other' is central to the Director's discourse, particularly towards the First Man.[66]
Whilst Beatriz Cortez argues that the dynamic between male bodies is indicative
of sadomasochism, the Director's verbal violence towards the First Man is not a
mutually gratifying exchange, but rather a cruel assault which is more indicative
of sadistic pleasure derived from the abasement of the other.[67] This is not a generic
rejection of homosexuality or certain types of homosexuality, as Jonathan Mayhew
finds in his reading of Lorca's poem 'Oda a Walt Whitman' (1929) [Ode to Walt
Whitman].[68] Rather, it is reflective of the Director's self-disgust and deep-seated
psychological problems as he struggles against his sexual desires, part of Lorca's
troubling of surface appearances in his theatre of poetry and of his expression of the
inner reality of his complex characters of bones-and-blood.

The Director's relationship with the First Man is a cruel and disgusted dynamic of desire and rejection. Whilst colour seems to be less evident in these verbal portrayals, it is an implicit part of these images of pierced and lacerated skin and of the drawing of blood. In Act One, the Director expresses a desire to embroider the First Man's skin as part of a cruel and painful rejection of his body:

> DIRECTOR *(Frío y pulsando las cuerdas)*   Gonzalo, te he de escupir mucho. Quiero escupirte y romperte el frac con unas tijeritas. Dame seda y aguja. Quiero bordar. No me gustan los tatuajes, pero lo quiero bordar con sedas [...]
> HOMBRE I. ° *(Llorando)*   ¡Enrique! ¡Enrique!
> DIRECTOR   Te bordaré sobre la carne. (p. 83)

> [DIRECTOR *(Cold and strumming the guitar strings)*   Gonzalo, I have to spit on you a lot. I want to spit on you and cut up your dinner jacket with some little scissors. Give me silk and needle. I want to embroider. I do not like tattoos, but I want to embroider you with silks [...]
> FIRST MAN *(Weeping)*   Enrique! Enrique!
> DIRECTOR   I will embroider your flesh.]

The Director's 'coldness' is contrasted with the weeping of the First Man, and his references to 'silk and needle', 'embroider' and 'tattoos' capture the piercing of naked male flesh with needles. Unlike the social ritual of tattooing, the Director's figurative 'sewing' of the First Man's skin is a sadistic image which contrasts craftsmanship with the infliction of suffering and pain. In the motif of embroidery Lorca captures a disturbing and possessive chromatic marking of the male body. The exchange between the Figure with Gold Bells (the Director) and Figure with Red Vine Leaves (the First Man) in Act Two depicts a similarly sadistic attack on the First Man's body, a struggle which uses objects in perverted and non-typical ways and which contrasts images of blood with the anti-mimetic red and gold costumes:

> FIGURA DE PÁMPANOS *(Con voz débil)*   [...] ¿Y si yo me convirtiera en un granito de arena?
> FIGURA DE CASCABELES   Yo me convertiría en un látigo.
> FIGURA DE PÁMPANOS   ¿Y si yo me convirtiera en una bolsa de huevas pequeñitas?
> FIGURA DE CASCABELES   Yo me convertiría en otro látigo. Un látigo hecho con cuerdas de guitarra.
> FIGURA DE PÁMPANOS   ¡No me azotes!
> FIGURA DE CASCABELES   Un látigo hecho con maromas de barco.
> FIGURA DE PÁMPANOS   ¡No me golpees el vientre!
> FIGURA DE CASCABELES   Un látigo hecho con los estambres de una orquídea.
> FIGURA DE PÁMPANOS   ¡Acabarás por dejarme ciego! (pp. 92–93)[69]

> [FIGURE WITH RED VINE LEAVES *(In a weak voice)*   [...] And if I turned into a grain of sand?
> FIGURE WITH GOLD BELLS   I would turn into a whip.
> FIGURE WITH RED VINE LEAVES   And if I turned into a sac of tiny eggs?
> FIGURE WITH GOLD BELLS   I would turn into another whip. A whip made of guitar strings.

Figure with Red Vine Leaves   Don't whip me!
Figure with Gold Bells   A whip made from ship rope.
Figure with Red Vine Leaves   Don't hit my stomach!
Figure with Gold Bells   A whip made from orchid stamens
Figure with Red Vine Leaves   You'll blind me!]

The repeated references to whips made of differing and anomalous materials — guitar strings, ship rope, and implicitly coloured (yellow?) orchid stamens — suggest the metaphorical laceration of the First Man's body. The different widths, textures, and strengths of these materials evoke wounds which are equally varied, creating an imaginary pattern of lacerations on the First Man's skin. Again, this is an excessive wounding of the male body. The First Man's fear of blindness suggests that the figurative whipping would not be limited to certain areas of the body, and captures the extreme nature of the Director's frenzied violence and the First Man's subsequent mental torment. The Director's passionless comments are contrasted with the First Man's trembling and 'weak voice' and with the move from the interrogative mood to the imperative mood in the First Man's speech, a pleading effect emphasised by exclamation marks. The Director's metaphorical torture of the First Man's body, and the 'real' psychological torment he causes, reveals a troubled and violent subjectivity rooted in the flagellation and puncturing of the object of his rejection or of his desire. Whether the Director is suffering and resisting his own homosexuality or whether he takes pleasure in cruelty and sadism, the result is a highly disturbing attack on the male body.

The overall effect of this verbal violence and implicit colour images for the audience is Barthes's original formulation of the punctum, especially when combined with other challenging elements of the play such as themes of bestiality and sexual sadism, the various levels of plot and metatheatre, and the multiple overlapping characters including animal protagonists and surreal, anti-mimetic characters. The idea of the punctum, explored by Barthes in *Camera Lucida,* offers ways of reading Lorca's theatre as both an affective act of piercing and as a literal puncturing of the male body. Whilst *jouissance* or colour bliss is an erotic, explosive force, as we saw in Chapter One, the punctum is more of a sharp shock, our emotive reaction to a small detail. Here, colour becomes more subtle, yet the mental images these violent depictions create are all centred on the implicit redness of blood. In *Camera Lucida*, Barthes distinguishes between two aspects of photography: 'studium' and 'the punctum'. 'Studium' is a neutral reaction to a photograph, a broad cultural or historical interest or 'a kind of general, enthusiastic commitment [...] without special acuity'.[70] In contrast, 'the punctum' is an aspect of a photograph 'which rises from the scene, shoots out of it like an arrow, and pierces me [...] it is that accident which pricks me (but also bruises me, is poignant to me)'.[71] The punctum is a sudden spark of affect which disturbs the studium; it is Nick Ut's photograph 'The Terror of War' (1972) where children run through napalm; it is the eye being sliced open in the film *Un Chien andalou* (1929) [An Andalusian Dog].[72] Barthes's theory of the punctum can be used to capture the specific affective quality of the piercing of the male body and spilling of corporeal colour in Lorca's theatre, particularly the way in which Lorca uses these perforations to 'prick' the audience's consciousness in his innovative theatre of poetry.

The lingering, bruising effect which we find in *Bodas de sangre* and *Yerma*, and in *Don Perlimplín*, to a lesser extent, is replaced by the repeated affective shocks of extreme violence against the body as Lorca translates the piercing of the body into the 'pricking' of the spectator. These effects are compounded by Lorca's portrayal of the Male Nurse's 'treatment' of the Red Nude in Scene Four of *El público* which is a rare example of the 'actual' piercing of the male body in this play and which brings the poetic theme of violence to the stage in material form. The scene opens with the Red Nude hanging from a perpendicular hospital bed, wearing a crown of blue thorns, his naked red skin evocative of spilled blood. Wright describes this portrayal as '[an] aestheticized, represented, mediated [...] spectacle of pain'.[73] The obvious Christological references are distorted and afforded surrealistic values by both the colour scheme and the aesthetics of the scene, which Lorca tells us is intended to mimic a 'primitive' painting. As McDermid observes, this is a 'perverted enactment of the Passion of Christ' which transports these religious motifs to a 'quasi-medical' environment and imbues the Biblical narrative with 'a surgical thread'.[74] The disturbing and 'piercing' nature of this scene is intensified by the Red Nude's medical 'treatment':

DESNUDO   Yo deseo morir. ¿Cuántos vasos de sangre me habéis sacado?
ENFERMERO   Cincuenta. Ahora te daré la hiel, y luego, a las ocho, vendré con
        el bisturí para ahondarte la herida del costado. (p. 130)

[MALE NUDE   I want to die. How many pints of blood have you taken?'
MALE NURSE   Fifty. Now I will give you bile then, at eight o'clock, I will
        come with the scalpel to widen the wound on your side.]

This is a surgical approach to the body, but one which is inverted and twisted in its focus on the draining of the patient's blood and the widening of his wound. Lorca's use of 'vaso' evokes 'vaso sanguíneo', blood vessel or vein, which intensifies this image of the draining of blood. The Male Nurse does not take pleasure from this draining and piercing of the male body. Rather, he is dispassionate and chillingly logical, and the Red Nude does not challenge his 'treatment'. The anti-mimetic colouring of the scene and its distorted perspective combines the sharp shock of these images with unsettling instances of material colour which challenge the audience. Like Lorca's portrayal of the Young Man's death in *Así que pasen*, the torture and death of the Red Nude is a stylised proxy of the brutal death of the First Man, who appears in agony on the reverse of the hospital bed as it rotates on its axis at the end of the scene. Rather than offering us mimetic depictions of human pain, Lorca elevates these moribund bodies to a poetic plane which rejects realism and uses the body and its colours to confront, and overturn the audience's expectations in visual terms.

Another important aspect of Lorca's theatre of poetry in *El público* is the materialisation of his quest for what lies beneath the surface. Lorca makes this poetic motif flesh in the staging — the X-ray windows, the transformative portable screen, and the vast range of coloured costumes — and through his troubling of the corporeal boundaries. Wright argues that the body in *El público* is one susceptible to infiltration and to piercing; it is 'open, vulnerable to attack, to assault, penetration and even to emptying out', producing bodily colour through blood and other bodily fluid and excretions.[75] Wright supports Andrew Anderson's reading of the play as a journey 'from outside the body to deep within it'[76] and traces the progression from the outer costumes and accoutrements, including cosmetics and hair, to representations of bare skin, flesh, blood, and bone.[77] We 'see' inside the body as we journey through various colours of skin, red flesh and muscle, yellow fat, red blood, white vomit, and white bone. For Wright, this is 'an impressively graphic configuration of the human body' which also creates 'a highly suggestive image of the body fragmented, broken, and dismembered', an important avant-garde motif which recurs in Lorca's drawings and in his film script *Viaje a la luna* (1929) [Journey to the Moon].[78] In *El público*, parts of the body also become costume-like, such as the Second Man's 'capa de músculos que utilizo cuando quiero' (p. 107) [a cape of muscles which I use when I want to] and the Black Horse's reference to 'el último traje de sangre' (p. 117) [the last costume of blood] in which the redness of the body is conflated with the chromatic materiality of the costumes. Conversely, the costumes become bodies; the discarded harlequin, pyjama and ballerina costumes become anthropomorphised ghosts, zombified bodies which lack an inner entity. Everything is removable and can be stripped away, including what Wright defines as 'the visual accoutrements to gender'.[79]

The troubling of gender identity which Wright and McDermid explore in *El público* is representative of Lorca's theatre more generally and has enjoyed sustained critical attention.[80] Through these depictions of male and female suffering in his theatre of poetry, Lorca exposes the psychological effects of the inflexible and harmful constraints of gender constructed and policed by society. His engagement with corporeal colour, found in the bruises, burns, sores, lacerations, and spilled blood, his penetration of the layers of the body, and his communication of inner subjective states, is an important part of this critique of a rigid vision of gender. Lorca's communication of the inner turmoil of female characters such as the Bride, the Mother, and Yerma — an anguish triggered by the marital and maternal demands of society and by the honour code, as we also see in *Bernarda Alba* — finds its counterpart in the penetration and exsanguination of his male protagonists. Rather than a sacrifice of manhood, as Carlos Feal and José Badenes suggest respectively, or even a reversal or re-appropriation of phallic power, the perforation of Lorca's male characters can be seen as part of a broader rejection of the restrictions of gendered and sexual categories and the accompanying boxing-in of individuals.[81]

Queering the Body through Colour

As well as expressing the inner pain of men and women dominated by rigid gender roles and social norms through the chromatic output of the wounded body, Lorca uses anti-mimetic bodily colour and materials to promote a disquieting queering of the body. The apparent 'emotional bruising' (female) and 'puncturing' (male) dialectic becomes troubled when we begin to consider the affective power of these portrayals and their mutual communication of pain though bodily colour. A 'queer' approach to Lorca's text captures this ambiguity and fluidity, an approach which Stuart Davis in his analysis of the possibility of 'queering' Hispanic Studies suggests 'looks beyond the explanatory and celebrates indeterminacy [...] and finds its strengths in its ambiguity, allowing and encouraging multiple meanings to be generated from the words that stand on the page'.[82] Laura Doan and Jane Garrity suggest that the parallels between queer theory and Modernism are significant as they both 'resist fixity, cross boundaries, and regard with fascination the transgressive, marginal, and liminal'.[83] Mayhew's re-evaluation of the possibilities of using queer theory to read Lorca, the understanding of sexual identity as fluid and changeable rather than as subscribing to fixed categories and gender binaries, is a timely challenge to the sustained critical emphasis on Lorca's own homosexuality in relation to portrayals of gender and sexuality in his work. Mayhew argues for a reading of sexuality in Lorca's work as 'an unstable textual construct rather than a biographical essence', highlighting the difference between a 'gay' approach and a 'queer' approach to Lorca. He suggests that the latter 'invok[es] more fluid textualities and identities'.[84] As I discussed in my Introduction, a 'gay' reading of Lorca's work risks placing too much emphasis on his personal sexuality and presumed understandings of his state of mind. Mayhew suggests that it is precisely the ambiguity and the lack of 'a single, unified approach towards sexuality' in Lorca's work which makes queer theory such an appropriate tool for evaluating Lorca's treatment of gender and sexuality.[85] This approach ties in with larger issues of Lorca's concern with representing the suffering of individuals as a result of societal restriction, the ambivalence and experimentation of his theatre of poetry, and the ways these are figured through colour.

We find the most explicit portrayals of this chromatic queering in *El público* and *Así que pasen*. In her analysis of *El público*, García distinguishes between physical violence, whether verbal or visual, and 'aesthetic violence' which she defines as 'the use of violent colours and sounds, violent emotions, shocking vocabulary and concepts, and breaking with the traditional conventions of the theatre'.[86] We find this 'violent' evocation of colour in *El público* in the bright red body of the Red Nude (p. 129), the grey skin of the Centurion (p. 95), Juliet's pink celluloid breasts (p. 108), and Elena's blue eyebrows (p. 84). Bodies also take on object properties and absorb non-human materials in a blending of sensate and insensate which reflects Lorca's rejection of verisimilitude in his theatre of poetry. As well as Julieta's 'celluloid' breasts, the Pyjama Costume's face is *'blanca, lisa y comba como un huevo de avestruz'* (p. 123) [white, smooth, and curved like an ostrich egg' and Elena's feet (p. 84) and the Figure with Red Vine Leaves's nude body (p. 97) are made of *'yeso'*, plaster, like the restrictive mask which the Director refers to in Act Three

(p. 118). These representations of literal whiteness subvert the colours of the real human body. In *Así que pasen* bodily colour is equally challenging, particularly in the representation of 'female' bodies. As well as disturbingly dehumanised female bodies, which Wright proposes represent 'images of femininity as frozen, static and stultified', these anti-mimetic portrayals continue Lorca's queering of the body through colour and materiality in his theatre of poetry.[87] The Mannequin's anti-mimetic grey and gold bodily colouring contrast with its ornate white wedding dress, train and veil in the stage directions, and the verbal references to whiteness in its dialogue:

> *Entra en la escena* EL VESTIDO DE NOVIA. *Este personaje tiene la cara gris y las cejas y los labios dorados como un* MANIQUÍ *de escaparate de lujo. Lleva peluca y guantes de oro. Trae puesto con cierto embarazo un espléndido traje de novia blanco, con larga cola y velo.* (p. 219)

> [The WEDDING DRESS enters the scene. This character has a grey face and gold eyebrows and lips like a luxury department store MANNEQUIN. It has a gold wig and gloves. It wears, with a certain embarrassment, a splendid white wedding dress, with a long train and veil.]

Its discourse has patent haptic values, referring to coloured and textured materials such as silver, sand, gold, mirrors, feathers, flesh, leaves, moss, snow, milk, and blood, with a particularly emphasis on the silk of its costume. This is a disturbing and ghostly evocation of 'femininity' which enhances Lorca's portrayal of the corporeal fading and exsanguination of the Young Man. This white, gold, and grey 'body' is fragmented and dismembered; in the final scene it is now missing its head and its hands. The First Mask is equally evocative of aesthetic violence and the dehumanised 'body' with its yellow silk hair and white plaster mask:

> *Ésta viste en un traje de 1900, amarillo rabioso, con larga cola, pelo de seda amarillo, cayendo como un manto, y máscara blanca de yeso con guantes hasta el codo, del mismo color. Lleva sombrero amarillo, y todo el pecho de tetas altas ha de estar sembrado de lentejuelas de oro. El efecto de este personaje debe ser el de una llamarada sobre el fondo de azules lunares y troncos nocturnos. Habla con un leve acento italiano.* (p. 239).

> [This character wears a costume from 1900, rabid yellow, with a long train, yellow silk hair, falling like a shawl, and a white plaster mask with elbow-length gloves, in the same colour. It wears a yellow hat, and its perky bosom should be covered in gold sequins. The effect of this character should be like a flame against the background of blue spots and nocturnal trunks. It speaks with a light Italian accent.]

This character is an explosion of yellow and gold which stands out against the setting. The costume and materials — silk, plaster, sequins — invade and replace human flesh, creating a queer and anti-mimetic body which forms part of Lorca's challenging theatre of poetry. Lorca's use of anti-mimetic bodily colour and materials to portray male, female and non-human characters moves beyond a male-female binary in favour of experimentation and a queer, Modernist body that challenges and troubles audience expectations and strengthens the combined effect of the affective 'bruising' and 'piercing' of the audience.

Throughout these works, Lorca's exploration of the bodily, 'human' dimensions of his theatre of poetry begins with an apparently gendered portrayal of corporeal colour which gives way to a more fluid approach to gender and sexuality that complements the ambivalence and experimentation of his theatre and his priority of depth over surface appearance. The initial symbolic values inherent in Lorca's depictions of white female body segue into a more complex probing that problematizes corporeal 'whiteness' and instead creates a discourse of deeply-rooted human suffering. This is rendered in somatic terms in the female characters' dialogue and the 'literal' stabbing of the male body, creating a lingering affective impact which leaves us figuratively black and blue. My discussion of the implicit colour of the wounded body and of the labile motifs of blood and milk reveals a highly material aspect of Lorca's colour-work which is often neglected and which is centred on the creative power of maternity and the destructive forces of exsanguination and death. The affective impact of eruptions of male blood on the audience is enhanced by the sharp, pricking effect of the punctum, a three-dimensional animation of the unsettling and piercing photographic detail which Barthes explores. These gendered depictions of suffering give way to a queering of the body through an exploration of anti-mimetic bodily colour and materials which creates a more stylised and disconcerting representation of poetry made human.

Notes to Chapter 2

1. Marina Warner, *From the Beast to the Blonde* (London: Vintage, 1995), p. 381 and p. 363.
2. Richard Dyer, *White: Essays on Race and Culture* (Oxford: Routledge, 1997), p. 77.
3. Dyer, p. 64.
4. Lorca's use of 'bride', 'doncella', and 'niña' are all female roles which imply sexual innocence. 'Doncella' is used in literary contexts to mean 'maid' in the virginal sense, or 'damsel', drawing again on the traditional fairy-tale relation of fairness and virginity. Paula Ortiz's award-winning re-imagining of the play — *La novia* [The Bride] (2015) — contrasts the actress Inma Cuesta's dark natural colouring with her white clothing. She takes Lorca's description of the Bride's white underwear on her wedding morning and extends it to at least one element of her clothing throughout the film: her nightdress, underwear, petticoats, shirt and, in contradistinction to the original play, her wedding dress.
5. In the play's premiere the Butterfly's costume consisted of a silk dress and shawl and a hood with curved antennae. A photograph of the original costumes is replicated in Alfonso Vázquez, 'El maleficio de la mariposa, primer estreno de Federico García Lorca: Del teatro eslava a la sala del mariano' [The Butterfly's Evil Spell, Federico García Lorca's First Première: From the Eslava Theatre to the Sala del Mariano], *Moon Magazine*, 16 March 2017, <https://www.moonmagazine.info/lorca-el-maleficio-de-la-mariposa-trece-gatos/> [accessed 3 May 2022]. Subsequent productions have continued to experiment with more anti-mimetic and insect-like ensembles. For example, in Mario Jaime and Yadiro Trejo's 2011 staging with the theatre group Cassandra Maledictio (Centro Cultura de la Paz, Baja California, Mexico), the Butterfly wore a white body suit and hood with long antennae; white, black, and bronze contoured make-up; and elaborate white silk wings painted with red and green patterns like real butterfly wings, which the actress controlled with sticks. See a recording of her monologue at: Elti Alejandro López Lora, 'El Maleficio de la Mariposa — Monologo de la Mariposa.wmv', *Youtube*, 25 August 2012, <https://www.youtube.com/watch?v=tı9EobıJ9Lo> [accessed 3 May 2022].
6. Paul McDermid, *Love, Desire and Identity in the Theatre of Federico García Lorca* (Woodbridge: Tamesis, 2007), p. 47.

7. These references to pomegranate are an unusual and important choice given the mythical and etymological links between the fruit and Granada, Lorca's birth place, reminding us of the setting of both *Mariana Pineda* and *Doña Rosita*.

8. These two representations of floral fading also evoke the core poetic motif of the mutable rose in *Doña Rosita*, as I explore in my discussion of object colour and theatre of poetry in Chapter Three. Rosita's costumes fade from pink to pale pink, to white throughout the course of the play in line with her growing age and hopelessness.

9. Dyer, p. 209.

10. Sarah Wright, *The Trickster Function in the Theatre of Federico García Lorca* (Woodbridge: Tamesis, 2000), p. 53.

11. McDermid, p. 80.

12. Warner, p. 363. The trope of the sexualised and erotic body of 'foreign' women or women of colour is a more common theme. Stephen Garton comments on how 'the Orient, the empire, "exotic races" and other tropes functioned within nineteenth-century Western culture to signify sexuality [...]. Idealised representations of otherness were saturated in sexual metaphors of allure, domination, temptation, luxury, voluptuousness, and death. These images depicted the East as a place of erotic fantasy and fulfilment, cementing the image of the Orient as a feminized and sexualized world, completely other to the chaste domestic world of European middle-class maternalism', *Histories of Sexuality: Antiquity to Sexual Revolution* (Oxford and New York: Routledge, 2014), p. 131.

13. This gustatory evocation of female whiteness also reminds us of Don Mirlo's description of the Zapatera in *La zapatera prodigiosa*: 'Zapaterilla blanca, como el corazón de las almendras, pero amargosilla también' [Little Shoemaker's wife, white like the heart of almonds, but a little bitter tasting too] (p. 205).

14. This passage mirrors Lorca's poem 'Serenata' [Serenade], which is dedicated to the Golden Age playwright Lope de Vega, in his poetry collection *Canciones* (1921–1924). Federico García Lorca, *Canciones* [1921–1924] [Songs] in *Obra completa I*, ed. by Miguel García-Posada (Madrid: Ediciones Akal, 2008, (p. 561).

15. The 'nardo' or tuberose flower is a recurring motif in Lorca's work, as found in his portrayal of Mariana's white neck in *Mariana Pineda*. There is a long-standing tradition of associating tuberose perfume with sexuality and the body. In her 2017 study on perfume in Victorian literature, Catherine Maxwell refers to tuberose as a 'carnal' flower associated with both the dead body and the erotic body, *Scents and Sensibility: Perfume in Victorian Literary Culture* (Oxford: Oxford University Press, 2017), p. 183. Exploring the motif of the tuberose flower in the work of Victorian poets Mark André Raffalovich, Mary Robinson, and Theodore Wratislaw, Maxwell suggests that 'the scent of the tuberose is bound up with dangerous or voluptuous pleasures, with love, eroticism, criminality, and death' (p. 13).

16. Dyer, p. 42. Indeed, seeking to capture hue whiteness in bodily form is a sad and dangerous trend. See Natasha Eaton, 'Anechoic White? Meta-colour in South Asia', in *Third Text*, <http://www.thirdtext.org/anechoic-white> [accessed 1 Aug 2021] regarding the side effects of skin-lightening cosmetics in India. For a discussion of the more historic use of white lead make-up see *Stage Makeup* ed. by Richard Corson, James Glavan, and Beverly Gore Norcross, 10th edn (Oxford: Routledge, 2016), p. 314 and Sara Downing, *Beauty and Cosmetics 1550 to 1950* (London: Bloomsbury, 2012), p. 29.

17. Dyer, p. 19.

18. See Carol Mavor on gastro-racism in Toni Morrison's novel *The Bluest Eye* (1970), including a discussion of milk and sugar. Mavor, *Blue Mythologies: Reflections on a Colour* (London: Reaktion Books, 2013), pp. 56–58. For an exploration of the colonial values of material colour, see also Michael Taussig *What Color is the Sacred?* (Chicago: University of Chicago Press, 2009), especially his probing of lapis lazuli in Chapter Eight (pp. 40–46) and of indigo in Chapter Nineteen (pp. 141–58); and Natasha Eaton, *Colour, Art and Empire: Visual Culture and the Nomadism of Representation* (London: I. B. Tauris, 2013).

19. In *La novia* Ortiz casts Inma Cuesta as the Bride and deliberately contrasts her dark hair, eyes, and skin with the fair colouring of other characters, including the First Girl, Second Girl, and

the Wife and her baby son, all of whom are also Hispanic. The differences between the bodily colouring of the Bride and that of the Wife and her child are even more striking given their genetic relationship as cousins, and the dark colouring of the baby's father, Leonardo. In fact, it is in Leonardo's body that we find the closest chromatic mirroring of the Bride's, a visual suggestion of their compatibility.

20. Whilst the black wedding gown might seem ominous or funereal, C. B. Morris reminds us that it was an old Galician tradition. *García Lorca: Bodas de Sangre* (London: Grant and Cutler, 1980), p. 54. This may stem from the Spanish Roman Catholic tradition within which the black wedding dress symbolised their dedication to that marriage until death. Rather than red-on-black, Paula Ortiz's and Carlos Saura's film versions of the play use a white dress for a greater visual impact, perhaps also playing into contemporary Western expectations of wedding dresses as white.

21. In *La novia*, Ortiz begins with this crucial final scene before moving back to the preceding events. Her version opens with the Bride lying corpse-like in grey clay against a white desertscape, her white clothing stained with blood and her head shrouded in white cloth. Her body is suffering: she struggles to move her feet in the slippery grey clay, groaning with pain and clutching her abdomen, her lips dry and cracked. Her natural bodily colour is stained with dust, clay, and blood, a more literal interpretation of this poetic image.

22. 'La noche de boda entraron cinco personas por los balcones. Cinco. Representantes de las cinco razas de la tierra. El europeo con su barba, el indio, el negro, el amarillo y el norteamericano,' [on the wedding night five people entered through the balconies. Five. Representatives of the five races of the earth. The European with his beard, the Indian, the Black, the Yellow, and the American], *Don Perlimplín* (p. 287).

23. Dyer, p. 3.

24. Sara Ahmed, 'A Phenomenology of Whiteness', *Feminist Theory*, 8:2 (2007), pp. 149–68 (p. 157). In this article, Ahmed considers 'whiteness' as an experience which is ' "real", material and lived' and explores 'the experiences of inhabiting a white world as a non-white body' and 'how whiteness becomes worldly through the noticeability of the arrival of some bodies more than others', p. 150. She observes that 'in a way, whiteness itself is a straightening device: bodies disappear into the "sea of whiteness" when they "line up" ', p. 159.

25. Steven Connor, *The Book of Skin* (New York: Reaktion Books, 2003), pp. 154–55.

26. Morris, *García Lorca: Bodas de sangre*, p. 36.

27. See Paul Julian Smith, *The Theatre of García Lorca: Text, Performance, Psychoanalysis* (Cambridge: Cambridge University Press, 1998), pp. 63–64.

28. In Ortiz's adaptation, glass becomes a central motif and twice the Bride coughs up pieces of bloodied glass in a visual representation of the metaphorical glass-pierced tongue.

29. Morris, *García Lorca: Bodas de sangre*, p. 40 and p. 42.

30. 'Cieno' is a particular quality of mud: silt, slime, or mire, which reminds us of Bernarda's description of village gossip in *Bernarda Alba*: 'Hay a veces una ola de fango que levantan los demás para perdernos' (p. 372) [Sometimes there is a wave of mud sent by others to engulf us].

31. Gwynne Edwards, *Lorca: Theatre Beneath the Sand* (London: Boyars, 1980), p. 155.

32. Lorca's use of 'raíz' here reminds us of Rosita's conflation of floral and human bodies in her dialogue in *Doña Rosita*. This metaphor also implies depth, enhancing the images of a suffering which has penetrated the very veins of the Mother's body.

33. Smith, *The Theatre of García Lorca*, p. 17.

34. Smith, *The Theatre of García Lorca*, p. 16.

35. Connor, *The Book of Skin*, pp. 148–49.

36. See McDermid, pp. 156–61. Despite his reading of bisexuality in Yerma, Smith still suggests that the play as a whole is explicitly focused on the female body and its reproductive functions, *The Theatre of García Lorca*, p. 17. Yerma's reproductive body has been the focus of several stagings of the play. Victor García's and Fabiá Puigserver's controversial 1971 adaptation of this play placed the audience inside Yerma's body in a womb-like trampoline set which Delgado proposes mimicked 'the stretchable tissue of the womb, serving as a visual metaphor for Yerma's childlessness'. Delgado, *Federico García Lorca*, p. 91. In a similar evocation of the female body,

Helen Kaut-Howson's 2006 production at London's Arcola Theatre contrasted a white set with 'a central vulva-shaped pool surrounded by rocks' as reviewer Sam Marlowe tells us. Sam Marlowe, 'Yerma at Arcola Theatre', *The Times*, 30 August 2006 <https://www.thetimes.co.uk/articleyerma-9cdvdkbbvqs> [accessed 1 August 2021]. Marlowe suggests that the set, designed by Lilja Blumenfeld, is as 'bleakly unyielding' as Yerma's terrible fate.

37. Andrew Anderson, *García Lorca: Yerma* (London: Grant and Cutler, 2003), pp. 98–99. This sense of imprisonment is compounded by Juan's repeated insistence that Yerma remain in the confines of their home and not stray from the female, domestic sphere: 'Las ovejas en el rédil y las mujeres en su casa. Tú sales demasiado' (pp. 457–58) [Sheep in their pen and women in their house. You go out too much].

38. McDermid, p. 152. There are clear gender divisions in terms of activities and spaces in *Yerma*, and womanhood is inseparable from maternity as this is the only role the women are granted. In Act Two, Scene Two, Yerma states: 'los hombres tienen otra vida: los ganados, los árboles, las conversaciones, y las mujeres no tenemos nada más que esta de la cría y el cuidado de la cría' (p. 459) [Men have another life: livestock, trees, conversations, and we women have nothing more than this matter of the child and raising the child]. Lorca's use of 'cría' reflects the play's agricultural discourse as this term also refers to animal offspring. We see this marked division of space and tasks by gender in *Bernarda Alba* in Act Two when the women, sat inside sewing, listen to the male reapers' song outside and lament the differences between the lives of men and women, and in Act One when Bernarda tells her daughters 'hilo y aguja para las hembras. Látigo y mula para el varón' (p. 320) [Needle and thread for the women. Whip and mule for the man]. As well as being a disapproving, colloquial term for a woman, 'hembra' is usually used to refer to the biological sex of an animal, reminding us of the discourse surrounding motherhood and women in *Yerma* in which women are paralleled with sheep and their children are described as their 'young'.

39. Anderson, *García Lorca: Yerma*, p. 75.

40. In his essay 'The Milk of Death', Georges Didi-Huberman explores milk in ways that depart from this affirmative, natural, and life-giving portrayal, arguing that milk is not necessarily 'pur' as it is 'toujours prés de tourner, de cailler, de "bleuir", de fermenter, de grumeler','Le Lait de la mort' in *Blancs soucis* [White Worries] (Paris: Minuit, 2005), pp. 9–65 (p. 31). 'Pure', 'always ready to turn, to curdle, to "turn blue", to ferment, to go lumpy'. English translation taken from Shalev-Gerz's website: 'Georges Didi Huberman: The "Blancs Soucis" of Our History', <http://www.shalev-gerz.net/wp-content/uploads/2014/08/Blancs_soucis_EN.pdf?> [accessed 1 August 2021]. See also Eric Robertson's useful discussion of this essay in ' "Le blanc souci de notre toile" ', pp. 328–29.

41. Despite claims that *Así que pasen* constitutes a hiatus in Lorca's theatre, along with *El público*, the wedding dress mannequin's dialogue is strongly evocative of this passage from *Yerma*, mimicking her fountains of milk and the wasp image in a discourse of blood, milk, and haunting: 'dos fuentes de leche blanca mojan mis sedas de angustia y un dolor blanco de abejas cubre de rayos mi nuca' (*Así que pasen*, p. 223) [two fountains of white milk dampen my silks of anguish and a white pain of bees covers my neck in lightning bolts]. The verbal whiteness in the mannequin's dialogue comes across as a hybrid of Lorquian women past and future. As well as *Yerma*, the mannequin evokes the Bride's crown of orange blossom in *Bodas de sangre* ('mi corona de azahar', [my crown of orange blossom], *Así que pasen*, p. 219); the 'frost' on Rosita's and the Manola sisters' bridal night gowns in *Doña Rosita* ('ropa interior que se queda helada de nieve oscura' [underwear that stays frozen with dark snow], *Así que pasen*, p. 220); and the foam in María Josefa's speech in Act Three of *Bernarda Alba* ('sin que los encajes puedan competir con las espumas' [without the lace being able to compete with foam], *Así que pasen*, p. 220).

42. Anderson, *García Lorca: Yerma*, p. 70.

43. Anderson, *García Lorca: Yerma*, p. 92.

44. Gwynne Edwards, 'Introduction', in *Federico García Lorca Yerma*, trans. by Gwynne Edwards (London: Methuen Drama, 2007), pp. v–lxv (p. xxviii).

45. Anderson, *García Lorca: Yerma*, p. 94 and pp. 80–81. Anderson proposes that the various female characters in the play — including María, the First Girl, the Second Girl, the Old Woman, and

the Washerwomen — allow Lorca to explore a range of views regarding marriage and maternity. For example, the Second Girl 'flouts authority' by claiming she does not want children and by having sexual intercourse with her boyfriend, whilst María 'clearly embodies the most balanced implementation of these teachings' and has 'a caring, faithful relationship with her husband'. Anderson, *García Lorca: Yerma*, pp. 30–31.

46. Carol Mavor, *Black and Blue: The Bruising Passion of 'Camera Lucida', 'La Jetée', 'Sans Soleil', and 'Hiroshima Mon Amour'* (Durham, NC: Duke University Press, 2012), p. 16. Mavor is quoting Sarah Turner here.

47. Mavor, p. 15 and p. 81.

48. Charles Spencer, 'A Woman's Pain Laid Bare', *The Telegraph*, 30 August 2006, <https://www.telegraph.co.uk/culture/theatre/drama/3654936/A-womans-pain-laid-bare.html> [accessed 1 August 2021]. He adds that: '[Kathryn] Hunter, physically diminutive but with an extraordinarily deep and expressive voice, captures all the impotent rage and frustration of a woman who feels deprived of her natural destiny [...] She brilliantly captures the complex mixture of delight, curiosity, sour jealousy and grief with which a childless woman regards the apparently effortless progeny of others'.

49. Ben Lawrence, 'Billie Piper Will Make You Numb with Pity: Review', *The Telegraph*, 5 August 2016 <https://www.telegraph.co.uk/theatre/what-to-see/billie-piper-will-make-you-numb-with-pity-in-yerma---review/> [accessed 11 September 2019]. For Lawrence, it is Piper's role as Yerma which invests this production with so much affective charge: 'Appearing in all but one scene, she snares you — uttering each line with an extraordinary spontaneity which in turn brings an emotional truth that Stone's production doesn't always deserve'. *Doña Rosita* has been described in similarly emotive terms: 'Our hearts break as we see a vivid young woman, fresh as one of her uncle's beloved roses, condemn herself to an arid life', Elyse Sommer, 'Doña Rosita the Spinster: A CurtainUp Review', *CurtainUp*, 11 January 2004 <http://www.curtainup.com/donarosita.html> [accessed 1 Aug 2021]. 'A searing drama of lost love and hope', Philip Fisher, 'Doña Rosita the Spinster', *British Theatre Review*, March 2004, <http://www.britishtheatreguide.info/reviews/donarosita-rev> [accessed 1 August 2021].

50. Robert Lima, 'Blood Spilt and Unspilt: Primal Sacrifice in Lorca's Bodas de sangre', *Letras peninsulares*, 8.2–3, (1995), 256–59 (p. 256).

51. Rupert Allen comments on the 'natural tendency to see the moon as an ax blade [...] or knife, since the analogy of form creates a sympathy between the moon and cutting instruments', *Psyche and Symbol in the Theater of Federico García Lorca: 'Perlimplín', 'Yerma', 'Blood Wedding'* (Austin: University of Texas Press, 1974), pp. 193–94.

52. Connor, *The Book of Skin*, p. 155.

53. Lima, p. 256.

54. Reed Anderson, *Federico García Lorca* (London: Macmillan, 1984), p. 100.

55. Lima, pp. 256–59.

56. The descriptions of the Mother lapping her son's blood and of the Moon imagining blood on its cheeks denote a vampiric digestion of redness, which is emphasised by the reference to 'sweetness' in the latter. In his discussion of portrayals of whiteness and death in Western visual culture, Dyer argues that colour is central to the vampire myth: 'Because vampires are dead, they are a pale cadaverous, white. They bring themselves a kind of life by sucking the blood of the living, and at such points may appear flushed with red, the colour of life' (p. 210).

57. Smith, *The Theatre of García Lorca*, p. 58.

58. Morris, *García Lorca: Bodas de sangre*, p. 51.

59. Morris, *García Lorca: Bodas de sangre*, p. 50–51.

60. Farris Anderson, 'The Theatrical Design of Lorca's Así que pasen cinco años', *Journal of Spanish Studies*, 7 (1979), 249–78 (p. 273).

61. Wright, *The Trickster Function*, pp. 82–83.

62. Wright, *The Trickster Function*, p. 83. Lorca is originally cited in Laffranque, *Teatro inconcluso*, p. 20.

63. Edwards, *Theatre Beneath the Sand*, p. 112.

64. See José Badenes, '"This Is My Body which Will Be Given Up for You": Federico García

Lorca's Amor de Don Perlimplín and the Auto Sacramental Tradition', *Hispania*, 92.4 (2009), 688–95, and Lyon, pp. 241–42. The auto sacramental was a type of Spanish morality play, usually with a religious theme, which was popular in the seventeenth and eighteenth centuries, such as Calderón's *El gran teatro del mundo* [The Great Theatre of the World] (c. 1634). The Eucharist sacrament was often an important feature. Badenes argues that Perlimplín's death evokes this religious rite as the Eucharist liturgy which refers to Christ's sacrifice of his body and of his blood comprises 'precisely the kind of self-sacrificing love found in Amor de Don Perlimplín' as 'it has to do with the oblation of the body for another out of love' (p. 691).

65. Kay García, 'Violence in Two Plays by Federico García Lorca', in *Violence in Drama*, ed. by James Redmond (Cambridge: Cambridge University Press, 1991), pp. 205–13 (p. 209).

66. Wright, *The Trickster Function*, pp. 110–11.

67. See Beatriz Cortez, 'Sadomasoquismo y travestismo en El público de Federico García Lorca: Un reto al heterosexismo compulsivo', *Hispanófila*, 133 (2001), 31–42.

68. See Jonathan Mayhew, 'Sexual Epistemologies: The Whitman Ode', in *Lorca's Legacy: Essays in Interpretation* (New York: Routledge, 2018), pp. 143–63. Mayhew argues that there are two types of homosexuality prevalent in the poem, the private and the public. He proposes that 'one of the things that bothers the speaker of the Ode the most is the public, *uncloseted* nature of urban homosexuality' (p. 153). Original emphasis.

69. See Carlos Jerez Ferrán, *Un Lorca desconocido: Análisis de un teatro 'irrepresentable'* [An Unknown Lorca: Analysis of an 'Unstageable' Theatre] (Madrid: Biblioteca Nueva, 2004) for an analysis of homosexuality and the avant-garde in *El público*, including this scene.

70. Roland Barthes, *Camera Lucida: Reflections on Photography*, trans. by Richard Howard (London: Vintage, 2000)), p. 26. For an examination of the impact of Barthes's changing perspectives regarding photography and visual representation on cultural and media studies, see Jean-Michel Rabaté (ed.), *Writing the Image after Roland Barthes* (Philadelphia, PN: Philadelphia University Press, 1997).

71. Barthes, *Camera Lucida*, p. 26.

72. Gwynne Edwards and Virginia Higginbotham have commented on the influence of this film on *Así que pasen*. See Edwards, 'Lorca and Buñuel: Así que pasen cinco años and Un chien andalou' [When Five Years Pass: A Literary Version of An Andalusian Dog], *García Lorca Review*, 9.2 (1981), 128–41, and Virginia Higginbotham, 'Así que pasen cinco años: Una versión literaria de Un chien andalou', *Cuadernos Hispanoamericanos*, 433–34 (1986), 343–50. Delgado and Smith also suggest that *An Andalusian Dog* heavily influenced Lorca's film script *Viaje a la luna*. See Smith, 'Reading Intermediality: Lorca's *Viaje a la luna* (Journey to the Moon, 1929) and *Un chien andalou* (Buñuel/Dalí, 1929)', *Modern Languages Open* (2014), 1–9, and Delgado, *Federico García Lorca*, pp. 128–29. The film's title supposedly refers to Lorca himself, which offended Lorca. According to Buñuel in his 1984 autobiography: 'Shortly before *Un chien andalou* Lorca and I had a falling-out; later, thin-skinned Andalusian that he was, he thought (or pretended to think) that the film was actually a personal attack on him. "Buñuel's made a little film, just like that!" he used to say, snapping his fingers. "It's called *An Andalusian Dog*, and I'm the dog!"' Luis Buñuel, *My Last Breath*, trans. by Abigail Israel (London: Vintage Digital, 2011), p. 157.

73. Wright, *The Trickster Function*, p. 122.

74. McDermid, p. 135 and pp. 138–39.

75. Wright, *The Trickster Function*, p. 116. For Wright, the body in *El público* is representative of Mikhail Bakhtin's 'grotesque body of carnival', which he explores in his 1965 study of Rabelais, as Lorca emphasises 'images of waste and excretions' and 'the lower bodily stratum, as well as the body's orifices', standing in contrast with the 'closed and individualised' Renaissance body. Wright, *The Trickster Function*, pp. 106–07. This sealed-off body is also found in *El público* in the depictions of plaster body parts which evoke Classical sculptures, including Elena's feet and the Emperor's hands, as I discuss later in this chapter. This lapidary whiteness takes us back to the realm of colour and architecture and to David Batchelor's comparison of Bakhtin's classical body and the art collector's ascetic white house. He notes 'the idea that anything might protrude, bulge, sprout or branch off from this sheer whiteness was inconceivable [...] this space was clearly a model for how a body ought to be: enclosed, contained, sealed'. Batchelor, *Chromophobia*, pp. 18–19.

76. Andrew A. Anderson, '"Un dificilísimo juego poético: Theme and Symbol in Lorca's *El público*', *Romance Quarterly*, 39.3 (1992), 331–46 (p. 332).

77. Wright, *The Trickster Function*, p. 108.

78. Wright, *The Trickster Function*, p. 108.

79. Wright, *The Trickster Function*, p. 90.

80. See Wright's discussion of androgyny in *El público*, *Así que pasen*, and *Bodas de sangre* in *The Trickster Function*, pp. 87–04; McDermid's exploration of masculinity and queering in *El público* (*Love, Desire and Identity*, pp. 126–32 and pp. 138–41), gender inversion in *Yerma* (pp. 150–60), and gender performance and camp in productions of *Bernarda Alba* (pp. 175–90); Paul Julian Smith's reading of *Yerma* as an intersexual type in *Text, Performance, Psychoanalysis*, pp. 24–33; and Bettina Knapp's analysis of hermaphroditism in *Bernarda Alba*, 'Federico Garcia Lorca's *The House of Bernarda Alba*: A Hermaphroditic Matriarchate', *Modern Drama*, 27.3 (1984), 382–94.

81. Carlos Feal reads the off-stage death of the men in *Bodas de Sangre* as a sacrifice of manhood before 'las fuerzas femeninas o maternales' [Feminine or maternal forces]. 'El sacrificio de la hombría en *Bodas de sangre*' [The Sacrifice of Manhood in *Blood Weddings*], *MLN*, 99 (1984), 270–87 (p. 287). In contrast, José Badenes suggests that throughout Lorca's plays 'embodied patriarchal heteronormative manhood is [...] immolated and sacrificed onstage' and instead a more androgynous homosexual masculinity is advocated. Badenes, 'Martyred Masculinities: Saint Sebastian and the Dramas of Tennessee Williams and Federico García Lorca', *Text and Presentation*, 5 (2008), 5–17, (p. 14).

82. Stuart Davis, 'Que(e)rying Spain: On the Limits and Possibilities of Queer Theory in Hispanism', in *Reading Iberia: Theory / History / Identity*, ed. by Helena Buffery, Stuart Davis, and Kirsty Hooper (Bern: Peter Lang, 2007), pp. 63–79 (p. 75).

83. Laura Doan and Jane Garrity, 'Modernism Queered', in *A Companion to Modernist Literature and Culture*, ed. by David Bradshaw and Kevin J. H. Dettmar (Oxford: Wiley-Blackwell, 2008), pp. 542–50, (p. 542).

84. Mayhew, p. 140. See also Miguel García López, *Queering Lorca's Duende: Desire, Death, Intermediality* (Cambridge: Legenda, 2021), which explores Lorca's concept of duende as the transgression of boundaries such as gender, sex, sexual identity, spatiotemporality, and media in poetry collections *Diván del Tamarit* (1934), and *Sonetos del amor oscuro* (1936) [Sonnets of Dark Love]; plays *Así que pasen* and *El público*; film script *Viaje a la luna*; and his drawings from 1930 to 1936.

85. Mayhew, p. 142.

86. García, p. 204.

87. Wright, *The Trickster Function*, p. 77. She sees this portrayal as rooted 'in outer accoutrements which signify an inner hollowness'. This depiction complements McDermid's reading of Julieta's celluloid breasts as 'hollow, transparent, flexible, and artificial'. McDermid, p. 120.

CHAPTER 3

❖

Object Colour:
From Page to Stage

This final chapter examines the role of object colour in Lorca's creation of a holistic theatrical experience that makes full use of the inter-relativity of the linguistic and material elements of the medium of theatre. I explore how Lorca 'makes poetry flesh' in his characters, particularly in the colours of their costumes, and examine the role of colour in the sets, lighting, and props in terms of the transference of key linguistic symbols and themes from page to stage as 'la poesía se levanta del libro y se hace humana' [poetry steps out of the book and becomes human].[1] I focus on Lorca's works that are guided by a central aesthetic vision in the title or subtitle: *Mariana Pineda*, *Don Perlimplín*, and, less explicitly, *Doña Rosita*, building on my discussion of the role of photography and the overarching visual and verbal conception of *Bernarda Alba* in Chapter One. I begin with an examination of the sensory and chromatic qualities of flowers in *Doña Rosita*, probing how Lorca communicates Rosita's emotional suffering through a blending of flowers and flesh that evokes the somatic discourse of *Bodas de sangre* and *Yerma* we saw in Chapter Two and exploring the role of 'the language of flowers' and her costume in this portrayal. In *Mariana Pineda*, I consider Lorca's use of costume colour to reflect or contrast with the colours of the sets, lighting, and props, weaving the hues of the *estampa* throughout the play, and his sensory engagement with the motif of the implicitly yellow quinces. The colours of the material staging in *Don Perlimplín* also reflect Lorca's aesthetic vision of the play, and act as a visual representation of Perlimplín's transformation from a stock figure to character of bones-and-blood. Similarly, I investigate the Shoemaker's Wife's visual presentation in *La zapatera prodigiosa* as the embodiment of the poetic themes and emotions of the play, and probe how Lorca creates a contrast between this character of bones-and-blood and others in the work. Throughout this chapter I consider how successful these portrayals are in terms of Lorca's aims in his theatre of poetry.

The personification of flowers or the attribution of floral qualities to the human body is a recurring theme in Lorca's theatre. Robert Havard, Sumner M. Greenfield, and Concha Zardoya have all commented on the paralleling of Mariana with flowers in *Mariana Pineda*,[2] whilst Margaret Rees draws our attention to the links between people and flowers in *La zapatera*, *Bodas de sangre*, and *Yerma*.[3] Belisa is also described as 'una azucena' (p. 269) [a lily] and 'encendida como un geranio'

(p. 295) [lit up like a geranium] in *Don Perlimplín*. Whilst flowers are an important motif throughout Lorca's theatre, in *Doña Rosita* they become integral. The range of flowers in *Doña Rosita* is astonishing, comprising over thirty species and leading Rees to comment on Lorca's botanical knowledge, comparing him to British horticulturalist Clay Jones.[4] The importance of the motif of flowers is emphasised in both the play's title — which refers to the nineteenth-century courtship tradition of communicating through the set symbols of a 'language of flowers' — and the subtitle which categorises the work as '[un] poema granadino del novecientos dividido en varios jardines, con escenas de canto y baile' [a nineteenth-century Granadan poem divided into various gardens, with scenes of song and dance]. In *Doña Rosita* the comparison between Rosita and the mutable rose forms a central part of the play's structure, its dialogue, and the characterisation of the eponymous protagonist. The rose is the 'poetic core' that guides Lorca's vision of a theatre of poetry in this play. The rose appears as a real flower in her Uncle's greenhouse until he fatefully cuts the stem in Act Two, symbolically foreshadowing Rosita's spiritual death, and in the form of the mutable rose poem in all three Acts.

Lorca divides the play into three temporally distinct Acts that reflect the three stages of the rose's life cycle: morning, afternoon, and evening. He also uses the mutable rose poem in a structural way by repeatedly linking it to Rosita's appearances on stage, and by using it as a way of questioning Rosita's location within the group of spinster sisters in Act Two. The colour aspect of this mutable rose aesthetic is explicit in Castilian due to the dual meaning of 'rosa' as both 'rose' and 'pink'. This pinkness is mirrored in the colours of Rosita's costumes. *Doña Rosita* is a prime example of how Lorca uses the visual presentation of his characters to reflect key linguistic themes and symbols, 'dressing' his characters of bones-and-blood in 'un traje de poesía' [a costume of poetry] as part of his theatre of poetry.[5] In an interview in 1935, Lorca tells us that 'yo pretendo hacer de mis personajes un hecho poético [...] Son una realidad estética' [I aim to make my characters a poetic fact [...] They are an aesthetic reality].[6] Lorca makes Rosita the embodiment of the aesthetic of the play by dressing her as the rose. Her costumes change from pink to pale pink to white throughout the play, and the varying styles of her dresses (leg-of-mutton sleeves in Act One, a bell-shaped skirt in Act Two) evoke the shapes of blossoms or petals. Lorca expands on this further when he describes the changing styles during the play: 'polisón, cabellos complicados, muchas lanas y sedas sobre las carnes, sombrillas de colores' [bustle, complex hairstyles, lots of wools and silks covering the flesh, coloured parasols] in Act One (set in 1885), 'talles de avispa, faldas de campanula' [wasp waists, bellflower skirts] in Act Two (set in 1900), and 'falda *entravée*' [hobble skirt] in Act Three (set in 1911).[7] However, this visual alignment is problematized by several factors. Whilst the chromatic values of 'rosa' as 'pink' are paralleled in Rosita's costumes, the mutable rose itself is described as 'roja como sangre' (p. 221) [as red as blood] in the morning and as turning white as evening falls. There is no visual alignment between Rosita and the first stage of the rose, as her costume is never red. Furthermore, the mutable rose is not explicitly described as pink; its pinkness is implied by what is assumed to be a gradual transition from red to white. Lorca himself contradicts this reading, describing the rose as '[una] flor que por la mañana es roja; más roja al mediodía; a la tarde, blanca, y con la noche se deshace' [a flower which is red in the morning; redder at midday; in the evening, white, and at nightfall it wilts and dies].[8] This is compounded by Lorca's use of the simple present tense when he describes the flower as turning white, which indicates a more sudden transformation than the present continuous tense or 'irse': '*se pone blanca, con blanco de una mejilla de sal*' (p. 221) [*it turns* white, as white as a cheek of salt (my emphasis)]. The reference to 'coral' in the poem, which seems to imply pinkness in Act One, is also challenged by the Uncle in Act Two when he suggests that 'en el mediodía, es roja como el coral' (p. 274) [in the afternoon, it is as red as coral]. Lorca does see Rosita in floral terms; he describes her as 'una doncella en flor, una doncella sin cortejo' [a maiden in flower, a maiden who has not been courted] and 'dura y fragrante como un nardo' [as firm and fragrant as a tuberose flower].[9] However, the pinkness of Rosita's costume points to a faded version of the rose motif; she already lacks the intense colours of the natural world when the play begins.[10] The poem exposes the burning pain and substance beneath the placid floral exterior of Rosita's name and costume in powerful embodied terms; she is 'la vida mansa por fuera y requemada por dentro de una doncella granadina' [the life of a Granadan maiden — placid on the outside and burning on the inside].[11]

The emotional reality of Rosita's spinsterhood and her role as a faded, less vital version of the mutable rose is also conveyed through the language of flowers, bringing the linguistic and material elements of the work together in Lorca's theatre of poetry. Much of the existing criticism on *Doña Rosita* focuses on the 'language of flowers' as having two distinct, competing components. Catherine Nickel comments on the contrast between a life of 'free creative expression', indicated by verse, and one of mundane repetition, reflected in the 'restricted standardized speech' of the prose passages.[12] Francie Cate-Arries reads the play as a juxtaposition of Rosita's 'repressed realm of unfulfilled wishes and passions' reflected in the mutable rose poem versus the 'socially condoned world of acceptable appearances' indicated by the traditional 'Lo que dicen las flores' [What the flowers say] song.[13] In contrast, María Pao suggests that the dichotomy of the play's language lies in the distinction between Rosita's stasis as the embodiment of the fixed, written word of the language of flowers tradition and the more transient oral/auditory dimension of the speech of the Aunt and the Housekeeper, which is evocative of action and a life fully lived.[14] Pao argues that the seemingly trivial, everyday conversations woven throughout the play are in fact of utmost importance as they capture 'the activities that fill in the space of this play', and offer insight into 'women's talk and women's concerns' and the realities of Granadan domestic life through the motifs of clothing, flowers, and food.[15] These are all persuasive readings given the plethora of poems and songs in the play and, of course, its structural poetic motif of the mutable rose. However, Noël Valis argues against binary readings of the language of flowers, such as conscious–unconscious and prose–poetry, suggesting instead that it has multiple, complex, and sometimes competing layers that defy such classification and which all form part of the expression of 'the deeper, less sayable meanings of the play'.[16]

Lorca tells us that the rose 'es como el símbolo del pensamiento que he querido que recoger [...] [un] pensamiento que la propia doncella repite una y otra vez' [is like the symbol of a thought I wanted to capture [...] a thought which the maiden herself repeats again and again].[17] Rather than a secondary element of the play, the language of flowers is the key to our understanding of Rosita's inner pain. Whilst there are two elements within the language of flowers — the song and the poem — they are neither competing nor autonomous; they work together as equally important aspects of the play's discourse and of Lorca's theatre of poetry.

Within the play's language of flowers, the primary manifestation is the mutable rose poem, which recurs throughout the play. Through these coloured textures, he seeks to create an embodied viewing experience that captures the corporeality of Rosita's role as the rose by inspiring mental pictures in the spectator's imagination. Elaine Scarry's study of mental re-creation in English literature suggests that the text can act as a guide for the reader as they re-picture this lush imagery in their imagination. The text acts as 'a set of instructions for mental composition — in something of the same way that a musical score provides a set of directions for how to reconstruct the music the composer heard long ago in his or her head'.[18] The concept of mental re-creation can also be used to refer to our reception of the dialogue in aural form, particularly when colours are explicitly stated or objects carry strong and unequivocal chromatic associations. In the poem, Lorca portrays the rose through red and white tones with strong haptic associations. Through his exploration of the sensory values of flowers, Lorca reinforces Rosita's poetic incarnation as the rose. The mutable rose poem is first introduced by Rosita's uncle at the beginning of Act One:

> Cuando se abre en la mañana,
> roja como sangre está.
> El rocío no la toca
> porque se teme quemar.
> Abierta en el mediodía
> es dura como el coral;
> el sol se asoma a los vidrios
> para verla relumbrar.
> Cuando en las ramas empiezan
> los pájaros a cantar
> y se desmaya la tarde
> en las violetas del mar,
> se pone blanca, con blanco
> de una mejilla de sal. (p. 221)

> [When it opens in the morning
> it is as red as blood.
> The dew doesn't touch it
> for fear of being burnt.
> In full bloom in the afternoon,
> it's as hard as coral.
> The sun peeks through the glass
> to see it shine.

When the birds begin
to sing on the branches
and evening falls
into the violets of the sea,
it turns white, as white
as a cheek of salt.]

The core images introduced by the first iteration of the poem reveal a wide range of natural object colours, both explicit ('red', 'white') and implied ('blood', 'violets', 'coral', 'salt'). The explicit colour terms are combined with objects that have clear colour associations, further emphasising the two core colours of the rose. These images also have strong sensory values, particularly in terms of texture. Rees has commented on both Lorca's tendency to attribute floral smells to people — the mother's deceased husband in *Bodas de sangre*, Yerma's longed-for child in *Yerma*, and the Mayor's description of women as scented roses and 'mujeres que les huele el pelo a nardos' (p. 224) [women whose hair smells of tuberose flowers] in *La zapatera* — and the unusual textures Lorca applies to flowers, such as 'camelias de escarcha' (p. 408) [camellias of frost] in *Bodas de sangre*.[19] Lorca's depiction of haptic experiences in the poem is equally potent. The changing textures of the mutable rose — blood, coral, and salt — are intertwined with implicit colour associations that complement Lorca's more explicit references to red and white. These object colours reflect the flower's transition from the glutinous haptic values of blood to the harder, more granular textures of coral and salt as the rose loses its succulence. Despite the lack of red in Rosita's costume, these mutating colour textures still reflect her deteriorating physical state as she wilts like the rose. The salt mimics the desiccation and preservation of a corpse, evoking what Valis calls Rosita's 'living death', a fate which the Housekeeper sees as worse than physical death: 'cuando enterré a mi niña fue como si me pisotearan las entrañas [...] Pero esto de mi Rosita es lo peor' (p. 282) [when I buried my girl it was as if somebody was trampling on my insides [...] But this thing with my Rosita is the worst].[20] Valis argues that 'something dies in Lorca's play — illusions, love — but something else persists like a ghost, haunting readers and spectators alike: the image of Doña Rosita herself'.[21] It is this 'haunting', lingering affect which I refer to in my discussions of emotional bruising and Mavor's reading of the residual impact of the punctum in Chapter Two. The reference to salt also has gustatory values, mirroring the bitterness of a life unlived. Through these colourful haptic images of the rose Lorca strengthens the parallels between this central motif and Rosita's own withering and spiritual death, the verbal aspects of his colour-work reinforced to some extent in her visual appearance. The sensory potency of the poem would be enhanced further by more explicit references to the rose in the staging, particularly in terms of redness in the first Act.

The language of the mutable rose poem also draws our attention to Rosita's emotional pain through a discourse of bodily wounding, emphasising the corporeal dimension of Rosita's portrayal as the poetic symbol of the rose made flesh through the haptic values of the red and white flower. Lorca's use of 'red as blood' and 'cheek of salt' reminds us that the poem actually narrates the decline of the human as well as floral body. This parallel is strengthened by his description of the 'fainting' violets in the poem, a comparison which invests flowers with human qualities and is similarly linked to blood flow. He also depicts the rose as 'encarnada' (p. 235) [red or flesh-coloured (from *carne*, flesh)] in the iteration of the poem at the end of Act One. This blending of flowers and flesh continues throughout the play, becoming increasingly evocative of bodily violence through the combination of the redness of blood with images of floral mutilation. There is an abundance of references to red and white in Rosita's dialogue with her fiancé (pp. 235–37) which perpetuate these flesh-like or bloody images and the colours of the mutable rose poem: the white of tuberose, foam, jasmines, doves, and the transparency of diamonds; and the reds of 'el llano carmesí' [the crimson plain], 'el clavel de su costado' [the carnation of [God's] side], and the 'jazminero desangrando' [jasmine bleeding to death]; and depictions of ice, snow, frost, fog, burning, and fire. One of the passages from this dialogue emphasises Rosita's alignment with the rose and with a bodily suffering expressed in floral terms:

> Una noche, adormilada
> en mi balcón de jazmines,
> vi bajar dos querubines
> a una rosa enamorada;
> ella se puso encarnada
> siendo blanco su color;
> pero, como tierna flor,
> sus pétalos encendidos
> se fueron cayendo heridos
> por el beso del amor.
> Así yo, primo inocente,
> en mi jardín de arrayanes
> daba al aire mis afanes
> y mi blancura a la fuente.
> Tierna gacela imprudente
> alcé los ojos, te vi
> y en mi corazón sentí
> agujas estremecidas
> que me están abriendo heridas
> rojas como el alhelí. (pp. 235–36)

> [One night, half asleep
> on my balcony of jasmine,
> I saw two cherubs land
> on a lovelorn rose;
> she turned red,
> white being her colour;
> but, like a tender flower,
> her burning petals
> were falling wounded
> by the kiss of love.
> So I, innocent cousin,
> in my garden of myrtle
> surrendered my desires to the air

and my whiteness to the fountain.
Tender imprudent gazelle
I raised my eyes, I saw you
and in my heart I felt
trembling needles
which opened up wounds on my body
as red as wallflowers.]

Similarly, the version of the poem that Rosita intersperses with the 'Lo que dicen las flores' song in Act Two temporarily introduces a more material, carnal dimension that affects the other characters as the Third Spinster sings: 'sobre tu largo cabello gimen las flores cortadas. Unas llevan puñalitos; otras, fuego, y otras, agua' (p. 268) [cut flowers groan in your long hair. Some carry little knives; others, fire, and others, water]. This image recurs in the Uncle's dialogue in Act Two when he compares the cutting of roses to the severing of his own fingers (p. 253), aligning the mutilation of flowers with human bodily properties and emphasising his personal distress through a discourse of corporeal suffering. The ways Lorca portrays flowers as experiencing physical pain through images centred on blood and the piercing of human flesh combine the motif of female bodily wounding as the expression of inner pain in the dialogue of the Bride and the Mother in *Bodas de sangre* and Yerma in *Yerma* with the portrayal of the stabbing and puncturing of the male body explored in Chapter Two. Rosita's bodily expression of her emotional pain, which is dominated by the redness of blood, offers us a powerful insight into her inner reality which leaves us emotionally bruised, to use Mavor's description of the emotional power of the filmic image, by the vision of her suffering. These images also have the effect of Barthes's punctum, like the wounding of the male body by sharp objects. Rees has noted that Lorca often transforms flowers from symbols of beauty into images of 'wounds, blood, death, and grief', and suggests that 'these metaphors that bring together wounds and blossoms are as much of a shock to the senses as the slit eyeball in Buñuel's *An Andalusian Dog*'.[22] Whilst these verbal images of stabbing are not as potent as the visual image like Rees suggests, they do have a 'piercing' impact on the spectator like the punctum created by the 'stabbing' of the male body. These corporeal images remind us that Rosita is not only floral on the surface as represented by name and costume; Rosita's body takes on the material properties of the rose. Rosita describes her feelings in terms of roots — 'tengo las raíces muy hondas' (p. 254) [my roots run very deep] — and, as the curtain falls and the flower loses its petals, she too loses her life source, fainting like 'la tarde en las violetas del mar' [the evening into the violets of the sea] as she repeats the last line of the poem. Despite the beauty of the images in the poem — the sensual coloured scents of the rose and the violets, and the dazzling qualities implied by 'relumbrar', 'quemar', 'vidrios', and 'estrellas' ['shine', 'burn', 'glass', and 'stars'] — Lorca's sensory and colourful portrayal of flowers exposes the mutable rose's lifespan as a distinctly human trajectory of decay and death. Through sensory and bodily evocations of object colour in the poem Lorca reminds us that Rosita is the flesh-and-blood version of the poetic symbol of the rose, and is thus capable of great physical and mental suffering.

The second core manifestation of the language of flowers is the 'Lo que dicen las flores' song in Act Two, which explores Rosita's inner reality through the contrast between the traditional, typified elements of the song and the more visceral expressive mode of the poem, a juxtaposition which is made flesh in the characters of Rosita and the Spinster sisters. The song draws on the traditional form of the language of flowers or floriography, originating in France in the late eighteenth century, which used floral imagery as a means of emotional expression. Initially, the traditional, recited elements of the song seem to stand in weak contrast to the powerful imagery of the poem which Rosita integrates within it, Lorca's more instinctive, embodied version of a language of flowers. Nickel suggests that despite the similarity in terms of form and theme, and the ways in which both invoke the symbolic, 'the rose poem does so in a highly original creative way while the flower ballad reiterates relationships which have been reduced by constant repetition through time to mere formulae' and is 'only a hollow approximation of the intense physical and emotional experience Rosita seeks'.[23] Similarly, Valis sees the language of the song as 'limited and highly typified'.[24] However, the deliberate tropes of the song are a crucial part of Lorca's characterisation of the Spinster sisters, especially as a contrast to Rosita. The two different forms and sources are an equal part of Lorca's version of a language of flowers indicated in the title, working together to communicate the struggle between individual and society and to capture these opposing and overlapping forces within it. The various gardens to which Lorca refers in the play's subtitle are not merely physical spaces but are also reflected at a linguistic level through the multiple layers of flower imagery. The traditional song acts as the outer floral border of the garden, framing the mutable rose at its centre. There is a marked contrast between the parts of the song based on the poem and those which are elements of the traditional song, both of which form part of Rosita's dialogue. If the poem of the mutable rose represents Rosita's true emotions and suffering in raw, somatic terms, then the more symbolic, typified aspects of the song are indicative of her stifling future as an artificial flower drained of passion and youth. In Act Two, the Housekeeper criticises the Uncle's obsession with his flowers, insisting that 'lo único que sirven las rosas es para adornar las habitaciones' (p. 253) [the only thing roses are good for is to decorate rooms]. The irony is that this is Rosita's fate. She is doomed to become 'mansa, sin fruto, sin objeto, *cursi...*' (my emphasis) [bland, fruitless, aimless, over-sentimental and tasteless] as Lorca describes, a decorative flower that withers and dies without bearing new fruit, a spectre compared to the lushness of the real mutable rose.[25]

Unlike the agency the poem gives Rosita in terms of personal expression, the song's restrictive symbolism, particularly in terms of colour, reduces the possibilities of a language of flowers to pre-determined codes. It is Rosita herself who recites these symbols: 'Las amarillas son odio; el furor, las encarnadas; las blancas son casamiento y las azules, mortaja' (p. 269) [the yellow ones are hatred; fury, the red ones; the white ones are marriage and the blue ones, a shroud]. These limited, generic colour symbols stand in stark contrast to the rich, haptic values of redness and whiteness in the poem. The vast range of floral motifs — such as 'heliotropo', 'flor de albahaca', 'violeta', 'rosa blanca', 'jazmín', 'clavel', 'jacinto', 'pasionaria', 'jaramago', 'lirio', 'nardo', 'madreselva', 'siempreviva', 'calambuca', 'dalia', and 'la gala de Francia' (pp. 267–69) [heliotrope, basil-flower, violet, white rose, jasmine, carnation, hyacinth, passion flower, mustard flower, iris, tuberose, honeysuckle, houseleek, Santa María tree flower, dahlia, and garden balsam or touch-me-not] — and their corresponding abundance of implicit colours and sensory values also invest the song with a superficiality that stands in relief to the primacy of the core image of the poem. This aspect of the language of flowers serves a different purpose. It reflects the contrast between Rosita and the Spinster sisters and their mother, whose excess is suggested in their costume and in their trivial concerns with social appearances and fashionable clothing: '¡Cuántas lágrimas, cuántas tristezas por una cinta o un grupo de bucles!' (p. 258) [So many tears, so much sadness over a ribbon or a cluster of ringlets!]. This excess of floral images adds to our impression of these gaudy, flamboyantly dressed characters:

> Entran las tres cursilonas y su mamá. Las tres solteronas vienen con inmensos sombreros de plumas malas, trajes exageradísimos, guantes hasta el codo con pulseras encima y abanicos pendientes de largas cadenas. La madre viste de negro pardo con un sombrero de viejas cintas moradas. (p. 255)[26]

> [The three "cursilonas" and their mother enter. The three spinsters are decked in huge hats with gaudy feathers, extremely exaggerated dresses, elbow-length gloves with bracelets on top, and fans hanging from long chains. Their mother wears dark brown with a hat with old purple ribbons.]

The potency of these mental images is diluted by its range of possible colours and textures, providing a weaker counterpoint to the concentrated haptic values of red and white in the poem. In the traditional elements of the song we must really stretch ourselves to 'see' the colours and get a sense of texture and scent as none of these associations are explicit, which provides a real challenge in performance when the dialogue must compete with the visual staging. However, this is precisely the point. Rosita is the flesh-and-blood rose who expresses herself through one floral image and with a greater depth of feeling. In contrast, the Spinsters are artificial flowers focused on appearances, who only seem to be able to communicate through this typified, symbolic language of spinsterhood which has little sensory and affective power. The Spinsters, who are also referred to as 'las tres cursilonas' [the three *cursilonas*], explicitly introduce the theme of 'cursilería', which has connotations of tackiness, over-sentimentality, tastelessness, and kitsch. Valis argues that Lorca gives the concept of 'cursilería' 'symbolic weight as the sign of women's sexual and emotional frustration and lack of freedom'.[27] This is not a play that merely mocks the pretensions of the advancing middle class. It is also, as Lorca himself tells us, a tragedy, a drama of repressed and desperate women in great emotional pain: 'es la tragedia de la cursilería española y provinciana' [the tragedy of provincial and Spanish *cursilería*'] and '[un] drama de la cursilería española, de la mojigatería española, del ansia de gozar que las mujeres han de reprimir por fuerza en lo más hondo de su entraña enfebrecida' [a drama of Spanish *cursilería*, of Spanish prudishness, of the desire that women have to repress by force in the deepest part of their feverish insides].[28] The language of flowers offers Rosita a way of trying to express this burning inner reality through bodily evocations of colour, yet at the same time she is perpetually re-defined and forced back into her role as the rose despite visual and corporeal contradictions in the form of her pink costumes and human body. Through his colourful exploration of floral imagery Lorca makes the poetic symbol of the rose and the theme of *cursilería* flesh in the characters of Rosita and the Spinster sisters in order to communicate the tragic fate of 'todas las doñas Rositas de España' [all of the Doña Rositas of Spain].[29] Throughout *Doña Rosita* Lorca uses the mutable rose and the language of the flowers to bring the central poetic themes to life within his vision of a theatre of poetry.

In *Mariana Pineda*, it is the *estampa* or engraved print that forms the backbone of the play's poetic core. Lorca brings the poetic symbols and themes to the material stage through the motif of the yellow quinces in Act One, and by reflecting the central colour images of the *estampa* and the lithograph settings throughout the play in Mariana's costumes and in the lighting. Whilst the sensory values of object colour are important in *Doña Rosita*, in *Mariana Pineda* this engagement is much more explicit in the visual staging, the actions of the characters, and the dialogue. The senses were a key consideration for Lorca. In his lectures on 'La imagen poética de Don Luis de Góngora' [The Poetic Image of Don Luis de Góngora], given between 1926 and 1930, he stressed that 'un poeta tiene que ser profesor en los cinco sentidos corporales [...] en este orden: vista, tacto, oído, olfato y gusto' [a poet has to be professor of the five senses [...] in this order: sight, touch, hearing, smell, and taste].[30] An appeal to the senses is also part of Lorca's creation of a humanised poetry that emphasises the corporeality of his characters and uses the somatic as a means of translating inner expression: '[los personajes] han de ser tan humanos [...] que se aprecien sus olores y que salga a los labios toda la valentía de sus palabras llenas de amor o de ascos' [the characters have to be so human [...] that we perceive their smells, and all of the courage of their words full of love or disgust can pour forth from their lips.].[31] Lorca's most sustained engagement with the sensory capacities of object colour in *Mariana Pineda* is found in his exploration of the implicitly yellow quinces throughout Act One. Indeed, Reed Anderson suggests that Lorca 'saw [this] work as one that would have a primary appeal to the senses'.[32] Whilst Paul McDermid has commented on Lorca's creation of a broader sense experience in this play and on the olfactory and gustatory values of the quinces, colour is also a key part of this sensory depiction, especially Lorca's blending of the visual and non-visual senses.[33] In *Mariana Pineda*, Lorca uses the material staging much more effectively than in *Doña Rosita* in his creation of an embodied theatre of poetry, appealing to the senses through the visual realm as well as through verbal prompts. These sense experiences are not restricted to touch in *Mariana Pineda*. Rather, Lorca uses the staging in Act One to create an embodied visuality which works with the dialogue to appeal to and to reinforce the spectators' memories of the real sense experiences in order to evoke textures, tastes, and smells through a non-interactive medium. Throughout Act One of *Mariana Pineda*, Lorca appeals to all of our senses through the visual abundance of the quinces in the staging and his portrayal of the characters' sensory experiences. In the opening stage directions there are quinces in a crystal bowl on the table, whilst others hang from the entire ceiling, creating a

powerful image of yellowness: '*Sobre una mesa, un frutero de cristal lleno de membrillos.*
Todo el techo estará lleno de la misma fruta, colgada' (p. 102) [on the table, a crystal
fruit bowl full of quinces. The whole ceiling will be covered with the same fruit,
hanging]. In Scene Two, Lorca combines the visual impact of the quinces with
Amparo's experience of their taste:

> *Amparo coge un membrillo y lo muerde.*
> LUCÍA (*enfadada*)   ¡Estáte quieta!
> AMPARO (*habla con lo agrio de la fruta entre los dientes*)   ¡Buen membrillo!
> *Le da un calofrío por lo fuerte del ácido, y guiña.* (p. 106)

> [*Amparo picks up a quince and bites into it.*
> LUCÍA (*angrily*)   Sit still!
> AMPARO (*speaking with the bitterness of the fruit between her teeth*)   What a delicious
>   quince!
> *The acidity of the fruit makes her shudder and she grimaces.*]

We see Amparo touch and bite the yellow quince and the bitterness of the fruit
is clear from her reaction; Amparo praises the taste of the quince — '¡Buen
membrillo!' — yet at the same time its acidity affects her in bodily ways. Like
other juxtapositions in the play — such as the beauty of Mariana's neck, which is
also the site of her horrific death — Amparo's experience of the yellow quinces is
contradictory and complex as it hovers on the brink between pleasure and disgust,
joy and melancholia. The 'agrio' taste of the quinces is reinforced by their colour,
which is evocative of sharpness like the yellowness of lemons. The sensory appeal
of the quinces is extended to the olfactory in Fernando's dialogue and in the stage
directions of the final act. As Fernando enters the house he exclaims: '¡Cómo me
gusta tu casa! Con este olor a membrillos' (p. 116) [How I love your house! With
that smell of quinces] and Lorca reinforces this verbal reference in the staging of
the final scene of the Act when '*el fino y otoñal perfume de los membrillos invade el
ambiente*' (p. 135) [the smooth and autumnal perfume of the quinces invades the
air]. The 'autumnal' scent of the quinces perpetuates the bittersweetness of the act
and creates a sense of things coming to an end. Whilst Mariana's friends Amparo,
Lucía, and Fernando are firmly rooted in the material realm — engaging with the
tastes and smells of the quinces — Mariana is wilting and dying, fading in body
and costume like Rosita. Lorca's use of 'invade' also suggests the dominance of
this yellow scent. Lorca's aim of literally filling the stage with the smell of quinces,
combined with their visual abundance and Fernando's emphasis on their scent as
he arrives, simultaneously captures the vivacity of the other characters and suggests
an oppressive, heady atmosphere that mirrors Mariana's feelings of claustrophobia
and of being watched. Far from a decorative element, the yellow quinces play a key
role in conveying the bittersweet, ominous atmosphere of the Act and in creating
a bodily theatre of poetry which extends linguistic imagery and symbolism to the
visual realm.

The second core way in which Lorca embodies poetic themes and symbols on
stage in this play is through his use of colour in terms of set, costume, and lighting.
Both McDermid and Zardoya have commented on how Lorca makes full use of

the different aspects of the theatrical medium, suggesting that he 'integrates speech, music, light, colour, settings and even smells to generate a sensorially holistic theatre work'[34] and that 'colores, formas, movimientos, gestos y palabras se integran en una unidad totalizadora, en una síntesis en que caben todos los ingredientes teatrales' [colour, forms, movements, gestures, and words are integrated in an all-encompassing whole, a synthesis in which all of the theatrical ingredients fit together] respectively.[35] However, colour in *Mariana Pineda* is not simply an element of Lorca's creation of a theatrical synthesis or a secondary part of his theatre of poetry. Rather, it is a central component and one of the factors which brings these aspects together through its complementary visual and verbal forms. Object colour is an important part of how Lorca transports the two-dimensional images of the *estampa*, a print or engraving, and the lithograph to the three-dimensional stage. Lorca uses the colours of Mariana's costumes and the lighting to reflect or contrast with the colours of the settings which evoke these plastic forms. In the prologue, Lorca describes the stage as:

> *Telón representando el desaparecido arco árabe de las Cucharas y perspectiva de la plaza Bibarrambla, en Granada. La escena estará encuadrada en un margen amarillento, como una vieja estampa, iluminada en azul, verde, amarillo, rosa y celeste. Una de las casas que se vean estará pintada con escenas marinas y guirnaldas de frutas. Luz de luna. Al fondo, las Niñas cantarán, con acompañamiento, el romance popular. (p. 98)*

> [Backdrop representing the disappeared Arabic arch of las Cucharas and a view of Bibarrambla square, in Granada. The scene will be framed in a yellowish border, like an old engraved print, lit up in blue, green, yellow, pink, and sky blue. One of the houses will be painted with maritime scenes and garlands of fruit. Moonlight. In the background, the Girls will sing, with accompaniment, the popular ballad.]

The 'yellowish' border of the scene invests the play with a visual sense of age which is reflective of the colour of old paper, an image also found in Lorca's description of Mariana's dress as '*un amarillo de libro viejo*' (p. 143) [an old-book yellow] in Act Two, Scene One. This suggestion of age reminds us that even in the prologue, set in 1850, the events of *Mariana Pineda* are already in the past. McDermid notes that the printing process is 'more antique than [...] the photographic recording of an event' and therefore adds a greater sense of temporal distance to the action of the play.[36] The yellow frame also acts as an anti-mimetic device, drawing our attention to the theatrical and illusory nature of the medium; the 'coarse lace', 'rigging', or 'bones' of theatre of poetry. The yellow frame, which should be a consistent part of the set throughout the production, and the yellow light of the prologue, are echoed in and reinforced by other aspects of the staging: the quinces in Act One, Mariana's costume in Act Two, and the '*inmenso arco de flores amarillas y plateadas de papel*' (p. 199) [immense arch of yellow and silver paper flowers] which frames the Our Lady of Sorrow statue at the convent in Act Three, Scene Seven. These visual instances of yellow are supported by verbal colour in the dialogue, for example Mariana's two references to yellow flowers and Pedro's allusions to yellow fever (p. 151) and to 'las viejas torres amarillas' (p. 158) [the old yellow towers]. The luminous colours of the *estampa* set in the prologue are also mirrored in the green and pink light as the play reaches its climax in Act Three, Scene Nine:

> *Toda la escena irá adquiriendo, hasta el final, una gran luz extrañísima de crepúsculo granadino. Luz rosa y verde entra por los arcos, y los cipreses se matizan exquisitamente, hasta parecer piedras preciosas. Del techo desciende una suave luz naranja, que se va intensificando hasta el final.* (pp. 208–09)

> [The whole scene gradually acquires a strong, strange Granadan twilight until the end. Pink and green light enters through the arches, and the cypresses become exquisitely tinged, until they look like precious stones. A soft orange light descends from the ceiling, which grows in intensity until the end.]

The pink, green, and orange light, combined with the burnished 'precious stone' appearance of the cypress trees, creates a powerful display of colour that grows in intensity throughout the scene, adding to the golden light that appears from Act Three, Scene Seven. Lorca's use of light in this Act — combined with the trembling topaz and amethyst candlelight in Act Two, Scene Seven — comprises his most varied engagement with luminous colour in his theatre. Lorca often uses coloured light in his plays: pink in *El maleficio*, gold in *Don Perlimplín*, orange and green in *La zapatera*, blue in *El público*, *Así que pasen*, *Bodas de sangre*, and *Yerma*, and silver, also in *El público*. The less mimetic colours such as blue, green, and silver often have a dream-like or eerie effect, moving towards a 'blissful' representation of colour. Some of these colours — pink, gold, and orange — can be attributed to sunlight or sunset. However, Lorca's use of adjectives such as '*fantásticamente*' [fantastically] to describe the pink light in *El maleficio* (p. 94) and his general description of the lighting in Act Two of *Don Perlimplín* as '*mágica*' (p. 303) [magic] as Perlimplín dies suggests a more meliorative, transformative effect which is more in line with the rich variety of the '*extrañísima*' [extremely strange] (p. 208), '*maravillosa*', and '*delirante*' (p. 211) [marvellous and delirious] coloured light in the final scene of *Mariana Pineda*. There is, of course, a symbolic level to this coloured light as in all three of these works the central protagonist has just died or, in Mariana's case, is about to die. Havard refers to this rainbow of light as a reversal of the darkening process throughout the play and 'the flooding light of salvation'.[37] He sees this scene as 'one of [Lorca's] finest theatrical sequences' and comments on Lorca's creation of 'an extremely pure climax, more uplifting than chilling, in which poetry fuses with the plastic elements of stagecraft to powerful and emotional effect'.[38] Instead of the gritty reality of Mariana's garrotting, we are left with the glittering, natural beauty of Granada and a glimpse into a sublime realm. However, these instances of coloured light also mark the climax of each play, representing an explosion of colour that does have more disruptive, sensual values and which creates a grand finale of coloured light as the plays come to a close. In *Mariana Pineda*, there is also a second moment of transportation: that of the audience being moved back to reality. The pink and green light in this final scene echoes that of the prologue when the *estampa* aesthetic is first introduced, creating a visual epilogue as we leave the world of the *estampa* and return through the yellow frame from 1831 to 1850 to the present day.

The colours of the *estampa* and the lithograph are also embodied in Mariana herself. Like Rosita, Mariana is the incarnation of the poetic themes of the play, and both corporeal colour and object colour are central to this aspect of Lorca's theatre of poetry. Lorca's declaration that he wanted to 'vestir [la historia] de poesía en la palabra y de emoción en el silencio y en las cosas que lo rodean' [to dress history in poetry of word and emotion within the silence and the things that surround it] in *Mariana Pineda* echoes the importance of the material presentation of his characters and their 'costumes of poetry' through which we can see the inner reality of bones-and-blood.[39] For McDermid, Lorca's statement means that 'the stage character should be the physical materialisation of the poetic story', an aspect of Lorca's theatre of poetry that we see in his visual portrayal of Mariana.[40] Zardoya suggests that colour is the guiding force beyond Lorca's carefully chosen costumes in *Mariana Pineda* and that 'siempre tiene en cuenta el papel que [el color del vestuario] ha de representar dentro del cuadro cromático general de la escena y [...] la correlación que ha de guardar con el espíritu del personaje' [he always bears in mind the role which the colour of the costumes plays within the general colour scheme of the scene and [...] the correlation that it must have with the essence of the character].[41] Mariana metaphorically reflects the yellow frame of the *estampa* in bodily ways. In Act One, Scene Eight she tells Fernando: 'me estoy poniendo amarilla como la flor del romero' (p. 132) [I am turning yellow like the rosemary flower], a verbal instance of colour which is materialised in her costume in the following Act. Mariana also personifies the visual framing of Act Two, in which Lorca describes the set as '*entonación en grises, blancos y marfiles, como una antigua litografía*' (p. 140) [grey, white, and marble tones, like an antique lithograph]. Lorca's use of 'entonación' implies both an artful application of colour and a subtly differentiated range of shades, which is emphasised by his use of plural colour nouns and by his very specific differentiation between 'white' and 'marble' tones. The use of 'marble' also evokes a very material depiction of colour which appeals to our sense of touch. The process of lithography relies on the absorption and repulsion of coloured ink and water, and is suggestive of the mobile capacity of colour. This bleaching of colour is reflected in the whiteness of Mariana's skin, particularly references to her neck, and in her white costume in the final act. However, Lorca also uses the colours of Mariana's costumes to capture the contrast between the yellow frame and various luminous colours of the *estampa* and the more austere, achromatic lithograph. When the lithograph image is introduced at the beginning of Act Two, Clavela is recounting a ballad to Mariana's two children about a young girl embroidering a red flag for the Duke of Lucena, a story which eerily evokes Mariana's own activities. When Mariana enters the scene in her faded, old-book-yellow costume, she provides a marked contrast to the grey, white, and marble tones of the lithograph set and interrupts the chromatic unity of the scene. There are very few examples of explicitly hued costumes in the play apart from Mariana's. Her adoptive mother Doña Angustias '*viste de oscuro*' (p. 102) [wears dark clothing]; Fernando wears a white shirt; the first three Conspirators have '*amplias capas grises*' (p. 155) [wide grey cloaks]; and Lorca describes Pedrosa as '*vestido de negro*' [dressed in black] in both Act Two, Scene Nine, and Act Three, Scene Six (p. 169 and p. 194). The contrast of Mariana's pale mauve and yellow dresses against the costumes of the other characters singles her out as the flesh-and-blood version of the *estampa* in Acts One and Two. By Act Three, she has been transformed into the bleached incarnation of the monochrome lithograph, now a faded spectre against the luminous *estampa* colours that resurge in the lighting of the final act.

Object colour is also an important part of the rich and often startling metaphorical language of the play. The quality of the dialogue of *Mariana Pineda* has often been called into question. Greenfield suggests that critics and biographers have generally seen the play as 'excessively melodramatic and much handicapped by dramatic commonplaces and static, superficial characterizations'.[42] However, Havard warns against 'the simplistic equation often made between Romanticism and shallow or immature emotionalism', particularly as Lorca did not share this view and praised Romantic drama in a 1935 interview.[43] Havard refutes the idea that there is 'too much poetry for the good of its dramatic effect', contending that 'the main threads of poetic imagery are necessary and effective in terms of creating the play's mood and promoting its themes'.[44] Reed Anderson also defends the lyricism of *Mariana Pineda*. He argues that Lorca had a 'keen awareness of the possibilities and limitations of this form', as shown by the ways he contrasts 'the detailed naturalism of the stage' with 'the artificiality of the verse dialogue', thus creating a tension between reality and artificial spectacle.[45] Far from lacking in depth, the language of *Mariana Pineda* corresponds to Lorca's artistic vision in his theatre of poetry, like the language of flowers in *Doña Rosita*. In several interviews in 1927, the year the play premiered, Lorca clearly states that his use of romantic clichés is deliberate, and that they serve a key purpose in the aesthetic of the play: '¿Que hay tópicos y trucos? ¡Claro! Como que componen bien en mi técnica de estampas escénicas' [Are there clichés and tricks? Of course! They work well within my technique of *estampas* for the stage].[46] There is what Havard calls a 'conscious artistry' in the lyricism and 'deliberate cliché' of *Mariana Pineda*, as we found with the language of flowers in *Doña Rosita*.[47] Beyond Lorca's engagement with the tropes of Romanticism and the creation of an effusive, elaborate discourse, there are multiple other effects of these remarkable colour images which demonstrate the importance of this seemingly typified language in Lorca's theatre of poetry. For example, in Amparo's account of the Ronda bullfight in Act One, Scene Four (pp. 112–13), she describes a world of motion and colour which emphasises Mariana's remoteness from the material world. Zardoya draws our attention to the abundance of colours in this passage, suggesting that 'su riqueza es tal que sugiere, a través de la palabra viva, un verdadero cuadro de fuertes tintes goyescas' [the richness is such that it suggests, through the live word, a real painting of strong Goya-esque tints].[48] These rich mental images are replete with colour and texture within the scene that Amparo describes: 'abanicos redondos bordados de lentejuelas' [round fans embroidered with sequins]; 'anchos sombreros grises' [broad grey hats]; '[un] traje color manzana bordado de plata y seda' [an apple-coloured costume embroidered with silver and silk]; 'toros de azabache con divisa verde y negra' [jet bulls with green and black ribbons]; the bullfighter as 'una gran mariposa de oro con alas bermejas' [a great butterfly of gold with auburn wings]; and the bullring as a macabre 'zodíaco de risas blancas y negras' [a zodiac of black and white laughter]. Like Amparo's sensory experience of the yellow quinces in this scene, her account of the bullfight suggests an engagement with life and with reality which stands in stark relief to Mariana's sequestered existence, first behind the walls of her house and later imprisoned in the convent. We never see Mariana outside except in the walled garden of the convent. The more startling colour images which combine abstracts nouns with concrete colour properties — such as the zodiac of white and black laughter in this passage, the 'pez de plata [que] finge rojo sueño' (Amparo, p. 109) [a silver fish which feigns red sleep] and the colour associations implied by 'el silencio me pesa mágicamente. Se agranda como un techo de violetas' (Mariana, p. 186) [the silence weighs me down magically. It expands like a roof of violets]' — also add a surreal, oneiric dimension and hint at another, more fantastical plane which lies beyond material reality. McDermid suggests that this is the dream-world of death, '[which] is continually breaking into reality', and that as her closeness to death increases so does 'the presence of the other world [that] pervades her existence'.[49] Havard has also commented on Mariana's 'curious intermediate state, partially dissociated with the world' in the final Act, which is full of reference to death, sleep, and 'morbid hallucinations'.[50] These depictions communicate Mariana's struggle between reality and fantasy, particularly in Act Three when she temporarily retreats into illusion and madness, unable to face the truth of her abandonment. Many of the colour metaphors in *Mariana Pineda* evoke the playful, surprising language of *Así que pasen*, including the Old Man's description of 'memory' as 'una palabra verde, jugosa' [a green word, juicy] (p. 166) and the Cat's 'voz de plata' (p. 181) [silver voice], problematizing the critical view that *El público*, *Así que pasen*, and Act Three, Scene One of *Bodas de sangre* comprise Lorca's only engagement with Surrealism in his theatre. However, Lorca's creation of a fantastical, multi-sensory world of object colour in the dialogue of *Mariana Pineda* is most powerful in textual form as the process of mental re-creation is very much a readerly process. In performance, Lorca's lush verbal colours lose their potency where they do not also appear in the stage directions in some form. Some of these mental pictures also problematize considerations of staging. Whilst stageability, surprisingly, was not always Lorca's main concern — in 1930 he admitted that he did not know if *El público* 'será muy representable en el orden material' [would be very stageable in the material world] — some of his verbal colour images pose even greater problems due to their abstract nature.[51] Unlike references to white, which are represented by Mariana's skin and her costume in the final Act, and to yellow, which are reflected in the sets and Mariana's costume in Act Two, many of these innovative mental pictures remain only oral-aural. This is compounded by the fact that in performance the text is more ephemeral in spoken form unless emphasised by constant repetition that and these mental images must also compete with the concrete reality of the staging. The sensory possibilities of the ballad of the bullfight are also much less effective than that of the yellow quince motif; too much imagination is required without visual direction. In *Mariana Pineda* the effect of many of the more complex and creative instances of mental colour are greatly reduced, if not lost altogether.

The idea of poetry made flesh in the colours of the central protagonists' costumes in my discussions of *Mariana Pineda* and *Doña Rosita* is also an important part of Lorca's theatre of poetry in *Don Perlimplín* and *La zapatera* respectively, particularly in terms of the metamorphosis of a puppet figure into a more human character which embodies the poetic themes of the work. Lorca subtitles *Don Perlimplín* as an *aleluya*, a type of popular comic strip with religious origins that was based on stock characters. From the mid-nineteenth century these characters included the figure of Don Perlimplín, who was traditionally depicted as 'feo, bajo, jorobado y chato' [ugly, short, hunch-backed, and snub-nosed], according to Margarita Ucelay.[52] The aesthetic of *Don Perlimplín* has proved problematic for critics due to the unusual perspectives and disconcerting visual elements in the staging, such as the green-and-black set, Perlimplín's golden antlers, the flocks of black paper birds, and the dining room table with a 'primitive' Last Supper painted on the surface:

> Casa de DON PERLIMPLÍN. *Paredes verdes, con las sillas y muebles pintados de negro. Al fondo, un balcón por el que se verá el balcón de* BELISA. PERLIMPLÍN *viste casaca verde y lleva peluca blanca, llena de bucles,* MARCOLFA, *criada, el clásico traje de rayas.* (Prologue, p. 263)

> [DON PERLIMPLÍN's house. Green walls, with chairs and furniture painted in black. In the background, a balcony from which BELISA's balcony can be seen. PERLIMPLIN wears a green dress coat and a white wig, full of ringlets, MARCOLFA, the maid, the classic striped costume.]

> Comedor de PERLIMPLÍN. *Las perspectivas están equivocadas deliciosamente. La mesa con todos los objetos pintados como en una cena primitiva.* (Scene Two, p. 287)

> [PERLIMPLIN's dining room. The perspectives are deliciously skewed. The table with all of the objects painted on like a primitive supper.]

In Scene Two, Lorca complicates this presentation further by playing with perspective. Wright has argued that the greater part of the play can be read as a dream space in which 'a gap is inserted between the representation and the reality it depicts', creating a world of visual trickery and disruptive perspectives.[53] The unsettling visual effects of *Don Perlimplín* can also be seen as the material embodiment of the *aleluya* as indicated in the subtitle, part of Lorca's creation of what María Delgado calls a 'patently synthetic' and 'two-dimensional, pseudo-cartoonish world'.[54] In his theatre of poetry Lorca makes the *aleluya* flesh through his playful experimentation with the material staging. Whilst Lorca draws on an established popular form, the discomfiting juxtaposition of 'aleluya' and 'erotic' in the play's subtitle points to a uniquely Lorquian vision of this traditional form in his theatre of poetry, in which he sought to 'subrayar el contraste entre lo grotesco y lo lírico y aun mezclarlos en todo momento' [to highlight the contrast between the grotesque and the lyrical and even mix them together at every moment].[55] The result is a work which consistently surprises us in terms of plot and staging, making full use of the startling effects of the visual realm.

McDermid argues that during the course of the play Perlimplín undergoes a transformation from a stock *aleluya* figure to a character of bones-and-blood as he gains agency and imagination.[56] This central change is reflected in the colours of the set, props, and costumes. In the prologue and Scene One, Perlimplín's character is firmly rooted in the *aleluya* puppet figure or the stock Golden Age types of the old man unsuitably married to a young girl and the cuckolded husband seeking to restore his honour. This fixed representation is reinforced by his green costume in the prologue and by his elaborate golden antlers in Scene One. First, in terms of the green costume, Ucelay sees the green of Perlimplín's frock coat and the green walls and black furniture of the set in the prologue as representative of the typical colours of the *aleluya*: black ink on green paper. She describes the green walls as 'color de pliego de aleluya' [the colour of the *aleluya* pamphlet] and argues that 'la fuerte impresión visual en verde y negro del decorado y el traje de Don Perlimplín responde también al color del papel de aleluyas' [the strong visual impression of green and black of the décor and Don Perlimplín's costume also correspond with the paper colour of the *aleluyas*].[57] These bold outlines are further reflected in the surreal image of '*una bandada de pájaros de papel negro*' (p. 271) [a flock of black paper birds] in the staging at the end of the prologue, which also refer back to the original materials of the *aleluya*.[58] However, there are problems with Ucelay's reading of green as evoking the *aleluya*, particularly as Ucelay herself notes that white and yellow paper was also used: '[La aleluya] queda restringid[a ...] a la combinación exclusiva de dos colores; a saber, negro-verde, o negro-amarillo, o negro-blanco' [the *aleluya* was restricted to [...] the exclusive combination of two colours: namely black-green, or black-yellow, or black-white].[59] In his 2011 study of the *aleluya* Antonio Martín suggests that in the nineteenth century the traditional white background gave way to a wide range of colours including yellow, blue, red, orange, and violet 'para captar mejor la atención y el interés de los niños' [to better capture the attention and interest of children], casting doubt on Ucelay's interpretation of green in *Don Perlimplín* as specifically representative of this medium.[60] On the other hand, the parallel Ucelay makes between Perlimplín's green coat and the Spanish idiom 'viejo verde' or 'dirty old man' is much more persuasive due to the established association.[61] We can see Perlimplín's role as the inappropriately old husband, a typical trope of the Golden Age *entremés* and *novela ejemplar*, reflected in the colours of his costume.[62] It is these stock Golden Age roles rather than the *aleluya* figure which are most explicitly reflected in Perlimplín's visual presentation.

The second and most significant example of this portrayal of object colour as the manifestation of Perlimplín as a stock Golden Age figure is represented by his ostentatious golden antlers in Scene One, which emphasise the poetic theme of infidelity in the material staging. When the Duendes pull back the curtain after Perlimplín and Belisa's wedding night, Lorca tells us in the stage directions:

> *Corren la cortina. Aparece* DON PERLIMPLÍN *en la cama con unos grandes cuernos dorados de ciervo en la cabeza.* BELISA *a su lado. Los cinco balcones del foro están abiertos de par en par. Por ellos entra la luz blanca de la madrugada.* (p. 283)[63]

[The curtain rises. DON PERLIMPLÍN appears in bed with large golden antlers on his head. BELISA by his side. The five balcony doors in the background are ajar. The white dawn light enters through them.]

The 'cuernos de ciervo' draw on the long-standing association between wearing horns and being cuckolded, as found in the use of the Spanish idioms 'poner los cuernos', 'llevar los cuernos', or 'sufrir el cuerno' to signify marital infidelity. Lorca's specific use of 'antlers' rather than other types of animal horns still captures the popular expression of unfaithfulness. However, the effect is much more exaggerated due to the multi-horned form and the size of the antlers, complementing the play's 'distorted' perspectives and exaggerated costumes, such as Belisa's Mother's wig which is adorned with beads and birds. It also adds a sense of comedy to the scene due to their ridiculousness, a joke in which the audience is complicit at Perlimplín's expense. Lorca's gilding of the antlers — which is reinforced even further by the influx of golden light — maximises the visual excess of this portrayal. Even though our assumption that Belisa has been unfaithful has not been subverted, Lorca confirms the 'truth' in exaggerated visual ways. However, this is a play where nothing is at it seems, a work which delights in 'the potential deceptiveness of the visual medium' as Wright observes.[64] Do the ostentatious golden antlers suggest that the interpretation of Perlimplín as an impotent cuckold is too simple, too obvious? Is this an example of the visual trickery that Wright identifies, making the joke at our expense? John Lyon sees the golden antlers as 'the visual confirmation of our prejudice', forming part of Lorca's aim of disturbing his audience and jolting us 'into a broader view of morality' whilst 'systematically frustrating the expectations [Lorca] has tempted [us] to formulate'.[65] Lorca suggested somewhat ambiguously:

> Don Perlimplín es el hombre menos cornudo del mundo. Su imaginación dormida se despierta con el tremendo engaño de su mujer; pero él luego hace cornudas a todas las mujeres que existen.[66]
>
> [Don Perlimplín is the least cuckolded man in the world. His dormant imagination awakens with his wife's vast deception; but then he makes cuckolds of all of the women in existence.]

McDermid suggests that Perlimplín 'becomes both cuckold and cuckolder' due to his creation of a new identity as the Young Man in the Red Cape.[67] Perlimplín's suicide then cruelly snatches the Young Man away from Belisa, however deliberately, and leaves her confused and betrayed by her husband, 'cornuda' in a different sense. Via the visual emphasis on the golden antlers, Lorca sets up, then dismantles, the Golden Age storyline, highlighting the moment in which our expectations of the old husband becoming a cuckold are seemingly fulfilled before they give way to an alternative vision and a more equivocal and human portrayal. Lyon sees Perlimplín as having an ambiguous, mutating identity that continually undermines our initial impression of him as a stock figure. He suggests that Perlimplín can be seen as equally motivated by the desire to teach Belisa the value of the spiritual over the carnal, the search for a release from the torment of Belisa's body, the rejection of judgemental social standards, and sadistic revenge for infidelity.[68]

In terms of Perlimplín's move away from this typified Golden Age, *aleluya* character, McDermid argues that Lorca's reference to the play as 'teatro de monigotes humanos' [theatre of human puppets] reflects this fleshing out of Perlimplín's character through his theatre of poetry as 'by providing an interiority of bones and blood, the poet gives depth, a third dimension, to a planar surface representation'.[69] The red velvet cape and the implicitly green emerald dagger are the agents of Perlimplín's transformation, reflecting his transition chromatically in terms of costume and props. McDermid emphasises that Lorca's version of Perlimplín represents 'a very important development from the stock [*aleluya*] character' as the red cloak gives him the means to hide his grotesque body and take on a new role, therefore 'offer[ing] him a mask of dignity and the means to transform his identity'.[70] By putting on the red velvet cloak, Perlimplín steps away from both the typical *aleluya* figure of ridicule and the Golden Age stereotypes as he becomes the driver of the play's plot; he is now a character of 'bones-and-blood' rather than a 'puppet' manipulated by Marcolfa and Belisa. It is Belisa who has the red cape in Scene One; she drapes it over the shoulders of her elaborate lace nightgown and Perlimplín covers her with '*un manto rojo*' [a red cloak or blanket] (p. 286) at the end of the scene following his grief-stricken epiphany. By covering her in the red cloak or blanket Perlimplín foreshadows Belisa's 'transformation' at the end of the play when she is soaked in his blood: 'Belisa, ya eres otra mujer... Estás vestida por la sangre gloriosísima de mi señor' (Marcolfa, p. 303) [Belisa, you are now another woman... You are dressed in the glorious blood of my lord]. For Marcolfa, who has become embroiled in Perlimplín's fantasy, this is a moment of sacred transformation. However, we are also witness to the confusion of a young girl who is soaked in her husband's blood, which points to the multi-faceted nature of the play and the central interplay between the lyrical and the grotesque. The multiple explicit mentions of the blood-red cape in the dialogue complement its material appearance and are an ominous indication of Perlimplín's bloody death in Scene Three. If the red velvet cloak is one of the tools of Perlimplín's metamorphosis, then the other is the emerald dagger which makes his transformation complete in that final scene. The 'puñal de esmeraldas' (p. 302) [emerald dagger] drives the play's resolution as the weapon with which Perlimplín stabs himself, simultaneously killing his alter-ego — the admirer — and instigating his own death. As McDermid notes, the emerald dagger is far more than a prop; it is 'highly ornamental [...] and symbolic' and has an important performative function.[71] Perlimplín's description of the murder weapon as '[un] ramo ardiente de piedras preciosas' (p. 302) [a burning bouquet of precious stones] captures the luminous quality of the green jewels, reminding us of the precious stone appearance of the cypress trees in the final scene of *Mariana Pineda*. This description of the emerald dagger adds to the chromatic and sensory richness of this scene: the soft red velvet cape, the hard, cold emeralds and the sharpness of the blade, and the warm, sticky redness of Perlimplín's actual spilled blood. Like the red cloak, the dagger is present in both the staging and the speech of this critical scene: it is mentioned twice in Perlimplín's dialogue and he shows Belisa '*el puñal clavado en el pecho*' (p. 302) [the dagger protruding from his chest] as he reveals his true identity and removes the cape. Whilst the moment of Perlimplín's stabbing occurs offstage, the visual image of the dagger in his chest emphasises the embodied dimension of the scene further. Through his suicide and his immersion in blood Perlimplín permanently becomes the Young Man, as emphasised by Marcolfa's declaration that 'ahora le amortajaremos con el rojo traje juvenil' (p. 303) [now we will shroud him in that youthful red costume] and by Belisa's confusion: 'Pero ¿dónde está el joven de la capa roja?' (p. 304) [But where is the young man in the red cloak?]. McDermid sees the reference to the emerald dagger as 'burning', as representative of 'the destructive and cleansing properties of fire', as it 'ends Perlimplín's physical life', suggestive of another level of transformation.[72] McDermid proposes that the dagger thus releases Perlimplín from 'the mask that the young man was'.[73] In contrast, the blood which Belisa is 'dressed' in is indicative of 'the adoption of another mask of layer or identity'.[74] First the puppet becomes flesh, then the character of bones–and–blood is reformed into a new identity which can only exist in fantasy and memory as Perlimplín's body is stripped back to what lies beneath: the ephemeral and unquantifiable essence of the human soul which no longer exists in the material world.

The contrast of characters of bones–and–blood with 'human puppets' and the exploration of characterisation through costume colour is also central to *La zapatera*. In his comparison of Lorca's treatment of love, imagination, and society in *Don Perlimplín* and *La zapatera*, Lyon suggests that both these plays encompass Lorca's concern with creating a self-conscious, theatrical quality.[75] He suggests that these plays are unique in terms of the ways that Lorca draws on his experiments with the puppet play genre to 'seek the same kind of spontaneous response while attempting to expand audience awareness and unsettle it'.[76] However, he warns us that neither are categorised as such, although they make use of the 'deliberate schematization of character, the stylisation of action, and the pruning of lyrical foliage in the dialogue' typical of the puppet play genre.[77] Andrew Anderson has a similar view of *La zapatera*, emphasising the importance of Lorca's theatre of poetry in any reading of the play, particularly in the ways that he uses stylisation to de-realise the spectating experience through music, patterned language, humour, character types, and self-conscious theatricality.[78] Anderson sees the Shoemaker's Wife as a fully fleshed-out character rather than a puppet figure. He suggests that she is 'a highly particularised, vividly brought to life example of that stock person and she is endowed with features which transcend the standard repertoire of the type'.[79] As with Perlimplín, Lorca elevates the Shoemaker's Wife from the puppet or stock figure to a character of bones–and–blood with a complex emotional interiority. Whilst Perlimplín undergoes a transformation during the play, the Shoemaker's Wife is already a fully developed character even before she comes on stage; we can hear her shouting offstage during the prologue and making furious demands as Lorca blurs the boundaries between fiction and reality. The Shoemaker's Wife stands in marked contrast to the other characters of the play, whom Anderson describes as 'depersonalised', 'mechanical', and 'puppet-like'.[80] Whilst Lyon has commented on her husband's transformation during the play,[81] Lorca himself tells us that the Shoemaker's Wife is the only true character:

> Los demás personajes le sirven en su juego escénico sin tener más importancia de lo que la anécdota y el ritmo del teatro requiere. No hay más personaje

que ella y la masa del pueblo que la circunda con un cinturón de espinas y carcajadas.[82]

[The other characters complement her in terms of staging without having any more importance than that which anecdote and theatrical rhythm require. There are no other characters except her and the mob which circles her with a belt of thorns and cruel laughter.]

Don Mirlo, Mr Blackbird, is a prime example of this contrast as Lorca juxtaposes his monochrome, jerky character with the Shoemaker's Wife's passion and vivacity. Don Mirlo's 'blackbird' character is embodied in his costume, reflecting the verbal colour associations in his visual portrayal: '*Viste de negro, frac y pantalón corto*' (p. 205) [he is dressed in black, frock coat and short trousers]. Lorca accentuates this portrayal further in his bobbing movement: '*Le tiembla la voz y mueve la cabeza como un muñeco de alambre*' (p. 205) [his voice trembles and he moves his head like a puppet on strings]. The anti-mimetic, stylised Don Mirlo is not a character of bones-and-blood like the Shoemaker's Wife, but rather a puppet without an inner dimension. In contrast, the Shoemaker's Wife is a protagonist who represents universal concerns and is a passionate, complex character brought to life by Lorca's theatre of poetry.

One of the ways in which Lorca makes the Shoemaker's Wife a character of bones-and-blood is through material colour, especially in her costumes, which complement and contrast with the dialogue, the set, and the movements of the characters. In an interview before the 1930 premiere, Lorca emphasised the importance of colour in terms of costume and characterisation:

[Son] escenarios y figurines míos. Son cosas, la concepción y el ambiente, tan unidos a los tipos, sus trajes, sus colores, que es casi imposible surja una compenetración entre el que los confecciona y el autor que los ha visto moverse y vivir mientras corría la pluma.[83]

[The sets and costumes are mine. They are things, the conception and the atmosphere, that are so much a part of the characters, their costumes, their colours, that it is almost impossible for an understanding to emerge between the person that makes them and the author that has seen them move and live whilst his quill sped across the page.]

For Lorca, the characters, costumes, and colours were so deeply interconnected that he insisted on designing the sets and outfits himself so that he could fully capture the atmosphere of the play and his material vision of the characters. Anderson suggests that the 'flamboyant' and 'colourful' costumes are 'determinedly anti-realistic', enhancing Lorca's theatre of poetry in which we can see the coarse lace, the rigging, the bones-and-blood.[84] This is particularly important in terms of the central protagonist. In the authorial prologue, Lorca refers to the Shoemaker's Wife as '[una] criatura poética que el autor ha vestido de zapatera' (p. 182) [a poetic creature which the author has dressed as a shoemaker's wife], which is deeply suggestive of his aim of creating characters of bones-and-blood dressed in 'costumes of poetry' as part of his vision of a theatre of poetry. The Shoemaker's Wife's passionate, lively personality is reflected in her personified red and green costumes. For example, in Act One:

> *Al levantarse el telón la* ZAPATERA *viene de la calle toda furiosa y se detiene en la puerta. Viste un traje verde rabioso y lleva el pelo tirante, adornado con dos grandes rosas. Tiene un aire agreste y dulce al mismo tiempo.* (p. 185)[85]

> [As the curtain rises, the SHOEMAKER's WIFE comes in from the street, in a fury, and stops at the door. She is wearing a furious green dress and has her hair tightly-styled, adorned with two big roses. She has an air of wildness and sweetness at the same time.]

In his description of her costume, Lorca invests the greenness of her dress with human qualities, seeking to capture the depth of the Shoemaker's Wife's emotions in her clothing and bring her inner reality to the stage in material form, what Gwynne Edwards sees as 'the visual statement of the youth and aggression of her character'.[86] The mixture of aggressiveness and sweetness in her character also indicates her complexity. The Shoemaker's Wife's costume in Act Two adds to this depiction:

> *La misma decoración. A la izquierda, el banquillo arrumbado. A la derecha un mostrador con botellas y un lebrillo con agua donde la* ZAPATERA *friega las copas. La* ZAPATERA *está detrás del mostrador. Viste un traje rojo encendido, con amplias faldas y los brazos al aire.* (p. 215)

> [The same decor. To the left, the discarded cobbler's bench. To the right a counter with bottles and an earthenware bowl full of water where the SHOEMAKER's WIFE washes the glasses. The SHOEMAKER's WIFE is behind the counter. She wears a burning red dress, with wide skirts, and her arms are bare.]

Both 'rabioso' — the green dress — and 'encendido' — the red dress — are indicative of anger. However, 'rabioso' also implies violence, particularly due to its associations with the dangerous and uncontrollable behaviour of rabid animals, whilst 'encendido' has the additional connotations of luminosity or a literal burning. Unlike the brutal attack on the body in *El público*, Kay García suggests that the physical violence of *La zapatera* is rooted in comedy and exaggeration, reflecting the combination of violence and farce in the play's subtitle. Instead, García sees Lorca's use of costume colour as indicative of what she calls 'aesthetic violence', the use of bold colours and visual effects. García observes that the 'violent green' of the Shoemaker's Wife's dress 'assaults the eye' as she enters the stage; it is a raging green that 'reflects her interior fury'.[87] Whilst Anderson sees the change of her costumes from 'budding (green)' to 'flowering (red)' as indicative of the Shoemaker's Wife achieving greater maturity, both costumes can be seen as the visual representation of her inner passion and fiery temper, an exposure of what lies beneath the surface, and the materialisation of the poetic theme of the play's subtitle as a 'violent farce' in three-dimensional form.[88]

This visual portrayal of anger, which would be challenging to convey by colour alone, is emphasised by the Shoemaker's Wife's movements and by her dialogue. She slams doors, slaps her forehead, stamps her feet, and is always bursting into tears or flying into a rage. In the stage directions, Lorca describes the Shoemaker's Wife as '*enfurecida*' (p. 186) [infuriated], '*saliendo furiosa*' (p. 194) [entering furiously], '*hecha una furia*' (p. 197) [full of fury, fuming mad], '*fiera*' (p. 197 and p. 217) [ferocious], and '*estallando furiosa*' (p. 225) [exploding furiously]. In terms of her discourse, we find reflections of the 'sharp' or 'knife-like' speech of Bernarda in *Bernarda Alba* explored in Chapter One, as the Shoemaker's Wife's dialogue is full of exclamations, imperatives, and insults, and is supported by violent bodily gestures. In contrast to the contradiction between Bernarda's 'colourful' speech and her obsession with material whiteness, the Shoemaker's Wife's abrasive dialogue is mirrored in her visual appearance through the 'loud' and striking colours of her costumes. The juxtaposition of the Shoemaker's Wife's costumes with the set also invests the vibrant colours of her dresses with a startling impact which complements her movements and her speech. Both Acts are set in the Shoemaker's Wife's house which Lorca tells us is a sparse white with grey accents, a precursor to the staging in Act Three, Scene Two of *Bodas de sangre* and all three sets in *Bernarda Alba*: '*Habitación completamente blanca [...] El foro es una calle también blanca con algunas puertecitas y ventanas en gris*' (p. 185) [A completely white room. [...] The background is street which is also white with some small doors and windows in grey]. The visual contrast between the white walls and the colours of the Shoemaker's Wife's dresses, compounded by '*una suave luz naranja de media tarde*' (p. 185) [a soft mid-afternoon orange light] in Act One, is not as unexpected as the intrusions of colour in the 'photographic documentary' aesthetic of *Bernarda Alba* in Chapter One. Nevertheless the parallel is striking, building on the disconcerting metatheatrical prologue which ended with a stream of water shooting out of the green glow of the author's top hat. This aesthetic violence is enhanced further by the Shoemaker's Wife's bold movements, including her dance in Act One, which invest colour with mobile qualities. This is a play rooted in motion, a work that Lorca described as 'casi un "ballet"' [almost a ballet] and 'musical [...] la música está en el ritmo de los movimientos, del diálogo que a veces termina, naturalmente, en canto' [musical [...] the music is in the rhythm of the movements, of the dialogue which sometimes finishes, naturally, in song].[89] The unexpected interruptions, exaggerated visual stylisation, and the inclusion of song and dance help Lorca to 'desrealizar la escena y quitar a la gente la idea de que "aquello está pasando de veras"' [to de-realize the scene and rid people of the idea that 'this is really happening'].[90] This portrayal of colour-in-motion is also emphasised by the chorus of female neighbours, who are defined by the material colours of their clothing rather than being given individual names: Red Neighbour, Purple Neighbour, Black Neighbour, Green Neighbour, and Yellow Neighbour. The Red Neighbour's daughters are defined in the same blanket terms: '*La acompañan sus hijas vestidas del mismo color*' (p. 192) [She is accompanied by her daughters dressed in the same colour]. At the end of Act One the neighbours descend on the Shoemaker's Wife, who has just learned of her husband's departure:

> *Por la puerta empiezan a entrar vecinas con trajes de colores violentos y que llevan grandes vasos de refrescos. Giran, corren, entran y salen alrededor de la zapatera que está sentada gritando, con la prontitud y ritmo de baile. Las grandes faldas se abren a las vueltas que dan.* (p. 213)[91]

> [Female neighbours dressed in loud colours and carrying large glasses of drink begin to enter through the door. They turn, run, come and go around the

Shoemaker's Wife, who is sat wailing, with the rapidity and rhythm of a dance. Their big skirts open up as they spin around.]

The colours of the neighbours' costumes serve several critical purposes in this scene. First, Lorca's description of their dresses as 'trajes de colores violentos' has a double meaning, referring to the connotation of 'violento' as 'loud' or 'garish' as a colour qualifier in Castilian and linking back to the Shoemaker's Wife's 'furious' green dress. These 'colores violentos' recur in the Shoemaker's *historia de ciego* near the end of Act Two (p. 233). Rather than developed characters in their own right, the neighbours act as a visual complement to the Shoemaker's Wife. Secondly, the dance creates a whirl of red, purple, black, green, and yellow circling around the weeping Shoemaker's Wife with her green dress, all against the white background of the set, greatly enhancing the visual contrast established at the beginning of the Act. This influx of colour fills the stage, acting as a grand visual finale to Act One. Throughout *La zapatera* Lorca uses material colour to reflect the Shoemaker's Wife's personality in physical form, bringing the stock puppet to life through his bold and stylised theatre of poetry.

Throughout these four plays Lorca makes poetry flesh in his theatre of poetry via the medium of object colour. Through the colours of costumes, sets, props, and lighting, he embodies the central themes and motifs of these works — the mutable rose, the *estampa*, the distorted *aleluya*, and the violent farce — in the physical staging in diverse and impactful ways which communicate key character experiences and transformations and challenge and stimulate the audience. The success of this material manifestation of poetic themes and emotions lies in the visual reflection of the verbal elements; even when images or colours are made explicit in the dialogue acts of mental re-creation cannot compete with the transient, visual nature of the live performance. Some instances — the sensory possibilities of the language of flowers in *Doña Rosita* and the unusual verbal metaphors in *Mariana Pineda* — are lost or overwhelmed when staged. However, other aspects of these plays reflected in the dialogue, the actors' movements, and the multiple aspects of the staging, such as the mutable rose (*Doña Rosita*), the yellow quinces and the *estampa* (*Mariana Pineda*), the green frock coat, golden antlers, emerald dagger, and the red velvet cloak (*Don Perlimplín*), and the violence of the Shoemaker's Wife's fury (*La zapatera*), reach their full potential in physical form.

Notes to Chapter 3

1. Federico García Lorca, *Prosa 1* in *Obras Completas VI*, ed. by Miguel García-Posada (Madrid: Ediciones Akal, 2008). *Prosa 1*, p. 730.

2. See Robert Havard, '*Mariana Pineda*: Politics, Poetry, and Periodization', in *Leeds Papers on Lorca and on Civil War Verse*, ed. by Margaret Rees (Leeds: University of Leeds, 1988), pp. 45–66 (pp. 53–54); Sumner M. Greenfield, 'The Problem of *Mariana Pineda*', *The Massachusetts Review*, 1.4 (1960), 751–63 (p. 757); and Concha Zardoya, '*Mariana Pineda*: romance trágico de la libertad' [Mariana Pineda: Tragic Ballad of Freedom], *Revista Hispánica Moderna*, 1.1–2 (1968), 471–97 (p. 492). Lorca compares Marina to irises, roses, jasmine, and yellow rosemary flowers in *Mariana Pineda*; women to poppies, roses, and tuberose in *La zapatera*; men, women, and the baby boy to carnations, dahlias, geraniums, lilies, pinks, sunflowers, and daisies in *Bodas de sangre*; and

Yerma's longed-for baby to jasmine in *Yerma*. Whilst Gwynne Edwards translates both 'lirio' and 'azucena' as 'lily', I read the former as 'iris' in line with Andrew Anderson's discussion of Lorca's differentiation between the two flowers in his article '"Lirio" and "azucena" in Lorca's Poetry and Drama', *Anales de la Literatura Española Contemporánea*, 11.1–2 (1986), 39–59. Whilst 'lirio' comes from the Latin root *lilium*, lily, and sometimes the two words can be synonymous, the Real Academia Española specifies that 'lirio' is of the *iridacae* genus.

3. Margaret Rees, '"Rosa y jazmín de Granada": The Role of Flowers in Lorca's Plays and Poetry' [Rose and Jasmine of Granada], in *Leeds Papers on Lorca and on Civil War Verse*, ed. by Margaret Rees (Leeds: University of Leeds, 1988), pp. 85–96 (pp. 89–91).

4. Rees, p. 86.

5. *Prosa 1*, p. 730.

6. *Prosa 1*, p. 716.

7. *Prosa 1*, p. 723. This extraordinary range of fabrics and textures is typical of Lorca's theatre. Different types of lacework are present in most of Lorca's works and he also incorporates acts of knitting, sewing, skein-making, and embroidery into the action of his plays, which emphasises the craft-like nature of his colour-writing through verbs such as 'tejer'. The range of coloured fabrics throughout Lorca's theatre — including 'terciopelo', 'seda', 'cuero', 'charol', 'pana', 'raso', 'lana', 'malla', 'muselina', 'popelinette', 'gasa', 'moaré', and 'armiño '[velvet, silk, leather, patent leather, velveteen or corduroy, satin, wool, tulle, muslin, poplinette, chiffon, moire (processed rippled silk), and ermine] — is enhanced by highly detailed embellishments — 'agremanes', 'borlas', 'espejitos', 'abalarios', 'botones', 'plumas', 'lentejuelas', 'flecos', 'cascabeles', 'clavos', 'bordados', and, of course, 'encajes' [brocade, tassels, mirrors, glass beads, buttons, feathers, sequins, fringe, bells, studs, embroidery, and lace] — not to mention the different shapes, cuts, and styles of clothing.

8. *Prosa 1*, p. 724.

9. Federico García Lorca, *Palabra de Lorca: Declaraciones y entrevistas completas*, ed. by Rafael Inglada (Barcelona: Ediciones Malpaso, 2017), p. 440.

10. The themes of unfulfillment and waiting, especially the use of 'marchita' or flower withering which we see in *Así que pasen*, *Bodas de Sangre*, *Yerma*, and *Doña Rosita* are also important in Lorca's poetry. For example, in 'Elegia' [Elegy] in *Libro de Poemas* [Book of Poems] (1918) Lorca describes the female protagonist as 'con la carne oscura de nardo marchito' [with the dark flesh of a wilted spikenard] and warns her that 'te marchitarás como la magnolia' [you will wither like the magnolia]. We also see a plethora of reds and whites in this poem that are distinctly evocative of *Doña Rosita*, as well as references to milk and childlessness which remind us of *Yerma*. See Federico García Lorca, *Libro de Poemas* [1918] in *Obra completa I*, ed. by Miguel García-Posada (Madrid: Ediciones Akal, 2008), pp. 195–97.

11. *Prosa 1*, p. 723.

12. Catherine Nickel, 'The Function of Language in García Lorca's *Doña Rosita la soltera*', *Hispania*, 66.4 (1983), 522–31 (p. 527).

13. Francie Cate-Arries, 'The Discourse of Desire in the Language of Flowers: Lorca, Freud, and *Doña Rosita*', *South Atlantic Review*, 57.1 (1992), 53–68 (p. 60).

14. See María Pao, 'Reading Rosita or the Language of Flowers', *Hispanic Research Journal*, 10.4 (2009), 321–35.

15. Pao, p. 323–24.

16. Noël Valis, 'The Culture of Nostalgia, or the Language of Flowers', in *The Culture of Cursilería: Bad Taste, Kitsch, and Class in Modern Spain* (Durham, NC: Duke University Press, 2002), pp. 244–76 (p. 259).

17. *Prosa 1*, p. 724.

18. Elaine Scarry, *Dreaming by the Book*, p. 244. In 'Colorsteps', Susan Harrow builds on Scarry's idea of imaginative re-creation and considers 'acts of chromatic imagining' in modern and contemporary French poetry, emphasising the potential for extending Scarry's concept specifically to colour. See Susan Harrow, 'Colorsteps in Modern and Contemporary French Poetry', *French Forum*, 37.1–2 (2012), 35–52 (p. 36).

19. Rees, p. 93.

20. Valis, p. 253.

21. Valis, p. 250.
22. Rees, pp. 93–94. Rees suggests that this shocking conflation of flowers and wounding 'should be no surprise, since the Surrealists of Lorca's generation, in their determination to jolt people out of their mental ruts, regularly compared the traditionally beautiful with the traditionally horrible or humdrum' (p. 93). However, Rees sees Lorca's floral imagery as equally influenced by the Baroque poet Luis de Góngora, whom Lorca praised in his lectures on 'La imagen poética de Don Luis de Góngora' (1926–1930) [The Poetic Image of Don Luis de Góngora]: 'When Góngora created images, says Lorca, the object as it is in nature was transformed in the camera obscura of the poet's brain and emerged as something new and individual. The same metamorphosis takes place when Lorca introduces flowers into his writings. They are mysterious, powerful forces of nature, sometimes surreal, sometimes violent, but portrayed with that delight in beauty on a miniature scale which Lorca himself says is typical of artists from Granada' (pp. 94–95).
23. Nickel, pp. 522–23.
24. Valis, p. 255.
25. *Prosa 1*, p. 724. *Cursi* refers to 'a person who pretends to be elegant or refined without success' or 'a thing with the appearance of elegance or wealth which is pretentious and tasteless' according to the Real Academia Española. I discuss the idea of *cursilería* in more depth later in this chapter.
26. This depiction reminds us of Belisa's mother in *Don Perlimplín* who appears in '*una gran peluca dieciochesca llena de pájaros, cintas y abalorios*' [a big eighteenth-century wig full of birds, ribbons, and glass beads] (p. 267) as part of Lorca's aim of blending of the lyrical and the grotesque in this play. These ostentatious costumes create bourgeois caricatures that revel in their grotesqueness. However, unlike Belisa's mother, the Spinsters are as much an object of pity as one of ridicule due to their stultified and restricted lives in which they struggle to maintain social appearances despite their growing poverty. These women are already that '*cosa grotesca y conmovedora*' [grotesque and moving thing] Lorca tells us Rosita is fated to become (*Prosa 1*, p. 723).
27. Valis, p. 253.
28. Lorca, *Palabra de Lorca*, p. 349 and p. 443.
29. Lorca, *Palabra de Lorca*, p. 444.
30. *Prosa 1*, p. 241.
31. *Prosa 1*, p. 730.
32. Reed Anderson, *Federico García Lorca* (London: Macmillan, 1984), p. 71
33. Paul McDermid, *Love, Desire and Identity in the Theatre of Federico García Lorca* (Woodbridge: Tamesis, 2007), p. 43.
34. McDermid, p. 40.
35. Zardoya, p. 489.
36. McDermid, p. 44.
37. Havard, 'Mariana Pineda', p. 63.
38. Havard, 'Mariana Pineda', p. 63.
39. *Prosa 1*, p. 612.
40. McDermid, p. 74.
41. Zardoya, p. 490.
42. Greenfield, 'The Problem of Mariana Pineda', pp. 754–55. Lorca had his own doubts about this work, describing it in 1929 as '[una] obra débil de principiante, y aun teniendo rasgos de mi temperamento poético, no responde ya en absoluto a mi criterio sobre el teatro', [a weak, beginner's work which, although it has traces of my poetic temperament, no longer corresponds in any way to my theatrical criteria] (*Prosa 1*, p. 374). Lorca's brother Francisco also tells us: 'Yo creo que Doña Rosita, escrita con grandes precauciones, vence el fracaso íntimo de Mariana Pineda' [I think that Doña Rosita, written with great caution, overcame the private failure of Mariana Pineda] 'Prólogo a una trilogía dramática' [Prologue to a Dramatic Trilogy], *FGL: Boletín de Federico García Lorca*, 7.13 (1993), 205–28 (p. 219). In a 1933 interview, the year the play premiered in Buenos Aires, Lorca seemed to change his mind about Mariana Pineda, at least in order to promote this new production, and praised the ways in which the play encapsulated his view of theatre as the fusion of emotion and poetry: 'El caudal de una verdadera poesía que fluía natural y constantemente, no sólo de los personajes, sino del ambiente que les rodea [...] de

Mariana Pineda éste es el concepto que más me satisfece' [The river of true poetry which flowed naturally and constantly, not only in the characters, but in the atmosphere around them [...] this is the concept in Mariana Pineda which satisfies me the most] (*Prosa 1*, p. 613).

43. Havard, 'Mariana Pineda', p. 46. Lorca stated 'del teatro romántico no queda nada. Y esa es la desgracia de la escena española', [Nothing remains of Romantic theatre. And this is the disgrace of the Spanish stage] (*Prosa 1*, p. 676).

44. Havard, 'Mariana Pineda', p. 53.

45. Reed Anderson, p. 70.

46. *Prosa 1*, p. 490. Lorca tells us that he borrowed selectively from the Romantic tradition to suit his vision of the play: 'He utilizado algunos [tópicos] — no todos los que quisiera — que le iban al ambiente de la obra a su carácter romántico, poco ironizado...' [I have used some romantic clichés — not all those I wanted — which complemented the atmosphere of the work and its romantic character, with little irony].

47. Havard, *Mariana Pineda*, p. 64.

48. Zardoya, p. 494.

49. McDermid, pp. 51–52.

50. Havard, *Mariana Pineda*, p. 62.

51. *Prosa 1*, p. 503.

52. Margarita Ucelay, 'Introducción', in Federico García Lorca, *Amor de Don Perlimplín con Belisa en su jardín*, ed. by Margarita Ucelay, 9th edn (Madrid: Ediciones Cátedra, 2010), pp. 9–232 (p. 20). Margarita is the daughter of Pura Ucelay, who worked closely with Lorca and staged the premiere of this play in a double bill with *La zapatera* in 1933.

53. Sarah Wright, *The Trickster Function in the Theatre of Federico García Lorca* (Woodbridge: Tamesis, 2000), p. 45.

54. María Delgado, *Federico García Lorca* (Oxford: Routledge, 2008), p. 66.

55. Prosa 1, p. 532.

56. See McDermid, pp. 74–79.

57. Ucelay, 'Introducción', p. 24.

58. This image recurs at the end of Scene One (p. 286), although in this instance their colour is not specified.

59. Ucelay, 'Introducción', p. 44.

60. See Antonio Martín, 'Las aleluyas, primera lectura y primeras imágenes para niños en los siglos XVIII–XIX. Un antecedente de la literatura y la prensa infantil en España' [Aleluyas, First Reading Matter and Images for Children in the 18th-19th Centuries. A precursor of Children's Literature and Magazines in Spain], *Estreno*, 47 (2011), no pagination. <https://webs.ucm.es/info/especulo/numero47/aleluya.html> [accessed 20 February 2022].

61. Margarita Ucelay 'Federico García Lorca y el Club Teatral Anfistora: El dramaturgo como director de escena' [Federico García Lorca and the Anfistora Theatre Club: The Playwright as Stage Director], in *Lecciones sobre Federico García Lorca: Granada, Mayo de 1986* [Lectures on Federico García Lorca: Granada, May 1986], ed. by Andrés Soria Olmedo (Granada: Comisión Nacional de Cincuentenario, 1986), pp. 49–64 (p. 44).

62. The entremés was a one-act comic sketch performed during the interlude of the main play. The *novelas ejemplares* [Exemplary Tales] were a series of short novels published by Cervantes in 1613.

63. Often Perlimplín is depicted as wearing horns, including wing-shaped ones in John Cobb's 2015 production at the Southwark Playhouse, London, huge, curved ones in Allison Rose Lloyd's staging at the Muhlenberg College New Visions Directors Festival in 2014, and even large, wooden ones protruding from a Viking helmet in the Portuguese television version starring Heitor Lourenço and Melânia Gomes in 2009. However, other productions have been more faithful to Lorca's specific reference to 'cuernos de ciervo', such as Andrés Zambrano's adaptation at La Guarida Colonial House, Cuenca, in 2018, although here they seem to lose their crucial golden colour.

64. Wright, *The Trickster Function*, p. 44.

65. John Lyon, 'Love, Imagination and Society in *Amor de don Perlimplín* and *La zapatera prodigiosa*', *Bulletin of Hispanic Studies*, 63.3 (1986), 235–45 (pp. 239–40).

66. Prosa 1, p. 532.

67. McDermid, p. 85.

68. Lyon, pp. 241–42.

69. McDermid, pp. 74–75. The original Lorca quote is in *Prosa 1*, p. 529.

70. McDermid, p. 76.

71. McDermid, p. 96.

72. McDermid, p. 86.

73. McDermid, p. 87.

74. McDermid, p. 87.

75. Lyon, p. 236.

76. Lyon, p. 236.

77. Lyon, p. 236.

78. Andrew Anderson, *García Lorca: La zapatera prodigiosa* (London: Grant and Cutler, 1991), pp. 101–02.

79. Anderson, *García Lorca: La zapatera prodigiosa*, p. 41.

80. Anderson, *García Lorca: La zapatera prodigiosa*, p. 97.

81. Lyon, p. 236.

82. Prosa 1, p. 481.

83. Prosa 1, p. 497. When Lorca speaks of the 'colour' of *La zapatera* as secondary, he is referring to 'local colour' and the Andalusian idioms in the dialogue, suggesting that the play has a universal appeal: 'El color de la obra es accesorio y no fundamental como en otra clase de teatro [...] La palabra y el ritmo pueden ser andaluces, pero no la sustancia' [The colour of the work is secondary and not fundamental like in other types of theatre [...] The words and rhythm can be Andalusian, but not the substance] (*Prosa 1*, p. 531).

84. Anderson, *García Lorca: Yerma* (London: Grant and Cutler, 2003), p. 57.

85. This green reminds us of the Friend's fan and the First Mask's dress in *Así que pasen*, which Lorca describes as 'rojo agresivo' [aggressive red] (p. 188) and 'amarillo rabioso' [rabid or furious yellow] (p. 239) respectively.

86. Gywnne Edwards, *Dramatists in Perspective: Spanish Theatre in the Twentieth Century* (Cardiff: University of Wales Press, 1985), p. 92.

87. Kay García, 'Violence in Two Plays by Federico García Lorca', in *Violence in Drama*, ed. by James Redmond (Cambridge: Cambridge University Press, 1991), pp. 205–13 (p. 204).

88. Anderson, *García Lorca: La zapatera prodigiosa*, p. 58.

89. *Prosa 1*, p. 592 and p. 598.

90. *Prosa 1*, p. 481.

91. Absolute Theatre's 1998 staging at the Festival de Almada in Lisbon made full use of the bright colours and full skirts depicted in Lorca's stage directions. See <http://www.absolutetheatre.co.uk/?p=237> [accessed 20 February 2022].

CONCLUSION

❖

Lorca's colour practice exceeds and unsettles purely symbolic readings and, instead, colour reveals itself to be a psychological, bodily, and inherently material force throughout his plays. From the affective impact of colour and the raw expression of individual suffering, to the colours of the body and the materialisation of poetic motifs, colour is a central element of Lorca's theatre of poetry. We must consider Lorca's colour practice in ways that recognise but move beyond symbolic values and which offer a more in-depth understanding of his varied and striking evocation of the chromatic throughout his theatre. It is also important to consider Lorca's theatre as a whole, rather than dividing his plays along stylistic or temporal lines, as such categorisations restrict and narrow the possibilities of his colour-work and undervalue his poetic vision and imagination. My focus on colour as the lens through which to examine these ten plays reveals Lorca's craftsmanship as well as his aesthetic and emotional engagement with the idea of a theatre of poetry.

In my study I have examined different facets of colour in Lorca's theatre of poetry: how colour sparks and reflects characters' mental states (Chapter One), the role of bodily recuperations of colour in terms of Lorca's exploration of character subjectivities and of implicit colours (Chapter Two), and the importance of object colour in terms of the materialisation of poetic themes and motifs (Chapter Three). In Chapter One, I focused on the psychological currency of colour in *Bernarda Alba*, which revealed powerful and complex reactions to colour on the part of the protagonists. Due to Bernarda's conflation of material whiteness with honour and hued colour with dishonour, she responds in extreme ways to intrusions of hued colour that threaten the ascetic white façade of her house. While intrusions of colour such as Adela's fan cause Bernarda to react in ways that are indicative of chromophobia, Adela, in contrast, desires colour, and the deathly whiteness of the house fills her with anxiety and horror. These competing and overlapping forces of colour were mirrored in the dialogue through silence, flatness, negation, and sparseness, on the one hand, and through verbal references to colour, emphatic gestures, exclamations, and colloquialisms on the other. However, Bernarda's dialogue is both 'white' and 'colourful', indicative of more ambivalent feelings that suggest the inner complexity of Lorca's characters and of the multi-faceted effect of colour on the psyche.

My analysis of Lorca's other plays in Chapters Two and Three showed Lorca's sustained preoccupation with character subjectivities, the reciprocity of key images in the dialogue and in the staging, and the impact of colour on the audience throughout his theatre. In Chapter Two, I explored the role of colour and corporeality related to Lorca's ideas of a poetry 'made human' in *El maleficio, Mariana Pineda, Don Perlimplín, El público, Así que pasen, Bodas de sangre*, and *Yerma*. The trope of female whiteness in *El maleficio, Mariana Pineda, Don Perlimplín*, and *Bodas de sangre*, which took the overlapping forms of the virginal, the dying, and the erotic, belied a much more ambivalent and complex portrayal, as we saw in *Bernarda Alba*. Rather than traditional, romanticised depictions of women, instead we find a visceral portrayal of suffering that is metaphorically inscribed on the female body and which has significant ramifications in terms of bodily colour. This discourse was especially important in *Bodas de sangre*, in the Bride's and the Mother's dialogue, and in *Yerma*, where the colours implied by references to blood and milk continually reinforce the experience of maternity that Yerma has been cruelly denied. Colour affect was also important for exploring of the repeated puncturing of the male body throughout Lorca's theatre. Through disquieting and violent portrayals of the metaphorical and literal puncturing of the male body, Lorca exposes the troubled mental states of the protagonists. These diverse and powerful portrayals of male and female suffering inscribed upon the body, either literally or metaphorically, stem from rigid and unrelenting moral and social codes constructed around gender. The combined effect of this visceral exploration of human suffering is a call for a more fluid approach to gender. This takes the form of a queering of the body through anti-mimetic bodily colour and materials in *El público* and *Así que pasen*. Through the pervasive and diverse colours of the body, Lorca creates a human 'poetry' which 'grita, llora y se desespera' [shouts, cries, and despairs] by inscribing the inner suffering of these restricted individuals on their very flesh.[1]

In Chapter Three, I examined how Lorca gives poetry physical form: how he uses object colour in the staging, including costumes, sets, lighting, and props, to convey a core poetic image. Like whiteness in *Bernarda Alba, Doña Rosita, Mariana Pineda*, and *Don Perlimplín* are all guided by an overarching aesthetic vision suggested in the title or subtitle: the *estampa* or engraved print, the *aleluya* or religious comic strip, and the language of flowers and mutable rose respectively. In *Doña Rosita*, there are important links to my discussion of female emotional pain and of affective bruising in the previous chapter. Through the blending of flowers and flesh in Rosita's discourse, Lorca uses the body to express her deep-rooted personal suffering. However, unlike *Bodas de sangre* and *Yerma, Doña Rosita* reveals a greater focus on the materialisation of poetic themes and motifs on the physical stage, namely the mutable rose. Through the colours and styles of Rosita's costumes, the tripartite structure of the play, and the language of flowers, which we see in the recurring mutable rose poem and the 'Lo que dicen las flores' [What the flowers say] song in Act Two, Lorca uses multiple elements of the performance to bring the mutable rose to life in human form. In *Mariana Pineda*, it is the *estampa* that Lorca animates through colour, as we see the central colours of the opening stage directions reflected in Mariana's costumes, the quinces, and other objects such as flowers, and the explosion of blissful coloured light as the play comes to a climax. Object colour in *Doña Rosita* and *Mariana Pineda* also highlighted the links between costume colour and characterisation, which are important elements of

Don Perlimplín and *La zapatera*. Whilst the decolouration of Rosita's and Mariana's bodies and costumes is indicative of one sort of journey, one of exsanguination and death, in *Don Perlimplín* Lorca explores another form of physical transformation through colour: Perlimplín's metamorphosis from a stock *aleluya* figure and a Punch-like puppet to a fully-developed and equivocal character of bones-and-blood. This journey is represented by the bold outlines of the green room with its black furniture in the prologue, the flocks of black paper birds, Perlimplín's green frock coat, and the golden antlers, on the one hand, and the red velvet cape and the green emerald dagger, which are the agents of his transformation, on the other. In contrast, in *La zapatera* the Shoemaker's Wife is already a character of bones-and-blood and Lorca uses costume colour to distinguish between her and other, more peripheral characters, like the interchangeable female neighbours and the figure of Don Mirlo. Whilst each of these chapters has a different focus — the psyche, the body, and the object — the affective and material qualities of Lorca's colour practice continually overlaps within each discussion as each of Lorca's plays is revealed to be part of his sustained experimentation with bringing poetry to the stage. Colour is found to be a unifying force that encompasses dialogue, sets, props, costumes, lighting, and characterisation.

Whilst I have considered some key performances of Lorca's plays, there is further scope for an exploration of what happens to his colour-work in practice in the rich history of his theatre in performance throughout the twentieth and twenty-first centuries, in Spain and across the globe. It would be interesting to reconsider Lorca's unfinished plays, 'juvenilia', and even his puppet plays and short plays within this framework in order to see whether these conclusions remain the same or whether the picture changes. A re-reading of colour in Lorca's prodigious and diverse poetic corpus is also overdue, particularly in light of these ideas of 'poetry' as a visceral portrayal of human suffering and a powerful emotive and material force, especially 'Romance sonámbulo' [Sleepwalking Ballad] (1927) and the poetry collection *Poeta en Nueva York* [Poet in New York] (1929). The ideas of affective and material colour explored in my study could also shed further light on colour in Hispanic poetry more broadly, especially by Rubén Darío, José Asunción Silva, and Rafael Alberti. Whilst Rosemary Lo Dato touches briefly on colour in her analysis of gems in Ramón del Valle-Inclán's, Darío's, and Asunción Silva's writing in her 1999 study, there is opportunity for a study of these writers' colour-work in its own right, including Valle-Inclán's prose writing, as José Manuel Pereiro Otero has begun to explore.[2] The burgeoning field of affective and material colour studies within French Studies — including the work of Susan Harrow, Emma Wilson, Georges Didi Huberman, and Elodie Ripoll — and Rey Conquer's *Reading Colour* (2019) in German and Austrian Studies, points to further unmined wealth in Hispanic Studies.

My reading of colour in Lorca's theatre also has wider implications for theatre studies as a whole, especially the difference between visual and verbal colour and how the two interact in performance, the affective impact of colour on the audience, the ways colour can be used to unite or create contrasts between different elements of the staging, and the possibilities of bringing the characters' mental states and key themes and images in the dialogue to the stage in physical form through colour. These ideas are especially important when we consider the role of colour in the experimental theatre that was developing in the early twentieth century, including Wassily Kandinsky's *Der Gelbe Klang* (1912) [The Yellow Sound] and Valle-Inclán's exploration of the *esperpento* in the plays *Luces de bohemia* [Bohemian Lights] (1920) and *Martes de carnival* [Carnival Tuesday] (1930).[3] There were also important ideas surrounding colour and the stage emerging in Italian Futurism, as Günter Berghaus explores in his study.[4] A research project that took into account the diverse chromatic landscape of theatre in early-twentieth-century Europe as a whole would be an excellent addition to the field of modern language studies. The implications of my colour study also reach beyond my temporal framework of 1920 to 1936 and provide a fruitful approach for looking at colour in other periods, such as the Golden Age. More broadly, I demonstrate how other areas of arts and humanities research and modern language research — both literary and visual — can nourish Hispanic studies in ways that are mutually beneficial and emphasise the inherently cross-disciplinary nature of both modern language studies and colour studies.

Notes to the Conclusion

1. Federico García Lorca, *Prosa 1*, in *Obras Completas VI*, ed. by Miguel García-Posada (Madrid: Ediciones Akal, 2008), p. 730

2. See Rosemary C. Lo Dato, *Beyond the Glitter: The Language of Gems in Modernista Writers Rubén Darío, Ramón del Valle-Inclán, and José Asunción Silva* (Lewisburg, NY: Bucknell University Press, 1999), and José Manuel Pereiro Otero, *La escritura modernista de Valle-Inclán: Orgía de colores* (Madrid: Editorial Verbum, 2009), Kindle edition.

3. Like Lorca, Valle-Inclán sought to renovate the stultified, bourgeois Spanish stage and expose the truth beneath the surface of things. The 'esperpento' acted as a distorting mirror, creating a grotesque portrayal of reality. The Real Academia Española defines Valle-Inclán's concept as '[un] género literario [...] en el que se deforma la realidad, recargando sus rasgos grotescos, sometiendo a una elaboración muy personal el lenguaje coloquial y desgarrado'. [A literary genre [...] in which reality becomes deformed, its grotesque features are exaggerated, and it is submitted to a very personal creation of colloquial and fragmented language].

4. See Günter Berghaus, *Italian Futurist Theatre, 1909–1944* (Oxford: Clarendon Press, 1998).

BIBLIOGRAPHY

❖

Editions of Primary Works

Plays

GARCÍA LORCA, FEDERICO, *Amor de Don Perlimplín con Belisa en su jardín* [The Love of Don Perlimplín with Belisa in his Garden], in *Obra completa III*, ed. by Miguel García-Posada (Madrid: Ediciones Akal, 2008 [1925])

——*Así que pasen cinco años* [When Five Years Pass], in *Obra completa V*, ed. by Miguel García-Posada (Madrid: Ediciones Akal, 2008 [1931])

——*Bodas de sangre* [Blood Weddings], in *Obra completa III*, ed. by Miguel García-Posada (Madrid: Ediciones Akal, 2008 [1932])

——*La casa de Bernarda Alba* [The House of Bernarda Alba], in *Obra completa IV*, ed. by Miguel García-Posada (Madrid: Ediciones Akal, 2008 [1936])

——*La casa de Bernarda Alba* (Barcelona: Ayma, 1964)

——*Doña Rosita la soltera o el lenguaje de las flores* [Doña Rosita the Spinster or the Language of Flowers], in *Obra completa IV*, ed. by Miguel García-Posada (Madrid: Ediciones Akal, 2008 [1935])

——*El maleficio de la mariposa* [The Butterfly's Evil Spell], in *Obra completa IV*, ed. by Miguel García-Posada (Madrid: Ediciones Akal, 2008 [1920])

——*Mariana Pineda*, in *Obra completa IV*, ed. by Miguel García-Posada (Madrid: Ediciones Akal, 2008 [1925])

——*El público* [The Audience], in *Obra completa V*, ed. by Miguel García-Posada (Madrid: Ediciones Akal, 2008 [1930])

——*Yerma*, in *Obra completa III*, ed. by Miguel García-Posada (Madrid: Ediciones Akal, 2008 [1934])

——*La zapatera prodigiosa* [The Prodigious Shoemaker's Wife], in *Obra completa III*, ed. by Miguel García-Posada (Madrid: Ediciones Akal, 2008 [1926])

Poetry

GARCÍA LORCA, FEDERICO, *Canciones* [Songs], in *Obra completa I*, ed. by Miguel García-Posada (Madrid: Ediciones Akal, 2008 [1921–1924])

——*Gypsy Ballads*, trans. by Robert Havard (Liverpool University Press: Liverpool, 1990)

——*Gypsy Ballads*, trans. by Jane Duran and Gloria García Lorca (Enitharmon Press: London, 2011).

——*Libro de Poemas* [Book of Poems], in *Obra completa I*, ed. by Miguel García-Posada (Madrid: Ediciones Akal, 2008 [1918])

Correspondence, Declarations, and Interviews

GARCÍA LORCA, FEDERICO, *Palabra de Lorca: Declaraciones y entrevistas completas*, ed. by Rafael Inglada (Barcelona: Ediciones Malpaso, 2017)

——*Prosa 1*, in *Obras Completas VI*, ed. by Miguel García-Posada (Madrid: Ediciones Akal, 2008)

——*Prosa 2*, in *Obras Completas VII*, ed. by Miguel García-Posada (Madrid: Ediciones Akal, 2008)

Secondary Works

Lorca Studies

AGUILAR PIÑAL, FRANCISCO, 'La honra en el teatro de García Lorca', *Revista de literatura*, 48.96 (1986), 447–54

ALLEN, RUPERT C., *Psyche and Symbol in the Theater of Federico García Lorca: 'Perlimplín', 'Yerma', 'Blood Wedding'* (Austin: University of Texas Press, 1974)

ANDERSON, ANDREW A., '"Lirio" and "azucena" in Lorca's Poetry and Drama', *Anales de la Literatura Española Contemporánea*, 11.1–2 (1986), 39–59

——*García Lorca: La zapatera prodigiosa* (London: Grant and Cutler, 1991)

——*García Lorca: Yerma* (London: Grant and Cutler, 2003)

——'"Un dificilísimo juego poético": Theme and Symbol in Lorca's *El público*', *Romance Quarterly*, 39.3 (1992), 331–46

ANDERSON, FARRIS, 'The Theatrical Design of Lorca's *Así que pasen cinco años*', *Journal of Spanish Studies*, 7.3 (1979), 249–78

ANDERSON, REED, *Federico García Lorca* (London: Macmillan, 1984)

BADENES, JOSÉ I., 'Martyred Masculinities: Saint Sebastian and the Dramas of Tennessee Williams and Federico García Lorca', *Text and Presentation*, 5 (2008), 5–17

——'"This Is My Body which Will Be Given Up for You": Federico García Lorca's *Amor de Don Perlimplín* and the Auto Sacramental Tradition', *Hispania*, 92.4 (2009), 688–95

CABRERA, VICENTE, 'Poetic Structure in Lorca's *La casa de Bernarda Alba*', *Hispania*, 61.3 (1978), 466–71

CATE-ARRIES, FRANCIE, 'The Discourse of Desire in the Language of Flowers: Lorca, Freud, and *Doña Rosita*', *South Atlantic Review*, 57.1 (1992), 53–68

CERQUEIRA, NELSON, 'Poetic Language in the Plays of Lorca and Cocteau', *Chiricú*, 3.2 (1983), 20–38

CORBIN, JOHN, 'Lorca's "Casa"', *The Modern Language Review*, 95.3 (2000), 712–27

CORTEZ, BEATRIZ, 'Sadomasoquismo y travestismo en El público de Federico García Lorca: Un reto al heterosexismo compulsivo', *Hispanófila*, 133 (2001), 31–42

DEAN-THACKER, VERONICA, and PEDRO GUERRERO RUÍZ, *Federico García Lorca: El color de la poesía* (Murcia: Universidad de Murcia, 1998)

DELGADO, MARIA M., *Federico García Lorca* (Oxford: Routledge, 2008)

DELGADO MORALES, MANUEL, and A. J. PROUST, (eds), *Lorca, Buñuel, Dalí: Art and Theory* (London: Associated University Presses, 2001)

DEVOTO, DANIEL, '*Doña Rosita la soltera*: Estructura y fuentes', *Bulletin Hispanique*, 69 (1969), 407–35

DOLAN, KATHLEEN, 'Time, Irony and Negation in Lorca's Last Three Plays', *Hispania*, 63.3 (1980), 514–22

EDWARDS, GWYNNE, *Lorca: The Theatre Beneath the Sand* (London: Boyars, 1980)

——'Lorca and Buñuel: *Así que pasen cinco años* and *Un chien andalou*', *García Lorca Review*, 9.2 (1981), 128–41

——*Dramatists in Perspective: Spanish Theatre in the Twentieth Century* (Cardiff: University of Wales Press, 1985)

——'Productions of *La casa de Bernarda Alba*', *Anales de la Literatura Española Contemporánea*, 25.3 (2000), 699–728

——'Introduction', in Federico García Lorca, *Yerma*, trans. by Gywnne Edwards (London: Methuen Drama, 2007), pp. v–lxv

——*Lorca, Buñuel, Dalí: Forbidden Pleasures and Connected Lives* (London and New York: I. B. Tauris, 2009)

FEAL, CARLOS, 'El sacrificio de la hombría en *Bodas de sangre*', *MLN*, 99 (1984), 270–87

FERGUSSON, FRANCIS, '*Don Perlimplín*: Lorca's Theatre-Poetry', *The Kenyon Review*, 17.3 (1955), 337–48

FERNÁNDEZ CIFUENTES, LUIS, *Garcia Lorca en el teatro: La norma y la diferencia* (Zaragoza: Universidad de Zaragoza, 1986)

GARCÍA, KAY, 'Violence in Two Plays by Federico García Lorca', in *Violence in Drama* ed. by James Redmond (Cambridge: Cambridge University Press, 1991), pp. 205–13

GARCÍA LÓPEZ, MIGUEL, *Queering Lorca's Duende: Desire, Death, Intermediality*, Studies in Hispanic and Lusophone Cultures, 49 (Cambridge: Legenda, 2021)

GARCÍA LORCA, FEDERICO, *Comedia sin título, seguida de "El sueño de la vida" de Alberto Conejero*, ed. by Emilio Peral Vega (Madrid: Ediciones Cátedra, 2018)

GIBSON, IAN, *Federico Garcia Lorca: A Life* (London: Faber and Faber, 1989)

GREENFIELD, SUMNER M., 'Poetry and Stagecraft in *La casa de Bernarda Alba*', *Hispania*, 38.4 (1955), 456–61

——'The Problem of *Mariana Pineda*', *The Massachusetts Review*, 1.4 (1960), 751–63

——'Lorca's Theatre: A Synthetic Re-examination', *Journal of Spanish Studies: Twentieth Century*, 5 (1977), 31–46

HARE, DAVID, *The House of Bernarda Alba* (London: Faber and Faber, 2005). Kindle edition

HARRIS, DEREK, 'Green Death: An Analysis of the Symbolism of the Colour "Green" in Lorca's Poetry', in *Readings in Spanish and Portuguese Poetry for Geoffrey Connell*, ed. by Nicholas Round and D. Gareth Walters (Glasgow: University of Glasgow Department of Hispanic Studies, 1985), pp. 80–97

HAVARD, ROBERT, 'The Symbolic Ambivalence of "Green" in García Lorca and Dylan Thomas', *Modern Language Review*, 67 (1972), 810–19

——'*Mariana Pineda*: Politics, Poetry, and Periodization', in *Leeds Papers on Lorca and on Civil War Verse*, ed. by Margaret Rees (Leeds: University of Leeds, 1988), pp. 45–66

HERNÁNDEZ VALCÁRCEL, MARÍA DEL CARMEN, 'Federico García Lorca', in *La expresión sensorial en cinco poetas del 27* (Murcia: Universidad de Murcia, 1978), pp. 197–248

HIGGINBOTHAM, VIRGINIA, '*Así que pasen cinco años*: Una versión literaria de *Un chien andalou*', *Cuadernos Hispanoamericanos*, 433–34 (1986), 343–50

—— *The Comic Spirit of Federico García Lorca* (Austin: University of Texas Press, 1976)

JEREZ FERRÁN, CARLOS, *Un Lorca desconocido: Análisis de un teatro "irrepresentable"* (Madrid: Biblioteca Nueva, 2004)

KNAPP, BETTINA, 'Federico Garcia Lorca's *The House of Bernarda Alba*: A Hermaphroditic Matriarchate', *Modern Drama*, 27.3 (1984), 382–94

LAFFRANQUE, MARIE, *Teatro inconcluso: Fragmentos y proyectos inacabados* (Granada: Universidad de Granada, 1987)

LIMA, ROBERT, 'Blood Spilt and Unspilt: Primal Sacrifice in Lorca's Bodas de sangre', *Letras peninsulares*, 8.2–3 (1995), 256–59

LYON, JOHN, 'Love, Imagination and Society in *Amor de don Perlimplín* and *La zapatera prodigiosa*', *Bulletin of Hispanic Studies*, 63.3 (1986), 235–45

MAYHEW, JONATHAN, 'Sexual Epistemologies: The Whitman Ode', in *Lorca's Legacy: Essays in Interpretation* (New York: Routledge, 2018), pp. 139–66

McDERMID, PAUL, *Love, Desire and Identity in the Theatre of Federico García Lorca* (Woodbridge: Tamesis, 2007)

MORLA LYNCH, CARLOS, *En España con Federico García Lorca: Páginas de un diario íntimo, 1928–1936* (Madrid: Aguilar, 1958)

MORRIS, C. B., *García Lorca: Bodas de Sangre* (London: Grant and Cutler, 1980)

—— 'The "Austere Abode": Lorca's *La casa de Bernarda Alba*', *Anales de la Literatura Española Contemporánea*, 11.1–2 (1986), 129–41

—— *García Lorca: La casa de Bernarda Alba* (London: Grant and Cutler, 1990)

NICKEL, CATHERINE, 'The Function of Language in García Lorca's *Doña Rosita la soltera*', *Hispania*, 66.4 (1983), 522–31

ORRINGER, NELSON R., 'Absence of Color: Its Erotic Connotations in the *Diván del Tamarit*', *García Lorca Review*, 3.1–2 (1975), 57–66

PAO, MARÍA, 'Reading Rosita or the Language of Flowers', *Hispanic Research Journal*, 10.4 (2009), 321–35

PERAL VEGA, EMILIO, *Pierrot/Lorca: White Carnival of Black Desire* (Woodbridge: Tamesis, 2015)

—— (ed.) *Federico García Lorca: 100 años en Madrid*, (Madrid: Comunidad de Madrid and Consejería de Cultura, Turismo y Deportes, 2019)

PROUT, RYAN, 'Greenery Blues: Synaesthesia, Landscape and Lorca's Lassitude in Vermont', *Bulletin of Hispanic Studies*, 77.3 (2000), 393–411

QUANCE, ROBERTA ANN, 'Los arquetipos de Venus y la Virgen: Un tema bordado', *Jardín deshecho: Lorca y al amor*, ed. by Christopher Maurer (Granada: Centro Federico García Lorca, 2019), pp. 88–105 (pp. 99–102), <https://www.centrofedericogarcialorca.es/es/publicaciones/catalogo-de-exposicion/17/jardin-deshecho-lorca-amor> [accessed 20 February 2022]

RAMSDEN, HERBERT, 'Introduction', in Federico García Lorca, *La casa de Bernarda Alba* (Manchester: University of Manchester, 1983), pp. vii–lix

REES, MARGARET, ' "Rosa y jazmín de Granada": The Role of Flowers in Lorca's Plays and Poetry', in *Leeds Papers on Lorca and on Civil War Verse*, ed. by Margaret Rees (Leeds: University of Leeds, 1988), pp. 85–96

SMITH, PAUL JULIAN, *The Theatre of García Lorca: Text, Performance, Psychoanalysis* (Cambridge: Cambridge University Press, 1998)

—— 'Reading Intermediality: Lorca's *Viaje a la luna* (Journey to the Moon, 1929) and *Un chien andalou* (Buñuel/Dalí, 1929)', *Modern Languages Open* (2014), 1–9

SOUFAS JR, C. CHRISTOPHER, 'Dialectics of Vision: Pictorial vs. Photographic Representations in Lorca's *La casa de Bernarda Alba*', *Ojancano*, 5 (1991), 52–66

—— *Audience and Authority in the Modernist Theater of Federico García Lorca* (Tuscaloosa, AL: University of Alabama Press, 1996)

STAINTON, LESLIE, *Lorca: A Dream of Life* (New York: Farrar, Straus and Giroux, 1999), Kindle edition

THOMPSON, MICHAEL, 'Poetry that Gets up off the Page and Becomes Human: Poetic Coherence and Eccentricity in Lorca's Theatre', in *Fire, Blood and the Alphabet: One Hundred Years of Lorca*, ed. by Sebastian Doggart and Michael Thompson (Manchester: Manchester University Press, 2010), pp. 67–79

UCELAY, MARGARITA, 'Federico García Lorca y el Club Teatral Anfistora: El dramaturgo como director de escena', in *Lecciones sobre Federico García Lorca: Granada, Mayo de 1986*, ed. by Andrés Soria Olmedo (Granada: Comisión Nacional de Cincuentenario, 1986), pp. 49–64

—— 'Introducción', in Federico García Lorca, *El amor de Don Perlimplín con Belisa en su jardín*, ed. by Margarita Ucelay, 9th edn (Madrid: Ediciones Cátedra, 2010), pp. 9–232

VALIS, NOËL, 'The Culture of Nostalgia, or the Language of Flowers', in *The Culture of Cursilería: Bad Taste, Kitsch, and Class in Modern Spain* (Durham, NC: Duke University Press, 2002), pp. 244–76

WADE BYRD, SUZANNE, *García Lorca: 'La Barraca' and the Spanish National Theater* (New York: Abrad Ediciones, 1975)

WRIGHT, SARAH, *The Trickster Function in the Theatre of Federico García Lorca* (Woodbridge: Tamesis, 2000)

——'Theatre', in *A Companion to Federico García Lorca*, ed. by Federico Bonaddio (Woodbridge: Tamesis, 2010), pp. 39–62

ZARDOYA, CONCHA, '*Mariana Pineda*: Romance trágico de la libertad', *Revista Hispánica Moderna*, 1.1–2 (1968), 471–97

ZIOMEK, HENRYK, 'El simbolismo del blanco en *La casa de Bernarda Alba* y en *La dama del alba*', *Symposium*, 24,1 (1970), 81–85

Colour Studies and Recommended Further Colour Reading

AHMED, SARA, 'A Phenomenology of Whiteness', *Feminist Theory*, 8:2 (2007), 149–68

BATCHELOR, DAVID, *Chromophobia* (London: Reaktion Books, 2000)

——*The Luminous and the Grey* (London: Reaktion Books, 2014)

BLASZCZYK, REGINA LEE, *The Color Revolution* (Cambridge, MA; London: MIT Press in association with Lemelson Center, Smithsonian Institution, 2012)

——'Chromophilia: The Design World's Passion for Colour', *Journal of Design History*, 27.3 (2014), 203–17

BROWN, SIMON, SARAH STREET, and LIZ WATKINS (eds), *Color and the Moving Image: History, Theory, Aesthetics, Archive* (Oxford: Routledge, 2013)

CONQUER, REY, *Reading Colour: George, Rilke, Kandinsky, Lasker-Schüler* (Oxford: Peter Lang, 2019)

DALY, NICHOLAS, 'The Woman in White: Whistler, Hiffenan, Courbet, Du Maurier', *Modernism/Modernity*, 12.1 (2005), 1–25

DIDI-HUBERMAN, GEORGES, *Blancs soucis* (Paris: Minuit, 2005)

DORAN, SABINE, *The Culture of Yellow: Or, The Visual Politics of Late Modernity* (London: Bloomsbury, 2013)

DYER, RICHARD, *White: Essays on Race and Culture* (Oxford: Routledge, 1997)

EATON, NATASHA, 'Anechoic White? Meta-colour in South Asia', in *Third Text*, <http://www.thirdtext.org/anechoic-white> [accessed 20 February 2022]

——*Colour, Art and Empire: Visual Culture and the Nomadism of Representation* (London: I. B. Tauris, 2013)

FOSSATI, GIOVANNA, VICTORIA JACKSON, BREGT LAMERIS, SARAH STREET, and JOSHUA YUMIBE (eds), *The Colour Fantastic: Chromatic Worlds of Silent Cinema* (Amsterdam: Amsterdam University Press, 2017)

GAGE, JOHN, *Colour and Culture: Practice and Meaning from Antiquity to Abstraction* (London: Thames and Hudson, 1993)

——*Colour and Meaning: Art, Science and Symbolism* (London: Thames and Hudson, 1999)

GASKILL, NICHOLAS, *Chromographia: American Literature and the Modernization of Colour* (Minneapolis, MN: University of Minnesota Press, 2018)

GUERIN, FRANCES, *The Truth is Always Grey: A History of Modernist Painting* (Minneapolis, MN: University of Minnesota Press, 2018)

HARROW, SUSAN, 'Zola: Colorist, Abstractionist', *Romanic Review*, 102.3–4 (2011), 465–84

——'Colorsteps in Modern and Contemporary French Poetry', *French Forum*, 37.1–2 (2012), 35–52

——'Thinking Colour-Writing: Introduction', *French Studies*, 71.3 (2017), 307–18

——*Colourworks: Chromatic Innovation in Modern French Poetry and Art Writing* (London: Bloomsbury, 2020)

IMBERT, CLAUDE, 'Manet: Effects of Black', *Paragraph*, 34.2 (2011), 187–98

JORDAN, SHIRLEY, 'Washes and Hues: Reading for Colour in Marie NDiaye,' *French Studies*, 71.3 (2017), 362–73

KRISTEVA, JULIA, 'Giotto's Joy', in *Desire in Language: A Semiotic Approach to Literature and Art* (Oxford: Basil Blackwell, 1981), pp. 210–36

LE CORBUSIER, 'A Coat of Whitewash: The Law of Ripolin', in *Essential Le Corbusier: L'Esprit Nouveau Articles*, trans. by James I. Dunnett (Oxford: Architectural Press, 1998), pp. 185–92

MAVOR, CAROL, *Black and Blue: The Bruising Passion of Camera Lucida, La Jetée, Sans Soleil, and Hiroshima Mon Amour* (Durham, NC: Duke University Press, 2012)

——*Blue Mythologies: Reflections on a Colour* (London: Reaktion Books, 2013)

MCLAUGHLIN, EMILY, '"et que faut-il penser | De ces pommes jaunes?": An Ecocritical Reading of Yves Bonnefoy's Punctual Colour Work', *French Studies*, 71:3 (2017), 348–61

O'CONNOR, CLÉMENCE, 'Colour, Desire, and Destruction in Béatrice Bonhomme's *La Maison abandonnée*', *French Studies*, 71:3 (2017), 374–87

PASTOUREAU, MICHEL, *Blue: The History of a Color*, trans. by Markus I. Cruse (Princeton: Princeton University Press, 2001)

——*Black: The History of a Color*, trans. by Jody Gladding (Princeton, NJ: Princeton University Press, 2009)

——*Green: The History of a Color*, trans. by Jody Gladding (Princeton, NJ: Princeton University Press, 2014)

——*Red: The History of a Color*, trans. by Jody Gladding (Princeton, NJ: Princeton University Press, 2017)

——*Yellow: The History of a Color*, trans. by Jody Gladding (Princeton, NJ: Princeton University Press, 2019)

PEREIRO OTERO, JOSÉ MANUEL, *La escritura modernista de Valle-Inclán: Orgía de colores* (Madrid: Editorial Verbum, 2009), Kindle edition

RILEY, CHARLES A., *Color Codes: Modern Theories of Color in Philosophy, Painting and Architecture, Literature, Music, and Psychology* (Lebanon, NH: University Press of New England, 1995)

RIPOLL, ELODIE, *Penser la couleur en littérature: Explorations romanesques des Lumières au réalisme* (Paris: Classiques Garnier, 2019)

ROBERTSON, ERIC, '"Le blanc souci de notre toile": Writing White in Modern French Poetry and Art', *French Studies*, 71.3 (2017), 319–32

SCOTT, HANNAH, '*Le Blanc et le Noir*: The Spectre Behind the Spectrum in Maupassant's Short Stories', *Nottingham French Studies*, 52.3 (2013), pp. 268–80

SHERINGHAM, MICHAEL, 'Language, Color and the Enigma of Everydayness' in *Sensual Reading: New Approaches to Reading in its Relations to the Senses*, ed. by Michael Syrotinski and Ian Maclachlan (Lewisburg, PA: Bucknell University Press, 2001), pp. 127–52

STREET, SARAH, and JOSHUA YUMIBE, 'The Temporalities of Intermediality: Colour in Cinema and the Arts of the 1920s', *Early Popular Visual Culture*, 11:2 (2013), pp. 140–57

TAUSSIG, MICHAEL T., *What Color is the Sacred?* (Chicago, IL: University of Chicago Press, 2009)

WATT, ADAM, 'Portraits by the Artists as Young Men: Proust, Valéry, Colour', *French Studies*, 71:3 (2017), 333–47

WILSON, EMMA, '*Three Colours: Blue*: Kieślowski, Colour and the Postmodern Subject', *Screen*, 39.4 (1998), 349–62

Other Works of Critical Thought and Theory

AKSOY ALP, EYLEM, 'De l'écriture blanche d'Albert Camus à l'écriture plate d'Annie Ernaux', *Frankofoni*, 27 (2015), 189–202

ANDERSON BLISS, JENNIFER, 'Writing as Flat as a Photograph: Subjectivity in Annie Ernaux's *La Place*', *Lit: Literature, Interpretation and Theory*, 24.2 (2013), 164–83

BARKER, JENNIFER, *The Tactile Eye: Touch and the Cinematic Experience* (Berkeley, CA: University of California Press, 2009)

BARTHES, ROLAND, *Writing Degree Zero*, trans. by Annette Lavers and Colin Smith (London: Cape, 1967)

——— *The Pleasure of the Text*, trans. by Richard Miller (New York: Hill and Wang, 1975)

——— *Camera Lucida: Reflections on Photography*, trans. by Richard Howard (London: Vintage, 2000)

——— 'Cy Twombly: Works on Paper', in *The Responsibility of Forms: Critical Essays on Music, Art and Representation*, trans. by Richard Howard (Berkeley: University of California Press, 1985), pp. 157–76

BERGHAUS, GÜNTER, 'A Theatre of Image, Sound and Motion: On Synaesthesia and the Idea of a Total Work of Art', *Maske und Kothurn*, 32.1–2 (1986), 7–28

——— *Italian Futurist Theatre, 1909–1944* (Oxford: Clarendon Press, 1998)

BUÑUEL, LUIS, *My Last Breath*, trans. by Abigail Israel (London: Vintage Digital, 2011)

COCTEAU, JEAN, *Théâtre 1* (Paris: Grasset, 1957)

CONNOR, STEVEN, *The Book of Skin* (New York: Reaktion Books, 2003)

CORSON, RICHARD, JAMES GLAVAN, and BEVERLY GORE NORCROSS (eds), *Stage Makeup*, 10th edn (Oxford: Routledge, 2016)

DAVIS, STUART, 'Que(e)rying Spain: On the Limits and Possibilities of Queer Theory in Hispanism', in *Reading Iberia: Theory / History / Identity*, ed. by Helena Buffery, Stuart Davis, and Kirsty Hooper (Bern: Peter Lang, 2007), pp. 63–79

DOAN, LAURA, and JANE GARRITY, 'Modernism Queered', in *A Companion to Modernist Literature and Culture*, ed. by David Bradshaw and Kevin J. H. Dettmar (Oxford: Wiley-Blackwell, 2008), pp. 542–50

DOUGHERTY, DRU, and MARÍA FRANCISCA VILCHES DE FRUTOS (eds), *El Teatro en España: entre la tradición y la vanguardia, 1918–1939* (Madrid: Consejo Superior de Investigaciones Científicas, Fundación Federico García Lorca, and Tabacalera, 1992)

DOWNING, SARA, *Beauty and Cosmetics 1550 to 1950* (London: Bloomsbury, 2012)

DOYLE GATES, LAURA, 'Jean Cocteau and "la poésie du théâtre"', *Romance Quarterly*, 35.4 (1988), 435–41

ERNAUX, ANNIE, *A Man's Place* trans. by Tanya Leslie (New York: Four Walls Eight Windows, 1992)

ERNAUX, ANNIE, and FRÉDÉRIC-YVES JEANNET, *L'écriture comme un couteau: Entretien avec Frédéric-Yves Jeannet* (Paris: Stock, 2003), Kindle edition

GARTON, STEPHEN, *Histories of Sexuality: Antiquity to Sexual Revolution* (Oxford: Routledge, 2014)

HAAS, BIRGIT, 'Staging Colours: Edward Gordon Craig and Wassily Kandinsky', in *Textual Intersections: Literature, History and the Arts in Nineteenth-century Europe*, ed. by Rachael Langford (Amsterdam: Rodopi, 2009), pp. 41–51

KIRSCHNER, TERESA, 'Typology of Staging in Lope de Vega's Theater', in *The Golden Age Comedia: Text, Theory, and Performance*, ed. by Charles Ganelin and Howard Mancing, pp. 358–71

LO DATO, ROSEMARY C., *Beyond The Glitter: The Language of Gems in Modernista Writers Rubén Darío, Ramón del Valle-Inclán, and José Asunción Silva* (Lewisburg, NY: Bucknell University Press, Associated University Presses, 1999)

LONDON, JOHN, 'Twentieth-Century Spanish Stage Design', *Contemporary Theatre Review*, 7.3 (1998), 25–56

MARTÍN, ANTONIO, 'Las aleluyas, primera lectura y primeras imágenes para niños en los siglos XVIII–XIX: Un antecedente de la literatura y la prensa infantil en España', *Espéculo*, 47 (2011), no pagination

MAXWELL, CATHERINE, *Scents and Sensibility: Perfume in Victorian Literary Culture* (Oxford: Oxford University Press, 2017)

MCKENDRICK, MALVEENA, 'Honour/Vengeance in the Spanish Comedia: A Case of Mimetic Transference?' *The Modern Language Review*, 79.2 (1984), 313–35

PERAL VEGA, EMILIO, 'Dos visionarios en escena: Edward Gordon Craig y Adrià Gual', *Hispanic Research Journal*, 17.6 (2016), 489–503

PÉREZ-SALES, PAU, *Psychological Torture: Definition, Evaluation and Measurement* (London: Routledge, 2017)

PODOL, PETER L., 'The Evolution of the Honor Theme in Modern Spanish Drama', *Hispanic Review*, 40.1 (1972), 53–72

RABATÉ, JEAN-MICHEL (ed.), *Writing the Image after Roland Barthes* (Philadelphia, PN: Philadelphia University Press, 1997)

SCARRY, ELAINE, *Dreaming by the Book* (New York: Farrar, Straus and Giroux, 1999)

SEATON, BEVERLY, *The Language of Flowers: A History* (London: University Press of Virginia, 2012)

SHANDLER-LEVITT, ANNETTE, 'Jean Cocteau's Theatre: Idea and Enactment', *Theatre Journal*, 45.3 (1993), 363–72

SOUFAS JR, C. CHRISTOPHER, *The Subject in Question: Early Contemporary Spanish Literature and Modernism* (Washington, D.C.: Catholic University of America Press, 2007)

VILCHES DE FRUTOS, MARÍA FRANCISCA, 'Directors of the Twentieth-Century Spanish Stage', *Contemporary Theatre Review*, 7.3 (1998), 1–23

WARNER, MARINA, *From the Beast to the Blonde* (London: Vintage, 1995)

Multimedia Resources

Film

La novia, dir. by Paula Ortiz (Get In The Picture Productions, Mantar Film, Cine Chromatix KG, TVE, 2015)

Newspaper articles

'Beatriz: *Bodas de sangre*', *ABC*, 9 March 1933

FISHER, PHILLIP, 'Doña Rosita at The Orange Tree Theatre', *British Theatre Guide*, March–April 2015 <https://www.britishtheatreguide.info/reviews/donarosita-rev> [accessed 20 February 2022]

——'Doña Rosita the Spinster', *British Theatre Review*, March 2004, <http://www.britishtheatreguide.info/reviews/donarosita-rev> [accessed 1 August 2021]

GARCÍA, ROCÍO, 'El teatro de Lorca retrata lo que más nos duele', *El País*, 15 January 2019 <https://elpais.com/cultura/2019/01/11/actualidad/1547217683_706159.html> [accessed 20 February 2022]

HAWORTH, SIMON, 'The House of Bernarda Alba, the Royal Exchange', *Manchester Review*, 3 February 2017 <http://www.themanchesterreview.co.uk/?p=7196> [accessed 20 February 2022]

HICKLING, ALFRED, 'The House of Bernarda Alba review — Hunter is a domestic dictator in anti-fascist classic', *The Guardian*, 8 February 2017 <https://www.theguardian.com/stage/2017/feb/08/the-house-of-bernarda-alba-review-kathryn-hunter-royal-exchange-manchester> [accessed 20 February 2022]

LAWRENCE, BEN, 'Billie Piper Will Make You Numb with Pity: Review', *The Telegraph*, 5 August 2016 <https://www.telegraph.co.uk/theatre/what-to-see/billie-piper-will-make-you-numb-with-pity-in-yerma---review/> [accessed 20 February 2022]

MARLOWE, SAM, 'Yerma at Arcola Theatre', *The Times*, 30 August 2006 <https://www.thetimes.co.uk/article/yerma-9cdvdkbbvqs> [accessed 20 February 2022]

SOMMER, ELYSE, 'Doña Rosita the Spinster: A CurtainUp Review', *CurtainUp*, 11 January 2004 <http://www.curtainup.com/donarosita.html> [accessed 1 August 2021]

SPENCER, CHARLES, 'A Woman's Pain Laid Bare', *The Telegraph*, 30 August 2006, <https://www.telegraph.co.uk/culture/theatre/drama/3654936/A-womans-pain-laid-bare.html> [accessed 20 February 2022]

Photographs

ALFONSO VÁZQUEZ, 'El maleficio de la mariposa, primer estreno de Federico García Lorca: Del teatro eslava a la sala del mariano', *Moon Magazine*, 16 March 2017. <https://www.moonmagazine.info/lorca-el-maleficio-de-la-mariposa-trece-gatos/> [accessed 3 May 2022]

Radio

'Lorca', *In Our Time*, BBC Radio 4, 4 July 2019

Videos

Absolute Theatre's 1998 staging of *La zapatera* at the Festival de Almada in Lisbon <http://www.absolutetheatre.co.uk/?p=237> [accessed 20 Feb 2022]

Mario Jaime and Yadiro Trejo's 2011 staging of *El maleficio* with the theatre group Cassandra Maledictio (Centro Cultura de la Paz, Baja California, Mexico), Butterfly's monologue at: Elti Alejandro López Lora, 'El Maleficio de la Mariposa — Monologo de la Mariposa. wmv', *Youtube*, 25 August 2012. <https://www.youtube.com/watch?v=t19EobIJ9L0> [accessed 3 May 2022].

INDEX

❖

www.ingramcontent.com/pod-product-compliance
Lightning Source LLC
Chambersburg PA
CBHW081418090426
42738CB00017B/3409